String Algorithms in C

Efficient Text Representation
and Search

Thomas Mailund

Apress®

String Algorithms in C: Efficient Text Representation and Search

Thomas Mailund
Aarhus N, Denmark

ISBN-13 (pbk): 978-1-4842-5919-1 ISBN-13 (electronic): 978-1-4842-5920-7
https://doi.org/10.1007/978-1-4842-5920-7

Managing Director, Apress Media LLC: Welmoed Spahr
Acquisitions Editor: Steve Anglin
Development Editor: Matthew Moodie
Coordinating Editor: Mark Powers

Cover designed by eStudioCalamar

Cover image by Jonathan J Castellon on Unsplash (www.unsplash.com)

Distributed to the book trade worldwide by Springer Science+Business Media New York, 233 Spring Street, 6th Floor, New York, NY 10013. Phone 1-800-SPRINGER, fax (201) 348-4505, e-mail orders-ny@springer-sbm.com, or visit www.springeronline.com. Apress Media, LLC is a California LLC and the sole member (owner) is Springer Science + Business Media Finance Inc (SSBM Finance Inc). SSBM Finance Inc is a **Delaware** corporation.

For information on translations, please e-mail booktranslations@springernature.com; for reprint, paperback, or audio rights, please e-mail bookpermissions@springernature.com.

Apress titles may be purchased in bulk for academic, corporate, or promotional use. eBook versions and licenses are also available for most titles. For more information, reference our Print and eBook Bulk Sales web page at http://www.apress.com/bulk-sales.

Any source code or other supplementary material referenced by the author in this book is available to readers on GitHub via the book's product page, located at www.apress.com/9781484259191. For more detailed information, please visit http://www.apress.com/source-code.

Printed on acid-free paper

Table of Contents

About the Author

Thomas Mailund is an associate professor in bioinformatics at Aarhus University, Denmark. He has a background in math and computer science. For the past decade, his main focus has been on genetics and evolutionary studies, particularly comparative genomics, speciation, and gene flow between emerging species. He has published *R Data Science Quick Reference*, *The Joys of Hashing*, *Domain-Specific Languages in R*, *Beginning Data Science in R*, *Functional Programming in R*, and *Metaprogramming in R*, all from Apress, as well as other books.

About the Technical Reviewer

Jason Whitehorn is an experienced entrepreneur and software developer and has helped many companies automate and enhance their business solutions through data synchronization, SaaS architecture, and machine learning. Jason obtained his Bachelor of Science in Computer Science from Arkansas State University, but he traces his passion for development back many years before then, having first taught himself to program BASIC on his family's computer while still in middle school.

When he's not mentoring and helping his team at work, writing, or pursuing one of his many side projects, Jason enjoys spending time with his wife and four children and living in the Tulsa, Oklahoma region. More information about Jason can be found on his website: `https://jason.whitehorn.us`.

CHAPTER 1

Introduction

Algorithms operating on strings are fundamental to many computer programs, and in particular searching for one string in another is the core of many algorithms. An example is searching for a word in a text document, where we want to know everywhere it occurs. This search can be exact, meaning that we are looking for the positions where the word occurs verbatim, or approximative, where we allow for some spelling mistakes.

This book will teach you fundamental algorithms and data structures for exact and approximative search. The goal of the book is not to cover the theory behind the material in great detail. However, we will see theoretical considerations where relevant. The purpose of the book is to give you examples of how the algorithms can be implemented. For every algorithm and data structure in the book, I will present working C code and nowhere will I use pseudocode. When I argue for the correctness and running time of algorithms, I do so intentionally informal. I aim at giving you an idea about why the algorithms solve a specific problem in a given time, but I will not mathematically prove so.

You can copy all the algorithms and data structures in this book from the pages, but they are also available in a library on GitHub: `https://github.com/mailund/stralg`. You can download and link against the library or copy snippets of code into your own projects. On GitHub you can also find all the programs I have used for time measurement experiments so you can compare the algorithm's performance on your own machine and in your own runtime environment.

Notation and conventions

Unless otherwise stated, we use x, y, and p to refer to strings and i, j, k, l, and h to denote indices. We use ϵ to denote the empty string. We use a, b, and c for single characters. As in C, we do not distinguish between strings and pointers to a sequence of characters. Since the book is about algorithms in C, the notation we use matches that which is used for strings, pointers, and arrays in C. Arrays and strings are indexed from zero,

© Thomas Mailund 2020
T. Mailund, *String Algorithms in C*, https://doi.org/10.1007/978-1-4842-5920-7_1

that is, $A[0]$ is the first value in array A (and $x[0]$ is the first character in string x). The ith character in a string is at index $i - 1$.

When we refer to a substring, we define it using two indices, i and j, $i \leq j$, and we write $x[i, j]$ for the substring. The first index is included and the second is not, that is, $x[i, j] = x[i]x[i + 1] \cdots x[j - 1]$. If a string has length n, then the substring $x[0, n]$ is the full string. If we have a character a and a string x, then ax denotes the string that has a as its first character and is then followed by the string x. We use a^k to denote a sequence of as of length k. The string $a^3 x$ has a as its first three characters and is then followed by x. A substring that starts at index 0, $x[0, i]$, is a *prefix* of the string, and it is a *proper prefix* if it is neither the empty string $x[0, 0] = \epsilon$ nor the full string $x[0, n]$. A substring that ends in n, $x[i, n]$, is a *suffix*, and it is a proper suffix if it is neither the empty string nor the full string. We will sometimes use $x[i,]$ for this suffix.

We use $\$$ to denote a *sentinel* in a string, that is, it is a character that is not found in the rest of the string. It is typically placed at the end of the string. The zero-terminated C strings have the zero byte as their termination sentinel, and unless otherwise stated, $\$$ refers to that. All C strings x have a zero sentinel at index n if the string has length n, $x = x[0]x[1] \cdots x[n - 1]0$. For some algorithms, the sentinel is essential; in others, it is not. We will leave it out of the notation when a sentinel isn't needed for an algorithm, but naturally include the sentinel when it is necessary.

Graphical notation

Most data structures and algorithmic ideas are simpler to grasp if we use drawings to capture the structure of strings rather than textual notation. Because of this, I have chosen to provide more figures in this book than you will typically see in a book on algorithms. I hope you will appreciate it. If there is anything you find unclear about an algorithm, I suggest you try to draw key strings yourself and work out the properties you have problems with.

In figures, we represent strings as rectangles. We show indices into a string as arrows pointing to the index in the string; see Figure 1-1. In this notation, we do not distinguish between pointers and indices. If a variable is an index j and it points into x, then what it points to is $x[j]$, naturally. If the variable is a pointer, y, then what it points to is $*y$. Whether we are working with pointers or indices should be clear from the context. It will undoubtedly be clear from the C implementations. We represent substrings by boxes of a different color inside the original string-rectangle. If we specify the indices defining the substring, we include their start and stop index (where the stop index points one after the end of the substring).

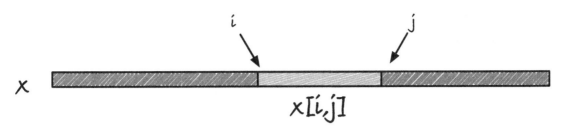

Figure 1-1. *Graphical string notation*

When we compare two strings, we imagine that we align the boxes representing them, so the parts we are comparing are on top of each other. For example, if we compare the character at index j in a string x with the character at index i in another string p, then we draw a box representing x over a box representing p, and we draw pointers for the two indices; see Figure 1-2. Since we are comparing the characters in the two indices, the two pointers are pointing at each other. Conceptually, we imagine that p is aligned under x starting at position $j - i$.

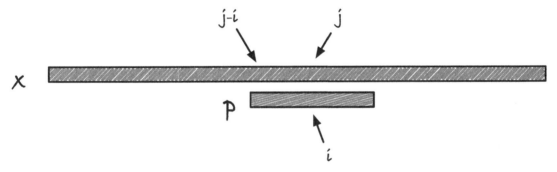

Figure 1-2. *Graphical notation for comparing indices in two different strings*

Code conventions

There is a trade-off between long variables and type names and then the line within a book. In many cases, I have had to use an indentation that you might not be used to. In function prototypes and function definitions, I will generally write with one variable per line, indented under the function return type and name, for example:

```
void compute_z_array(
    const unsigned char *x,
    uint32_t n,
    uint32_t *Z
);
```

```
void compute_reverse_z_array(
    const unsigned char *x,
    uint32_t m,
    uint32_t *Z
);
```

If a return type name is long, I will put it on a separate line:

```
static inline uint32_t
edge_length(struct suffix_tree_node *n) {
    return range_length(n->range);
}
struct suffix_tree *
mccreight_suffix_tree(
    const unsigned char *string
);
struct suffix_tree *
lcp_suffix_tree(
    const unsigned char *string,
    uint32_t *sa,
    uint32_t *lcp
);
struct suffix_tree_node *
st_search(
    struct suffix_tree *st,
    const char *pattern
);
```

I make an exception for functions that take no arguments, that is, have void as their argument type.

There are many places where an algorithm needs to use characters to look up in arrays. If you use the conventional C string type, char *, then the character can be either signed or unsigned, depending on your compiler, and you have to cast the type to avoid warnings. A couple of places we also have to make assumptions about the alphabet size. Because of this, I use arrays of uint8_t with a zero termination sentinel as strings. On practically all platforms, char is 8 bits so this type is, for all intents and purposes, C strings. We are just guaranteed that we can use it unsigned and that the alphabet size is 256. Occasionally it is necessary to cast a uint8_t * string to a C string. A direct cast, (char *)x, will most likely work unless you are on an exotic platform. If it doesn't, you have to build a char buffer and copy characters byte by byte. It has to be a *very* exotic platform if you cannot store 8 bits in a char! Because I assume that you can always cast to char *, I will use the C library string functions (with a cast) when this is appropriate. It is a small matter to write your own if it is necessary.

I will use uint32_t for indices, assuming that strings are short enough that we can index them with 32 bits. You can change it as needed, but I find it a good trade-off between likely lengths of strings and the space I need for data structures. I work in bioinformatics, so hundreds of millions of characters are usually the longest I encounter.

Reporting a sequence of results

In search algorithms, we report each occurrence of a pattern. This sounds straightforward, but there is a design choice in how we report the occurrences. Consider the following algorithm. It is the Boyer-Moore-Horspool (BMH) algorithm that you will see in the next chapter. It takes a string, *x*, and a pattern, *p*, and searches for all occurrences of *p* in *x*. First, it does some preprocessing, and then it searches. This is a general pattern for the algorithms in the next chapter. In the search, when it has found an occurrence of *p*, it reports the position by calling the REPORT(j) function.

```c
void bmh_search(
    const uint8_t *x,
    const uint8_t *p
) {
    uint32_t n = strlen((char *)x);
    uint32_t m = strlen((char *)p);

    // Preprocessing
    int jump_table[256];

    for (int k = 0; k < 256; k++) {
        jump_table[k] = m;
    }
    for (int k = 0; k < m - 1; k++) {
        jump_table[p[k]] = m - k - 1;
    }
```

```
    // Searching
    for (uint32_t j = 0;
         j < n - m + 1;
         j += jump_table[x[j + m - 1]]) {

        int i = m - 1;
        while (i > 0 && p[i] == x[j + i])
            --i;
        if (i == 0 && p[0] == x[j]) {
            REPORT(j);
        }
    }
}
```

If a global report function is all you need in your program, then this is an excellent solution. Often, however, we need different reporting functions for separate calls to the search function. Or we need the report function to collect data for further processing (and preferably not use global variables). We need some handle to choose different report functions and to provide them with data.

One approach is using callbacks: Provide a report function and data argument to the search function and call the report function with the data when we find an occurrence. In the following implementation, I am assuming we have defined the function type for reporting, report_function, and the type for data we can add to it, report_function_data, somewhere outside of the search function.

```
void bmh_search_callback(
    const uint8_t *x,
    const uint8_t *p,
    report_function report,
    report_function_data data
) {
    uint32_t n = strlen((char *)x);
    uint32_t = strlen((char *)p);

    // Preprocessing
    uint32_t jump_table[256];
```

```
for (int k = 0; k < 256; k++) {
    jump_table[k] = m;
}
for (int k = 0; k < m - 1; k++) {
    jump_table[p[k]] = m - k - 1;
}

// Searching
for (uint32_t j = 0;
       j < n - m + 1;
       j += jump_table[x[j + m - 1]]) {

    int i = m - 1;
    while (i > 0 && p[i] == x[j + i])
        --i;
    if (i == 0 && p[0] == x[j]) {
        report(j, data);
    }
}
}
```

Callback functions have their uses, especially to handle events in interactive programs, but also some substantial drawbacks. To use them, you have to split the control flow of your program into different functions which hurts readability. Especially if you need to handle nested loops, for example, iterate over all nodes in a tree and for each node iterate over the leaves in another tree where for each node-leaf pair you find occurrences… (the example here is made up, but there are plenty of real algorithms with nested loops, and we will see some later in the book).

We can get the control flow back to the calling function using the iterator design pattern. We define an iterator structure that holds information about the loop state, and we provide functions for setting it up, progressing to the next point in the loop, and reporting a match and then a function for freeing resources once the iterator is done.

The general pattern for using an iterator looks like this:

```
struct iterator iter;
struct match match;
iter_init(&iter, data);
```

```
while (next_func(&iter, &match)) {
    // Process occurrence
}
iter_dealloc(&iter);
```

The iterator structure contains the loop information. That means it must save the preprocessing data from when we create it and information about how to resume the loop after each time it is suspended. To report occurrences, it takes a "match" structure through which it can inform the caller about where matches occur. The iterator is initialized with data that determines what it should loop over. The loop is handled using a "next" function that returns true if there is another match (and if it does it will have filled out match). If there are no more matches, and the loop terminates, then it returns false. The iterator might contain allocated resources, so there should always be a function for freeing those.

In an iterator for the BMH, we would keep the string, pattern, and table we build in the preprocessing.

```
struct bmh_match_iter {
    const uint8_t *x; uint32_t n;
    const uint8_t *p; uint32_t m;
    int jump_table[256];
    uint32_t j;
};
struct match {
    uint32_t pos;
};
```

We put the preprocessing in the iterator initialization function

```
void init_bmh_match_iter(
    struct bmh_match_iter *iter,
    const uint8_t *x, uint32_t n,
    const uint8_t *p, uint32_t m
) {
    // Preprocessing
    iter->j = 0;
    iter->x = x; iter->n = n;
    iter->p = p; iter->m = m;
```

```
    for (int k = 0; k < 256; k++) {
        iter->jump_table[k] = m;
    }
    for (int k = 0; k < m - 1; k++) {
        iter->jump_table[p[k]] = m - k - 1;
    }
}
```

and in the next function we do the search

```
bool next_bmh_match(
    struct bmh_match_iter *iter,
    struct match *match
) {
    const uint8_t *x = iter->x;
    const uint8_t *p = iter->p;
    uint32_t n = iter->n;
    uint32_t m = iter->m;
    int *jump_table = iter->jump_table;

    // Searching
    for (uint32_t j = iter->j;
        j < n - m + 1;
        j += jump_table[x[j + m - 1]]) {

        int i = m - 1;
        while (i > 0 && p[i] == x[j + i]) {
            i--;
        }
        if (i == 0 && p[0] == x[j]) {
            match->pos = j;
            iter->j = j +
                    jump_table[x[j + m - 1]];
            return true;
        }
    }
    return false;
}
```

We set up the loop with information from the iterator and search from there. If we find an occurrence, we store the new loop information in the iterator and the match information in the match structure and return true. If we reach the end of the loop, we report false.

We have not allocated any resources when we initialized the iterator, so we do not need to free anything.

```c
void dealloc_bmh_match_iter(
    struct bmh_match_iter *iter
) {
    // Nothing to do here
}
```

Since the deallocation function doesn't do anything, we could leave it out. Still, consistency in the use of iterators helps avoid problems. Plus, should we at some point add resources to the iterator, then it is easier to update one function than change all the places in the code that should now call a deallocation function.

Iterators complicate the implementation of algorithms, especially if they are recursive and the iterator needs to keep track of a stack. Still, they greatly simplify the user interface to your algorithms, which makes it worthwhile to spend a little extra time implementing them. In this book, I will use iterators throughout.

CHAPTER 2

Classical algorithms for exact search

We kick the book off by looking at classical algorithms for exact search, that is, finding positions in a string where a pattern string matches precisely. This problem is so fundamental that it received much attention in the very early days of computing, and by now, there are tens if not hundreds of approaches. In this chapter, we see a few classics.

Recall that we use iterators whenever we have an algorithm that loops over results that should be reported. All iterators must be initialized, and the resources they hold must be deallocated when we no longer need the iterator. When we loop, we have a function that returns true when there is something to report and false when the loop is done. The values the iterator reports are put in a structure that we pass along to the function that iterates to the next value to report. For the algorithms in this chapter, we initialize the iterators with the string in which we search, the pattern we search for, and the lengths of the two strings. Iterating over all occurrences of the pattern follows this structure:

```c
struct iterator iter;
struct match match;
iter_init(iter, x, strlen(x), p, strlen(p));
while (next_func(&iter, &match)) {
    // Process occurrence
}
iter_dealloc(&iter);
```

When we report an occurrence, we get the position of the match, so the structure the iterator use for reporting is this:

```c
struct match {
    uint32_t pos;
};
```

T. Mailund, *String Algorithms in C*, https://doi.org/10.1007/978-1-4842-5920-7_2

Naïve algorithm

The simplest way imaginable for exact search is to iteratively move through the string x, with an index j that conceptually runs the pattern p along x, and at each index start matching the pattern against the string using another index, i (see Figure 2-1). The algorithm has two loops, one that iterates j through x and one that iterates i through p, matching $x[i+j]$ against $p[i]$ along the way. We run the inner loop until we see a mismatch or until we reach the end of the pattern. In the former case, we move p one step forward and try matching again. In the second case, we report an occurrence at position j and then increment the index so we can start matching at the next position. We stop the outer loop when index j is greater than $n - m$. If it is, there isn't room for a match that doesn't run past the end of x.

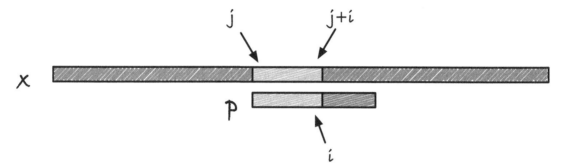

Figure 2-1. *Exact search with the naïve approach*

We terminate the comparison of $x[i+j]$ and $p[i]$ when we see a mismatch, so in the best case, where the first character in p never matches a character in x, the algorithm runs in time $O(n)$ where n is the length of x. In the worst case, we match all the way to the end of p at each position, and in that case, the running time is $O(nm)$ where m is the length of p.

To implement the algorithm using an iterator, the iterator needs to remember the string to search in and the pattern to search for—so we do not need to pass these along each time we increment the iterator with potentials for errors if we use the wrong strings—and we keep track of how far into the string we have searched.

```
struct naive_match_iter {
    const uint8_t *x; uint32_t n;
    const uint8_t *p; uint32_t m;
    uint32_t current_index;
};
```

When we initialize the iterator, we remember the two strings and set the current index to zero—before we start iterating we are at the beginning of the string.

```
void init_naive_match_iter(
    struct naive_match_iter *iter,
    const uint8_t *x, uint32_t n,
    const uint8_t *p, uint32_t m
) {
    iter->x = x; iter->n = n;
    iter->p = p; iter->m = m;
    iter->current_index = 0;
    iter->current_index = 0;
}
```

When we increment the iterator, we follow the algorithm as described earlier except that we start the outer loop at the index saved in the iterator. We search from this index in an outer loop, and at each new index, we try to match the pattern with an inner loop. We break the inner loop if we see a mismatching character, and if the inner loop reaches the end, we have a match and report it. Before we return, we set the iterator index and store the matching position in the match structure.

```
bool next_naive_match(
    struct naive_match_iter *iter,
    struct match *match
) {
    uint32_t n = iter->n, m = iter->m;
    const uint8_t *x = iter->x;
    const uint8_t *p = iter->p;

    if (m > n) return false;
    if (m == 0) return false;

    for (uint32_t j = iter->current_index; j <= n - m; j++) {
        uint32_t i = 0;
        while (i < m && x[j+i] == p[i]) {
            i++;
        }
```

```
    if (i == m) {
        iter->current_index = j + 1;
        match->pos = j;
        return true;
    }
  }

  return false;
}
```

The code

```
if (m > n)  return false;
if (m == 0) return false;
```

makes sure that it is possible to match the pattern at all and that the pattern isn't empty. This is something we could also test when we initialize the iterator. However, we do not have a way of reporting that we do not have a possible match there, so we put the test in the "next" function.

We do not allocate any resources when we initialize the iterator, so we do not need to do anything when deallocating it either. We still need the deallocator function, however, so we always use the same design pattern when we use iterators. To make sure that if we, at some point in the future, need to free something that we put in an iterator, then all users of the iterator (should) have added code for this.

```
void dealloc_naive_match_iter(
    struct naive_match_iter *iter
) {
    // Nothing to do here...
}
```

Border array and border search

It is possible to get $O(n + m)$ running times for both best and worst case, and several algorithms exist for this. We will see several in the following sections. The first one is based on the so-called *borders* of strings.

Borders and border arrays

A border of a string is any substring that is both a prefix and a suffix of the said string; see Figure 2-2. For example, the string $x = ababa$ has borders aba, a, and the empty string. There is always at least one border per string—the empty string. It is possible to list all borders by brute force. For each index i in x, test if the substrings $x[0, i]$ matches the string $x[n - i, n]$. This approach makes time $O(n)$ per comparison, and we need it for all possible borders which means that we end up with a running time of $O(n^2)$. It is possible to compute the longest border in linear time, as we shall see. The way we compute it shows that sometimes more is less; we will compute more than the length of the longest suffix. What we will compute is the *border array*. This is an array that for each index i holds the length of the longest border of string $x[0, i]$. Consider $x = ababa$. For index 0 we have string a which has border a, so the first element in the border array is 1. The string ab only has the trivial, nonempty border, so the border array value is zero. The next string is aba with border a, so we get 1 again. Now $abab$ has borders ab, so the border array holds 2. The full string $x = ababa$ with border aba so its border array looks like ba = [1, 0, 1, 2, 3].

X

Figure 2-2. *A string with three borders*

We can make the following observation about borders and border arrays: The longest border of $x[0, i]$ is either the empty string or an extension of a border of $x[0, i - 1]$. If the letter at $x[i]$ is a, the border of $x[0, i]$ is some string y followed by a. The y string must be both at the beginning and end of $x[0, i - 1]$ (see Figure 2-3), so it is a border of $x[0, i - 1]$. The longest border for $x[0, i]$ is the longest border of $x[0, i - 1]$ that is followed by a (which may be the empty border if the string x begins with a) or the empty border if there is no border we can extend with a.

Another observation is that if you have two borders to a string, then the shorter of the two is a border of the longer; see Figure 2-4.

The two observations combined gives us an approach to computing the border array. The first string has the empty border as its only border, and after that, we can use the border array up to $i-1$ to compute the length of the longest border of $x[0, i]$. We start by testing if we can extend the longest border with $x[i]$, and if so, $ba[i] = ba[i-1] + 1$. Otherwise, we look at the second-longest border, which must be the longest border of $x[0, ba[i-1]]$. If the character after this border is $x[i]$, then $ba[i] = ba[ba[i-1]] + 1$. We continue this way until we have found a border we can extend (see Figure 2-5). If we reach the empty border, we have a special case—either we can extend the empty border because $x[0] = x[i]$, in which case $ba[i] = 1$, or we cannot extend the border because $x[0] \neq x[i]$, in which case $ba[i] = 0$.

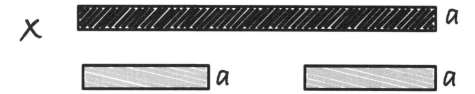

Figure 2-3. *Extending a border*

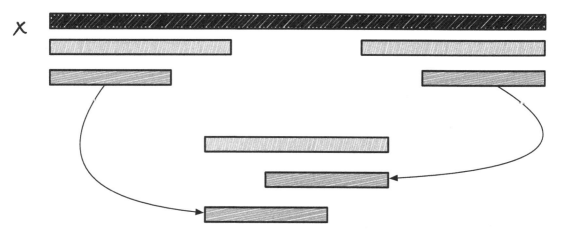

Figure 2-4. *A shorter border is always a border of a longer border*

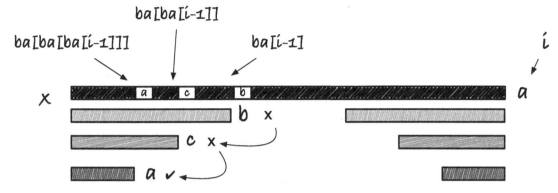

Figure 2-5. *Searching for the longest border we can extend with letter a*

An implementation of the border array construction algorithm can look like this:

```
ba[0] = 0;
for (uint32_t i = 1; i < m; ++i) {
    uint32_t b = ba[i - 1];
    while (b > 0 && x[i] != x[b])
        b = ba[b - 1];
    ba[i] = (x[i] == x[b]) ? b + 1 : 0;
}
```

The running time is m for a string x of length m. It is straightforward to see that the outer loop only runs m iterations but perhaps less easy to see that the inner loop is bounded by m iterations in total. But observe that in the outer loop, we at most increment b by one per iteration. We can assign $b + 1$ to ba[i] in the last statement in the inner loop and then get that value in the first line of the next iteration, but at no other point do we increment a value. In the inner loop, we always decrease b—when we get the border of $b - 1$, we always get a smaller value than b. We don't allow b to go below zero in the inner loop, so the total number of iterations of that loop is bounded by how much the outer loop increase b. That is at most one per iteration, so we can decrement b by at most m, and therefore the total number of iterations of the inner loop is bounded by $O(m)$.

Exact search using borders

The reason we built the border array was to do an exact search, so how does the array help us? Imagine we build a string consisting of the pattern we search for, p, followed by the string we search in, x, separated by a sentinel, $ character not found elsewhere in the two strings, $y = p\$x$. The sentinel ensures that all borders are less than the length of p, m, and anywhere we have a border of length m, we must have an occurrence of p (see Figure 2-6). In the figure, the indices are into the $p\$x$ string and not into x, but you can remap this by subtracting $m + 1$. The start index of the match is $i - m + 1$ rather than the more natural $i - m$ because index i is at the end of the match and not one past it.

We can construct the string $p\$x$ in linear time and compute the border array—and report occurrences in the process—in linear time, $O(m + n)$. You don't need to create the concatenated string, though. You can build the border array for p and use that when computing the border array for x. You pretend that p is prepended to x. When you do this, the sentinel between p and x is the null-termination sentinel in the C-string p.

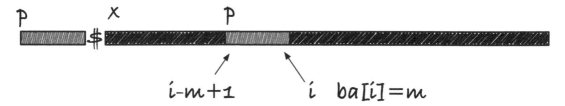

Figure 2-6. *Searching using a border array*

An iterator that searches a string with this algorithm must contain the border array of p, the index into x we have reached, and the b variable from the border array construction algorithm.

```
struct border_match_iter {
    const uint8_t *x; uint32_t n;
    const uint8_t *p; uint32_t m;
    uint32_t *border_array;
    uint32_t i; uint32_t b;
};
```

When we initialize the iterator, we set its index to zero. That, after all, is where we start searching in x. We also set the iterator's b variable to zero. We imagine that we start the search after a sentinel, so the longest border at the start index for x has length zero. We then allocate and compute the border array.

```
void init_border_match_iter(
    struct border_match_iter *iter,
    const uint8_t *x, uint32_t n,
    const uint8_t *p, uint32_t m
) {
    iter->x = x; iter->n = n;
    iter->p = p; iter->m = m;
    iter->i = iter->b = 0;

    uint32_t *ba = malloc(m * sizeof(uint32_t));
    compute_border_array(p, m, ba);
    iter->border_array = ba;
}
```

Since we allocated the border array when we initialized the iterator, we need to free it again when we deallocate it.

```
void dealloc_border_match_iter(
    struct border_match_iter *iter
) {
    free(iter->border_array);
}
```

A third of my implementation for incrementing the following iterator is setting up aliases for the variables in the iterator, so I don't have to write iter->b and iter->m for variables b and m, respectively. Other than that, there are the tests for whether it is possible at all to have a match, that we also saw in the previous section, and then there is the border array construction algorithm again, except that we never update an array but instead report when we get a border of length m.

```
bool next_border_match(
    struct border_match_iter *iter,
    struct match *match
) {
    const uint8_t *x = iter->x;
    const uint8_t *p = iter->p;
    uint32_t *ba = iter->border_array;
    uint32_t b = iter->b;
    uint32_t m = iter->m;
    uint32_t n = iter->n;

    if (m > n) return false;
    if (m == 0) return false;

    for (uint32_t i = iter->i; i < iter->n; ++i) {
        while (b > 0 && x[i] != p[b])
            b = ba[b - 1];
        b = (x[i] == p[b]) ? b + 1 : 0;
        if (b == m) {
            iter->i = i + 1;
            iter->b = b;
            match->pos = i - m + 1;
            return true;
        }
    }

    return false;
}
```

When we report an occurrence, we naturally set the position we matched in the report structure, and we remember the border and index positions.

Knuth-Morris-Pratt

The Knuth-Morris-Pratt (KMP) algorithm also uses borders to achieve a best- and worst-case running time of $O(n + m)$, but it uses the borders in a slightly different way. Before we get to the algorithm, however, I want to convince you that we can, conceptually, move the pattern p through x in two different ways; see Figure 2-7. We can let j be an index into x and imagine p starting there. When we test if p matches there, we use a pointer into p, i, and test $x[j + i]$ against $p[i]$ for increasing i. To move p to another position in x, we change j, for example, to slide p one position to the right we increment j by one. Alternatively, we can imagine p aligned at position $j - i$ for some index j in x and an index i into p. If we change i, we move $j - i$ so we move p. If, for example, we want to move p one step to the right, we can decrement i by one. To understand how the KMP algorithm works, it is useful to think about moving p in the second way. We will increment the j and i indices when matching characters, but when we get a mismatch, we move p by decrementing i.

The idea in KMP is to move p along x as we would in the naïve algorithm, but move a little faster when we have a mismatch. We use index j to point into x and i to point into p. We match $x[j]$ against $p[i]$ as we scan along x and the pattern is aligned against x at index $j - i$. We can move p's position by modifying either i or j. Consider a place in the algorithm where we have matched $p[0, i]$ against $x[j - i, j]$ and see a mismatch. In the naïve algorithm, we would move p one step to the right and start matching p again at that position. We would set i to zero to start matching from the beginning of p, and we would decrement j to $j - i + 1$ to match at the new position at which we would match p. With KMP we will skip positions where we know that p cannot match, and we use borders to do this.

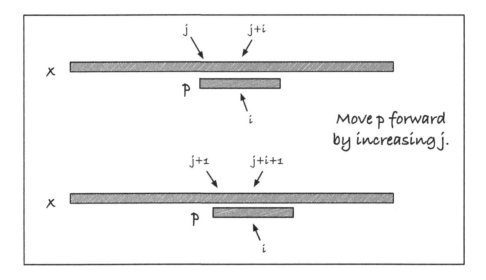

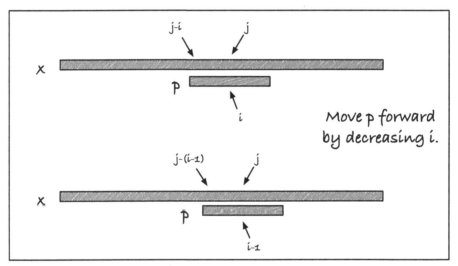

Figure 2-7. *Two ways to conceptually look at matching*

If we have matched p up to index i and then had a mismatch, we know that the only next position at which we could possibly have a match is one where we match a border of $p[0, i-1]$ against a suffix of the string we already matched $x[j-i, j-1]$; see Figure 2-8. It has to be a border of $p[0, i-1]$ and not $p[0, i]$, although that might look like a better choice from the figure. However, we know that $p[0, i]$ doesn't match at the last index, so we need a border of the pattern up to index $i-1$. When we move p, we must be careful not to slide it past possible matches, but if we pick the longest border of $p[0, i-1]$, then this cannot happen. Aligning the longest border moves the pattern the shortest distance where a border matches a suffix of $x[j-i, j-1]$. When we have a mismatch at index i, we move p up to the next possible match by decreasing i to $ba[i-1]$. See Figure 2-9 for a visualization of this idea.

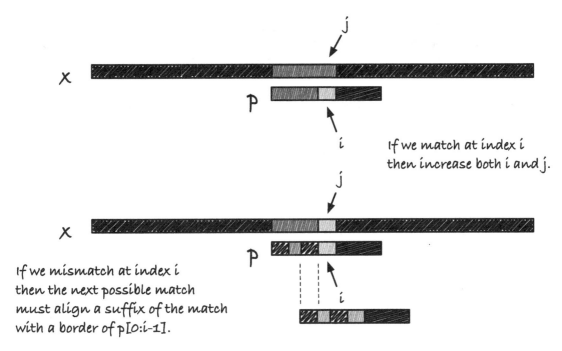

Figure 2-8. *Borders and the observation underlying the KMP algorithm*

When we move p to match a border to the string we already matched, there is a chance that the character following the border doesn't match $x[j]$ either. It is not straightforward to pick a border where we are sure that the next character matches, but we can easily avoid that we mismatch on exactly the same character as before. We need to modify the border array, so we do not include borders where the next character matches the character that follows the border. A border array where we have removed the borders $p[0, ba[i]]$ and $p[i - ba[i], i]$ where $p[ba[i] + 1] = p[i + 1]$ is what we call a *restricted border array*. We can compute this restricted array by scanning the border array from left to right and skipping a border if the characters match. The longest border of the skipped border will not be followed by the same character as the border we skip. If it did, we would have skipped past it when we processed the longer border.

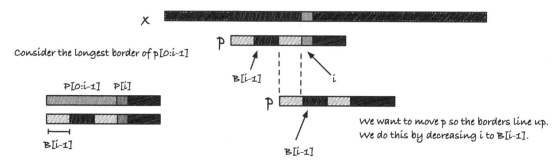

Figure 2-9. *Calculations for how much we should jump at a mismatch*

```
for (uint32_t i = 0; i < m - 1; i++) {
    if (ba[i] > 0 && pattern[ba[i]] == pattern[i + 1])
        ba[i] = ba[ba[i] - 1];
}
```

An iterator for the KMP algorithm needs to hold the border array and the indices *i* and *j*.

```
struct kmp_match_iter {
    const uint8_t *x; uint32_t n;
    const uint8_t *p; uint32_t m;
    uint32_t *ba;
    uint32_t j, i;
};
```

The initialization consists of computing the border array and modifying it to avoid borders that are followed by the same characters.

```
void compute_border_array(
    const uint8_t *x,
    uint32_t m,
    uint32_t *ba
) {
    ba[0] = 0;
    for (uint32_t i = 1; i < m; ++i) {
        uint32_t b = ba[i - 1];
        while (b > 0 && x[i] != x[b])
            b = ba[b - 1];
```

```
        ba[i] = (x[i] == x[b]) ? b + 1 : 0;
    }
}

void computed_restricted_border_array(
    const uint8_t *x,
    uint32_t m,
    uint32_t *ba
) {
    compute_border_array(x, m, ba);
    for (uint32_t i = 0; i < m - 1; i++) {
        if (ba[i] > 0 && x[ba[i]] == x[i + 1])
            ba[i] = ba[ba[i] - 1];
    }
}

void init_kmp_match_iter(
    struct kmp_match_iter *iter,
    const uint8_t *x, uint32_t n,
    const uint8_t *p, uint32_t m
) {

    iter->x = x; iter->n = n;
    iter->p = p; iter->m = m;
    iter->j = 0; iter->i = 0;

    uint32_t *ba = malloc(m * sizeof(uint32_t));
    ba[0] = 0;
    computed_restricted_border_array(p, m, ba);

    iter->ba = ba;
}
```

Since we allocate memory for the border array, we must also free it in the deallocation function.

```
void dealloc_kmp_match_iter(
    struct kmp_match_iter *iter
) {
    free(iter->ba);
}
```

The next function gets its information from the iterator. It then iterates as long as index j hasn't reached a point where no more matches can occur, or until we have a match that we report. We scan the text and pattern, by increasing i and j as long as we have a match, and if i reaches m, we know that we have a match. To move p to the next position, we increase j by one if i is zero (so we need to match from the beginning of p), or we decrease i if i is not zero using the border array. If we have a match to report, we update the iterator with the current loop state and return the position where we had the match, $j - m$.

```
bool next_kmp_match(
    struct kmp_match_iter *iter,
    struct match *match
) {
    // Aliases to make the code easier to read...
    uint32_t j = iter->j;
    uint32_t i = iter->i;
    uint32_t m = iter->m;
    uint32_t n = iter->n;
    const uint8_t *x = iter->x;
    const uint8_t *p = iter->p;

    if (m > n) return false;
    if (m == 0) return false;

    // Remember that j matches the first i
    // items into the string, so + i.
    while (j <= n - m + i) {
        // Match as far as we can
        while (i < m && x[j] == p[i]) {
            i++; j++;
        }
```

```
        // We need to check this
        // before we update i.
        bool we_have_a_match = i == m;

        // Update indices
        if (i == 0) j++;
        else i = iter->ba[i - 1];

        // If we have a hit...
        if (we_have_a_match) {
            // ...yield new match
            iter->j = j; iter->i = i;
            match->pos = j - m;
            return true;
        }
    }
    return false;
}
```

The reason we have a Boolean for when we have a match is that we need to update the indices whether we have a match or not. I chose this solution to avoid duplicated code, but you could also have the update code twice instead.

To see that the algorithm runs in linear time, we need two observations. First, the index j never decreases and this bounds it to maximal n steps. This variable does not increase in each iteration, but when j doesn't increase, i decreases instead. When i decreases, we conceptually move p toward the right by increasing $j - i$, where the beginning of p sits under x. We never move p to the left, so the number of steps we can move p forward is also bounded by n. So, in each iteration we either increment j or move p, and both operations are bounded by n steps. This means that we have a linear bound on the KMP algorithm.

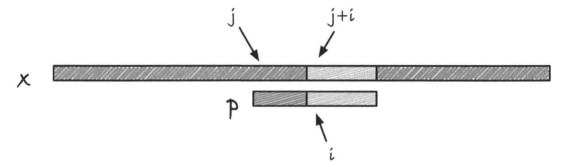

Figure 2-10. *Matching from right to left*

Boyer-Moore-Horspool

With the Boyer-Moore-Horspool (BMH) algorithm, we are back to a worst-case running time of $O(nm)$, but now with a best-case running time of $O(n/m + m)$, that is, a potential sublinear running time. The trick to going faster than linear is to match the pattern from right to left (see Figure 2-10), which lets us use information about the match after the current position of p. If we have a mismatch before we reach the first character in p, that is, before we reach index j in x, we might be able to skip past the remaining prefix of $x[j, j+m]$ without looking at it.

The idea in the BMH algorithm is straightforward. To have a match, at the very least, the last character of p, $p[m-1]$, should match the last character in the substring we are trying to match p against, that is, $x[j + m - 1]$. If we see a mismatch, we do not simply increment j by one. Instead, we move p to the next position where the rightmost occurrence of $x[j + m - 1]$ occurs in p; see Figure 2-11. We cannot include the last character since if that matches we will not move anywhere, so "rightmost" really means the rightmost that is not the last character. As a preprocessing step, we want to build a "jump table" that, whenever we have a mismatch (or get to the beginning of p), moves us to the next position where we match $x[j + m - 1]$. If the rightmost occurrence of this last character is at index k in p, we want to move p $m - 1 - k$ positions; see Figure 2-12.

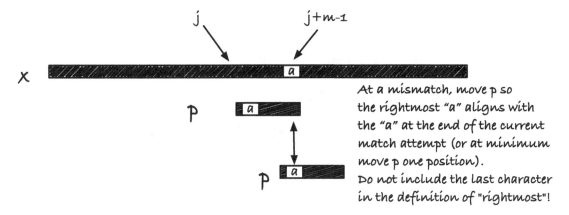

At a mismatch, move p so the rightmost "a" aligns with the "a" at the end of the current match attempt (or at minimum move p one position).
Do not include the last character in the definition of "rightmost"!

Figure 2-11. *Observation that lets us jump ahead after a mismatch*

When we build the jump table, we cannot include the last character in p, $p[m-1]$, since jumping to align this one might leave us at the same position as we are already at. Excluding it means that p will always jump at least one position to the right, that is, when j is updated with the jump table, it will always increase. When we build the jump table, we start by setting all entries to m. If a character is not in p, this will let us jump entirely past the current $j + m - 1$ position. We then iterate through p and insert the position where we see a character into the table. If a character occurs more than once, it will be the last position that is in the table because we update the table from left to right.

```
for (uint32_t k = 0; k < 256; k++) {
    jump_table[k] = m;
}
for (uint32_t k = 0; k < m - 1; k++) {
    jump_table[pattern[k]] = m - k - 1;
}
```

It should be obvious that the preprocessing is done in $O(m)$.

In our BMH iterator, we need to store the current position of p in x, j, and we need to store the jump table.

```
struct bmh_match_iter {
    const uint8_t *x; uint32_t n;
    const uint8_t *p; uint32_t m;
    uint32_t jump_table[256];
    uint32_t j;
};
```

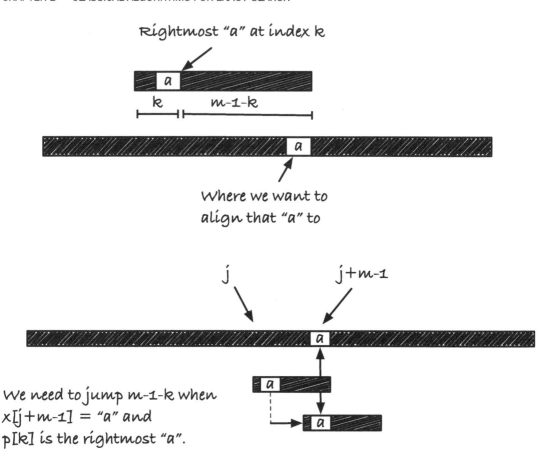

Figure 2-12. *The length to jump at a mismatch*

When we initialize the iterator, we set j to the first position in x and we compute the jump table for the pattern.

```
void init_bmh_match_iter(
    struct bmh_match_iter *iter,
    const uint8_t *x, uint32_t n,
    const uint8_t *p, uint32_t m
) {
    iter->j = 0;
    iter->x = x; iter->n = n;
    iter->p = p; iter->m = m;
    for (uint32_t k = 0; k < 256; k++) {
        iter->jump_table[k] = m;
    }
```

```
    for (uint32_t k = 0; k < m - 1; k++) {
        iter->jump_table[pattern[k]] = m - k - 1;
    }
}
```

The jump table is not heap allocated, we know its size at compile time, so we do not need to free it when we deallocate the iterator.

```
void dealloc_bmh_match_iter(
    struct bmh_match_iter *iter
) {
    // Nop
}
```

When we increment the iterator, we search from the current j, but instead of incrementing the index by one in each iteration, we increment it with the value in the jump table. For each position of j, we try to match p starting from the last character and moving toward the first. If we have a match, we report the matching position and increment j to the position where the next search should start.

```
bool next_bmh_match(
    struct bmh_match_iter *iter,
    struct match *match
) {
    // Aliasing to make the code easier to read...
    const uint8_t *x = iter->x;
    const uint8_t *p = iter->p;
    uint32_t n = iter->n;
    uint32_t m = iter->m;
    uint32_t *jump_table = iter->jump_table;

    if (m > n)  return false;
    if (m == 0) return false;

    for (uint32_t j = iter->j;
         j < n - m + 1;
         j += jump_table[x[j + m - 1]]) {

        uint32_t i = m - 1;
```

```
    while (i > 0 && p[i] == x[j + i]) {
        i--;
    }
    if (i == 0 && p[0] == x[j]) {
        match->pos = j;
        iter->j = j + jump_table[text[j + m - 1]];
        return true;
    }
  }
  return false;
}
```

To see that the worst-case running time is $O(nm)$, consider a string and a pattern that has only one character, $x = aaa \cdots a$, $p = aaa \cdots a$. With these two strings, we never have a mismatch, the rightmost occurrence of a (excluding the last character in p as we do) is $m - 2$, so we jump $m - 1 - k$ with $k = m - 2$, which moves us one position to the right. So at each position in x, we match m characters, which gives us a running time of $O(nm)$. For the best-case running time, consider $x = aaa \cdots a$ again but now the pattern $p = bbb \cdots b$. We will always get a mismatch at the first character we see, and then we need to move to the rightmost occurrence of a in p. There isn't any a in p, so we move p all the way past position $j + m - 1$. This means that we only look at every mth character and we, therefore, get a running time of $O(n/m + m)$, where the m is for the preprocessing. These two examples are, of course, extreme, but with random strings over a large alphabet, or with natural languages, the rightmost occurrence can be far to the left or even not in the string, and we achieve running times close to the best case bound.

There is another observation we can make that won't change the worst-case running time but might let us jump faster along x. If we have matched to index i and have a mismatch there, there is no reason to place p at a location where the same character will mismatch. We have the mismatching character and know where the rightmost occurrences of characters are in p, so we can jump p to a position where $p[i]$ and $x[j + i]$ will match. If the rightmost occurrence of $x[j + i]$ is at position k in p, then we can jump by $i - k$; see Figure 2-13. If the rightmost occurrence of $x[j + i]$ is to the right of i in p, then the jump would be negative, which we do not want since that moves our search backward and can in the worst case lead to an infinite loop. But if we jump the maximal length given both of the rules above, then the jump rules will always move us at least one character forward.

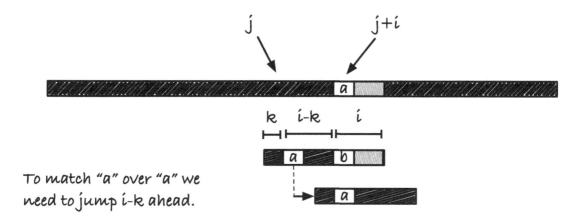

To match "a" over "a" we
need to jump i-k ahead.

Figure 2-13. *Second jump rule for BMH*

We cannot make a jump table for this rule since the length we have to jump
depends on *i* as well as the character where the mismatch occurs. So instead we store
the "rightmost occurrence" array in the iterator. We can compute both jump rules from
this. We need a way to handle characters that are not in the pattern, so we use a signed
value. That way, these characters can have index -1. Here, we assume that the length of
the pattern cannot be more than half of the string we are searching in, but this is not an
unreasonable assumption and is unlikely ever to be a problem.

```
struct bmh_match_iter {
    const uint8_t *x; uint32_t n;
    const uint8_t *p; uint32_t m;
    // Signed so we can indicate no occurrence
    int32_t rightmost[256];
    uint32_t j;
};
```

Computing the array is straightforward. We initialize the array with -1 which is what
the entries should be if a character is not found in *p*. We then run from left to right and
insert indices by their character.

```
void init_bmh_match_iter(
    struct bmh_match_iter *iter,
    const uint8_t *x, uint32_t n,
    const uint8_t *p, uint32_t m
) {
```

```
    iter->j = 0;
    iter->x = x; iter->n = n;
    iter->p = p; iter->m = m;
    for (uint32_t k = 0; k < 256; k++) {
        iter->rightmost[k] = -1;
    }
    for (uint32_t k = 0; k < m - 1; k++) {
        iter->rightmost[pattern[k]] = k;
    }
}
```

The expression for jumping occurs twice in the algorithm but is quite cumbersome to write and not informative about what is really happing, so it is a good idea to define a macro to handle it.

```
static inline uint32_t MAX(uint32_t a, uint32_t b) {
    return (((a) > (b)) ? (a) : (b));
}
#define BMH_JUMP() \
    MAX(i - iter->rightmost[x[j + i]], \
        (int32_t)m - iter->rightmost[x[j + m - 1]] - 1)
```

The various variables in the macro are not arguments but hardwired to be used inside the algorithm. This makes it easier to see what the intent of the macro is inside the function and is an approach I will often take in this book.

The function that increments the iterator uses the macro instead of the jump table from earlier, it uses a signed value for i so we can handle -1 when we get it from the rightmost array, but otherwise, there are no changes compared to the version from earlier.

```
bool next_bmh_match(
    struct bmh_match_iter *iter,
    struct match *match
) {
    // Aliasing to make the code easier to read...
    const uint8_t *x = iter->x;
    const uint8_t *p = iter->p;
```

```
uint32_t n = iter->n;
uint32_t m = iter->m;
int32_t  *rightmost  = iter->rightmost;

if (m > n) return false;
if (m == 0) return false;

// We need to handle negative numbers, and we have already
// assumed that indices into the pattern can fit into
// this type.
int32_t i = m - 1;
for (uint32_t j = iter->j;
     j < n - m + 1;
     j += BMH_JUMP()) {

    i = m - 1;
    while (i > 0 && p[i] == x[j+i]) {
        i--;
    }
    if (i == 0 && p[0] == x[j]) {
        match->pos = j;
        iter->j = j + BMH_JUMP();
        return true;
    }
}
return false;
}
```

Extended rightmost table

The two components work well for jumping along x, but the first only looks at the last match of p in x and the other only contributes to jumping if the rightmost occurrence of the mismatched character is to the left of i. We can do better than this and jump to the rightmost position *to the left of i* every time we have a mismatch. To do this, we need a table where we can look up by character and by index. If the alphabet has size k, we would have a $k \times m$ table. We can do this as still be in $O(nm)$ worst case and $O(n/m + m)$

running time, but we can save some space by having a linked list per character, and look up indices in it. Let us add such an array of lists to the iterator:

```
struct index_linked_list {
    struct index_linked_list *next;
    uint32_t data;
};
struct bmh_match_iter {
    const uint8_t *x; uint32_t n;
    const uint8_t *p; uint32_t m;
    int32_t rightmost[256];
    struct index_linked_list *rightmost_table[256];
    uint32_t j;
};
```

There is nothing unique in how a linked list is implemented. See the Appendix. We will need prepend to lists and to free them, so we write functions for that.

```
static inline struct index_linked_list *
new_index_link(
    uint32_t val,
    struct index_linked_list *tail
) {
    struct index_linked_list *link =
        malloc(sizeof(struct index_linked_list));
    link->data = val; link->next = tail;
    return link;
}

void free_index_list(
    struct index_linked_list *list
) {
    while (list) {
        struct index_linked_list *next = list->next;
        free(list);
        list = next;
    }
}
```

When we initialize an iterator, we append each position to the list found at the position's character. When we are done, each list will contain all the occurrences of the character they are associated with.

```c
void init_bmh_match_iter(
    struct bmh_match_iter *iter,
    const uint8_t *x, uint32_t n,
    const uint8_t *p, uint32_t m
) {
    iter->j = 0;
    iter->x = x; iter->n = n;
    iter->p = p; iter->m = m;
    for (uint32_t k = 0; k < 256; k++) {
        iter->rightmost[k] = -1;
        iter->rightmost_table[k] = 0;
    }
    for (uint32_t k = 0; k < m - 1; k++) {
        iter->rightmost[p[k]] = k;
        iter->rightmost_table[p[k]] =
            new_index_link(k,
                iter->rightmost_table[p[k]]);
    }
}
```

We allocate list links in the initializer, so we must free them again in the deallocator.

```c
void dealloc_bmh_match_iter(
    struct bmh_match_iter *iter
) {
    for (uint32_t k = 0; k < 256; k++) {
        free_index_list(iter->rightmost_table[k]);
    }
}
```

The positions in each list are in descending order, so if we search for the rightmost occurrence to the left of an index i, we scan until we find a position that is less than i.

```
static int32_t find_rightmost(
    struct index_linked_list *list,
    int32_t i
) {
    while (list) {
        if (list->data < i) {
            return list->data;
        }
        list = list->next;
    }
    return -1;
}
```

The iteration function doesn't change, but the BMH_JUMP() macro does. Instead of the table lookup to find the rightmost occurrence in the entire string, we use the find_rightmost() function. Otherwise, nothing is new.

```
#define BMH_JUMP() \
    MAX(i - find_rightmost( \
        iter->rightmost_table[text[j+i]], i), \
        (int32_t)m - iter->rightmost[text[j+m-1]] - 1)
```

You might object, now, that the search in the lists is not constant time, so the running time now potentially exceeds $O(nm + m)$ in the worst case. To see that this isn't so, consider how many links we have to search through. The only indices that are larger than i are those $m - i$ we scanned past before a jump. The first link after that will have an index smaller than i and we return that immediately. This means that the search in the list is not more expensive than the scan we just did in the string, so the running time is at most twice as many operations as without the lists, so worst case $O(nm + m)$ and best case $O(n/m + m)$.

Boyer-Moore

The *Boyer-Moore* (BM) algorithm adds two additional jump rules to the BMH algorithm. These exploit that we have information about a suffix of the pattern that we have matched against a substring of x. If we have matched the pattern suffix $p[i, m]$ against $x[j + i, j + m]$, then we can use knowledge about where $p[i, m]$ occurs, or partly occurs, in the pattern. We have one rule for when $p[i, m]$ occurs somewhere in p at some

$p[k, k + m - i]$. If one or more of such substrings exist, then we should move the rightmost occurrence such that it aligns with the matched part. For p to match in x, it must at least match on the $p[i, m] = p[k, k + m - i]$. Picking the rightmost matching substring means that we move the minimal distance where such a match is possible, guaranteeing that we do not skip past a potential match. Since we have a mismatch at $p[i - 1] \neq x[j + i - 1]$, we will also require that $p[i - 1] \neq p[k - 1]$. Without this requirement, we might shift to a position where we get exactly the same mismatch in the next comparison. See Figure 2-14 for the intuition for the first jump rule.

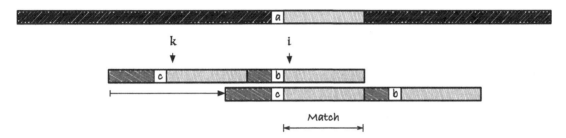

Figure 2-14. *Jump rule one*

As you can see from the figure, we shift p to the right to match up a substring with a suffix. This suffix is a border of the string $p[k, n]$. The border array we used in the first, nontrivial, algorithm gives us, for each i the longest border of $p[0, i + 1]$, and this border is a prefix of the string. We need a suffix, so we use a corresponding border array computed from the right. We call it the *reversed border array*. Since we want the preceding characters to mismatch, we modify the reversed border array the same way as for the usual border array, but from the right to take care of preceding characters. Let us call this the *restricted reversed border array*, just to have something to call it. We shall use a variant of this array to compute the first jump table. There will not always be an occurrence of $p[i, m]$ to the left of the suffix $p[i, m]$, in which case this jump rule cannot be used. When this is the case, we set the jump rule to zero. Since the character rules in the BMH algorithm ensure that we always step at least one position to the right, and we will take the largest step possible between the two rules in this section and the two rules in the previous section, we will always move forward.

The second jump table is used when the string $p[i, m]$ does not occur to the left of the suffix. If we cannot match such an occurrence against $x[j + i, j + m]$, then we can try to match a suffix of $x[j + i, j + m]$ against a border of p; see Figure 2-15. If there is no nontrivial border of p, we set the jump table distance to zero. The character-based rules will ensure that we always move forward by at least one character.

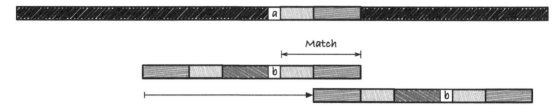

Figure 2-15. *Jump rule two*

Jump rule one

To build the jump table for the first case, it might be tempting to try to use a border array to build a jump table. For each position i in the string p, the border array tells us how long a match we have with a prefix, that is, the length of the longest string that is both a prefix and a suffix of $p[0, i]$. If we build a border array from the right instead of from the left, we know, for each position i, the length of the longest string that is both a prefix and a suffix of $p[i, m]$.

```
void compute_reverse_border_array(
    uint32_t *rba,
    const uint8_t *x,
    uint32_t m
) {
    rba[m - 1] = 0;
    for (int32_t i = m - 2; i >= 0; --i) {
        uint32_t b = rba[i+1];
        while (b > 0 && x[i] != x[m - 1 - b])
            b = rba[m - b];
        rba[i] = (x[i] == x[m - 1 - b]) ? b + 1 : 0;
    }
}
```

Here, it is easy to modify the algorithm to run from right to left instead of left to right, but in general, if you want to have a border-like structure where you can compute the left-to-right version and want the right-to-left version, you can reverse the string, build the left-to-right array, and then reverse that array. For the reverse border array, it would look like this:

```
void compute_border_array(
    const uint8_t *x,
    uint32_t m,
    uint32_t *ba
) {
    ba[0] = 0;
    for (uint32_t i = 1; i < m; ++i) {
        uint32_t b = ba[i - 1];
        while (b > 0 && x[i] != x[b])
            b = ba[b - 1];
        ba[i] = (x[i] == x[b]) ? b + 1 : 0;
    }
}

static void intarray_rev_n(uint32_t *x, uint32_t n)
{
    uint32_t *y = x + n - 1;
    while (x < y) {
        uint32_t tmp = *y;
        *y = *x;
        *x = tmp;
        x++ ; y--;
    }
}

void compute_reverse_border_array(
    const uint8_t *x,
    uint32_t m,
    uint32_t *rba
) {
    uint8_t x_copy[m];
    strncpy((char *)x_copy, (char *)x, m);
    str_inplace_rev_n(x_copy, m);
```

```
    computed_border_array(x_copy, m, rba);
    intarray_rev_n(rba, m);
}
```

Here, I have split the computation into multiple functions to make it clear what each step is. I prefer the reverse-compute-reverse strategy in most cases, because though it is slightly less efficient it greatly minimizes the work necessary to implement both directions and reduces the risk of errors since there are fewer lines of code.

You can also calculate the reversed restricted border array this way. Recall that the restricted border array is the border array where we exclude from the array the borders that are followed by the character $p[i + 1]$; we only keep borders where the letter that follows them differs. If we reverse the string, compute the restricted border array, and then reverse the result, we get the *restricted reversed border array*:

```
void computed_restricted_border_array(
    const uint8_t *x,
    uint32_t m,
    uint32_t *ba
) {
    compute_border_array(x, m, ba);
    for (uint32_t i = 0; i < m - 1; i++) {
        if (ba[i] > 0 && x[ba[i]] == x[i + 1])
            ba[i] = ba[ba[i] - 1];
    }
}

void compute_reverse_restricted_border_array(
    const uint8_t *x,
    uint32_t m,
    uint32_t *rba
) {
    uint8_t x_copy[m];
    strncpy((char *)x_copy, (char *)x, m);
    str_inplace_rev_n(x_copy, m);
    computed_restricted_border_array(x_copy, m, rba);
    intarray_rev_n(rba, m);
}
```

Now, when we have the restricted reverse border array, we can scan from left to right and make a pointer from where a suffix ends (where we might have a mismatch in the algorithm) to the position of the border inside the pattern—perhaps something like this (see Figure 2-16):

```
for (uint32_t i = 0; i < m - 1; i++) {
    jump[n - xrba[i] - 1] = n - xrba[i] - i;
}
```

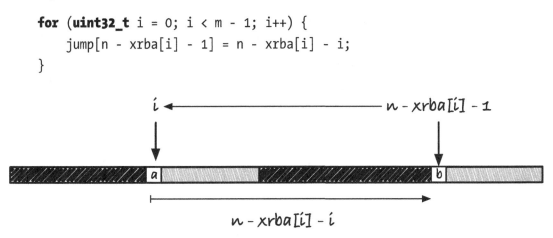

Figure 2-16. *Jump table based on reverse borders*

We go from left to right and let each suffix that also occurs internally in *p* and know about the position where it occurs. We do not add the matching part of the suffix to the jump table since we want to jump when we have a mismatch, so we get the index at the position left of the matching suffix. At the matching suffix, we insert in the jump table the length we should jump, $n - \text{xrba}[i] - i$. Because we do this from left to right, if there is more than one occurrence, we will get the rightmost one.

That this algorithm computes the jump table sounds convincing, and I have seen this implemented numerous times, which is why I mention it. There is a problem, however: several borders can end at the same rightmost index. Consider the string *dabcacabca*. Figure 2-17 shows the reverse border array on the left and the restricted reverse border array on the right (the reverse border array where the previous character differs between the suffix and the border). If we build a jump table from the reverse border array, we would get a jump for the two nonzero values; see the two arrows on the top of Figure 2-18. We would not see the jump at the bottom because it jumps to an index where a longer border starts.

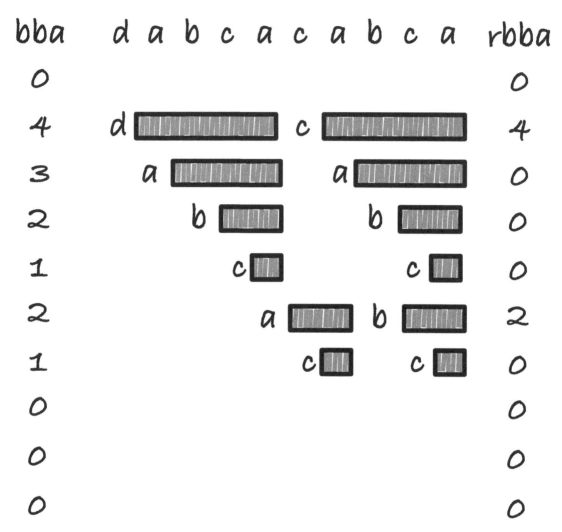

Figure 2-17. *Example of backward border array and restricted backward border arrays*

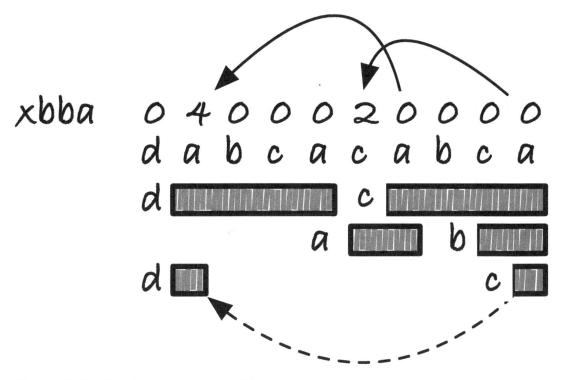

Figure 2-18. *Border array jump table*

Each index in our pattern can be the endpoint of multiple borders. If we follow the preceding idea, we only set a jump pointer to the longest border. If there are several suffixes of the pattern where the rightmost occurrence in the pattern starts at the same position, then only the longest match will get a jump rule. These borders, however, will have different endpoints; see Figure 2-19.[1] These are unique—two different borders can't have the same endpoint. Imagine two borders with the same endpoint and consider their start points. Where the shortest starts, there must be a mismatch between the start point and the border at the suffix. If not, the border would be longer and the start point further to the left. This, however, contradicts that the longer border must match, or it would be shorter. See Figure 2-20. If the longer light-gray string is a border, then it must

---

[1]If we were looking simply at borders, then the shorter substrings would not be rightmost in the figure. The shorter strings are borders of the longer borders and thus found at both ends of these. Therefore, there are occurrences before the end of string, namely, at the left end of the longer borders. The rightmost occurrences are therefore not those that match the start index. With the *restricted* border arrays, however, it *is* possible to be in the situation illustrated in the figure.

match the "a" in the suffix. The character that precedes the shorter string must therefore also be "a", contradicting that it could be another character. So while start points for rightmost occurrences of suffixes are not unique, the endpoints are.

Figure 2-19. *Point to border endpoints rather than start points*

Figure 2-20. *Uniqueness of endpoints*

There is an array, called the *Z array*, that captures the essence of the start point/ endpoint difference. The array is very similar to the border array, but at each index i, it stores the length, k, of the longest string $p[i, i + k]$ that starts in index i (not ends, as the border array) and is a prefix of p, that is, $p[0, k] = p[i, i + k]$; see Figure 2-21. We do not want an array of strings that matches prefixes but rather one that matches suffixes, that is, we want an array Z' where $Z'[i]$ contains the length of the longest substring $[i - k, i]$ that matches a suffix of p, that is, $p[i - k, i] = p[n - k, n]$. This is the reverse of the Z array of the reversed string p, so we can compute it assuming we have a function `compute_z_ array()` that computes the Z array.

```
void compute_reverse_z_array(
    const uint8_t *x,
    uint32_t m,
    uint32_t *Z
) {
    uint8_t x_copy[m + 1];
    strncpy((char *)x_copy, (char *)x, m); x_copy[m] = 0;
    str_inplace_rev_n(x_copy, m);
    compute_z_array(x_copy, m, Z);
    intarray_rev_n(Z, m);
}
```

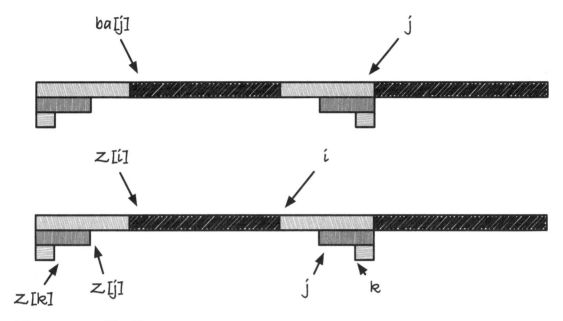

Figure 2-21. *The Z array*

In the Z array, $p[0, Z[i]] = p[i, i + Z[i]]$ is the longest border of $p[0, i + Z[i]]$. We cannot extend it to the longest border of $p[0, i + Z[i]+1]$ because $p[Z[i]+1] \neq p[i + Z[i]+1]$ since otherwise the longest string starting in i that matches a prefix of p would be at least one longer. With the Z array, we get the "restricted border" effect for free in this sense. For the reversed Z array, the same is true but for the letter that precedes the border strings.

Computing the Z array

The trivial algorithm for computing the Z array simply matches the string at each position against the first part of our string, giving us an $O(n^2)$ running time.

```
uint32_t match(
    const uint8_t * s1,
    const uint8_t * s2
) {
    uint32_t n = 0;
    while (*s1 && *s2 && (*s1 == *s2)) {
        ++s1;
        ++s2;
        ++n;
    }
```

```
        return n;
}

void trivial_compute_z_array(
        const uint8_t *x,
        uint32_t n,
        uint32_t *Z
) {
        Z[0] = 0;
        for (uint32_t i = 1; i < n; ++i) {
                Z[i] = match(x, x + i);
        }
}
```

The match() function works on pointers to strings and compares them as long as they haven't reached the null sentinel and as long as they agree on the current character. If our string consists of only one character, $x = a^n$, then match() will run through the entire string $x[i, n]$ which averaged over all the indices as $O(n)$, giving us a total running time of $O(n^2)$. We can do better!

In a linear-time construction algorithm, we iteratively consider indices $k = 0, 1, ..., n - 1$ and compute $Z[k]$ using the previously computed values. We let l and r denote the leftmost index and one past the right index, respectively, of the rightmost string we have seen so far. As invariants in the algorithm, we have for all $k' < k$ that $Z[k']$ is computed and available and that l and r index the rightmost string $r[l, l + Z[l]]$ seen so far.

There are three cases to consider; see Figure 2-22. The first is when the index we are computing is to the right of r. We can get in this situation if we have seen a rightmost string pointed to by l and r, but the following ks gave us empty borders. To get $Z[k]$ we must compare x with $x + k$ to get the matching length. If this length is zero, we set $Z[k]$ to zero and move to $k + 1$. If the match result is greater than zero, we set $Z[k]$ to the value and move l to k and r to $k + Z[k]$; the rightmost string we have seen is now then one starting in k, and the updated indices will point at it.

In the other two cases, k is between l and r. This means that the string $x[l, r]$ contains information about the string starting in k that we can exploit. Let $k' = k - l$ and $r' = r - l$. If we look at $Z[k']$—which, by the invariant, is available—there are two possibilities. Either $Z[k'] < r'-k' = r-k$ in which case the string starting in k' stops before index r'. This means that there is a mismatch between $x[Z[k'] + 1]$ and $x[k' + Z[k'] + 1]$; see the middle case in

Figure 2-22. Since $x[l, r]$ is a prefix of x, the mismatching character will also follow the string $x[k, k + Z[z']]$ which means that the longest string matching a prefix and starting in k will have the length $Z[k']$. We update $Z[k] = Z[k']$ and leave l and r alone; the string pointed to by l and r is still the rightmost.

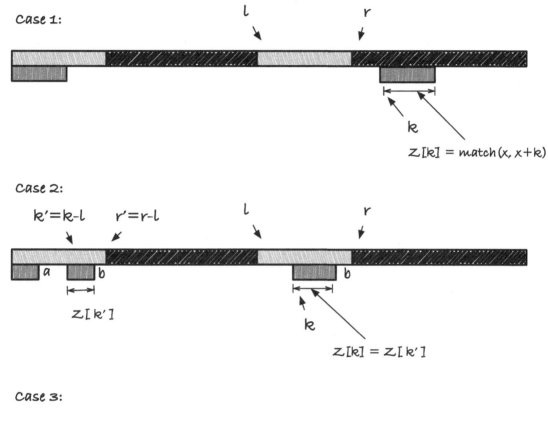

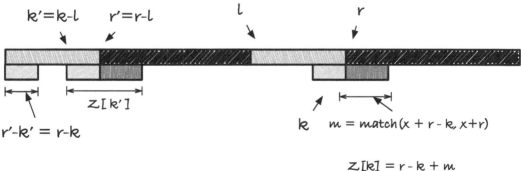

Figure 2-22. *The three cases for the Z array construction algorithm*

Case three is when the string starting at index k' continues past index r'. In this case, we know that a prefix of the string matches a suffix of the string $x[l, r]$, but we do not know how much further the prefix will match the string starting at index k. To find out where, we must do a character-by-character match. We do not need to start this search at index 1 and k, however. We know that the first $r - k$ characters match, so we can start our match at indices $r - k$ and r; see case three in Figure 2-22. When we have found the right string, we update the left pointer to point at the start of it, $l = k$, and we set the right pointer to the end of the string $r = k + Z[k]$.

An implementation can look like this:

```
void compute_z_array(
    const uint8_t *x,
    uint32_t n,
    uint32_t *Z
) {
    Z[0] = 0;
    if (n == 1) return; // special case
    Z[1] = match(x, x + 1);
    uint32_t l = 1;
    uint32_t r = l + Z[1];

    for (uint32_t k = 2; k < n; ++k) {
        // Case 1:
        if (k >= r) {
            Z[k] = match(x, x + k);
            if (Z[k] > 0) { l = k; r = k + Z[k]; }

        } else {
            uint32_t kk = k - l;
            if (Z[kk] < r - k) {
                // Case 2:
                Z[k] = Z[kk];
            } else {
```

```
                // Case 3
                Z[k] = r - k + match(x + r - k, x + r);
                l = k;
                r = k + Z[k];
            }
        }
    }
}
```

To see that the running time is linear, first ignore the calls to match(). If we do, we can see that there are a constant number of operations in each case, so without matching, we clearly have a linear running time. To handle match(), we do not consider how much we match in each iteration—something that depends on the string and that we do not have much control over. Instead, we consider the sum of all matches in a run of the algorithm. We never call match() in the second case, so we need only to consider cases one and three. Here, the key observation is that we only search to the right of r and never twice with the same starting position.

In case one, we either have a mismatch on the first character, or we get a new string back. In the first case, we leave l and r alone and immediately move to the next k, which we will use as the starting point for the next match. As long as we are not getting a string back from our matching, we use constant time for match() calls for each k, and we never call match() on the same index twice. If we get a string, we move the right pointer, r, to the end of this string. We will never see the indices to the left of r again because both case one and three never search to the left of r. In the search in case three and a nontrivial result in case one, we always move r past all indices we have started a search in earlier.

Z-based jump table

The jump rule needs to slide p to the rightmost position where we potentially have a match. If i is where the rightmost occurrence sits, then index $i - rZ[i]$ is the character just before the start of the occurrence. If there is no occurrence, we set the jump distance to zero, which leaves it up to one of the other jump rules. The prefix it matches starts at position $n - rZ[i]$, and it is when we have a mismatch $p[i - rZ[i]] \neq p[n - rZ[i] - 1]$

we should move p. Therefore, we want to store the jump distance for index $n-rZ[i]-1$ in our jump table. The distance we need to jump is the one that places $i-rZ[i]$ at position $n-rZ[i]-1$, so $n-rZ[i]-q-(i-rZ[i]) = n-i-1$. See Figure 2-23 for an illustration of the jump rule and Figure 2-24 for a concrete example.

We build the jump table as follows: We first set all the entries to zero—the default that will give the other jump rules control of the jump—and after that, we compute the reverse Z array and set the jump values as described earlier.

```
uint32_t rZ[m];
compute_reverse_z_array(iter->pattern, m, rZ);
uint32_t jump1[m];
for (uint32_t i = 0; i < m; i++) {
    jump1[i] = 0;
}
for (uint32_t i = 0; i < m; i++) {
    jump1[m - rZ[i] - 1] = m - i - 1;
}
```

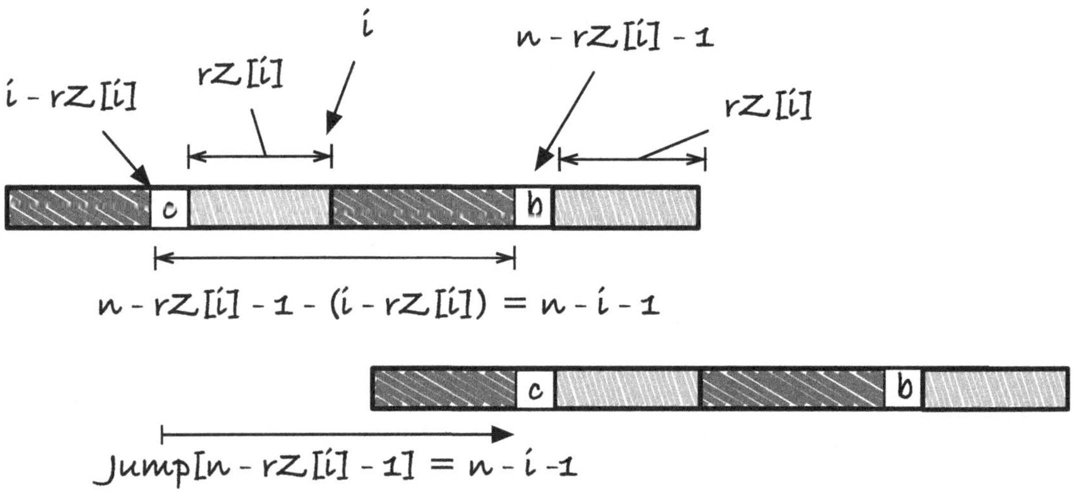

Figure 2-23. *First jump rule for Boyer-Moore*

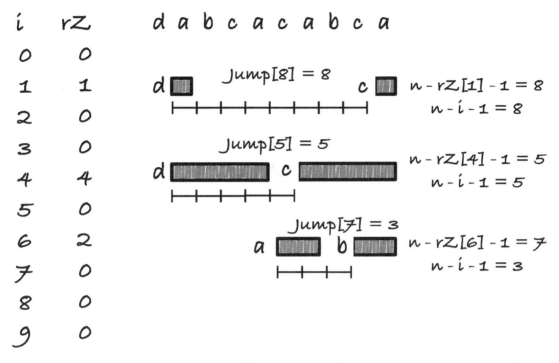

Figure 2-24. *Boyer-Moore jump table one example*

We do this in the iterator initialization. We will see the full initialization later when we have seen the second jump table as well.

We do not test for whether the reverse Z value is zero. In this case, we want the jump to be zero (so we will use one of the other jump rules), but whenever Z *is* zero, the loop will update the last index, $n - rZ[i] - 1 = n - 1$. In the final iteration, we will write $n - i - 1 = n - (n - 1) - 1 = 0$ there, exactly as desired.

Second jump table

The second jump rule is used where there are no occurrences of the matched string inside the pattern. When this is the case, we should move the minimal amount necessary to match a prefix of the pattern with a suffix of the matched text; see Figure 2-15. If we have the border array for the pattern, then the longest border of the entire string is ba[$m - 1$], the second-longest border is ba[ba[$m - 1$]], and so on. When we have a mismatch, we need to jump such that the longest border possible matches the longest suffix of the text we already matched. If we have matched more than ba[$m - 1$] characters, then we should align the longest border with the matched string. If we have matched less than ba[$m - 1$], then we should not align this border; it will only give us a mismatch at the same position we just mismatched on. Instead, we should use the second-longest border for the jump. In general, every time we have a mismatch between borders b_i and b_{i+1} (with b_{i+1} the shortest), then we should use the shorter of the two, b_{i+1}; see Figure 2-25. The distance we need to move when using border b is m minus its length, that is, $m - b$.

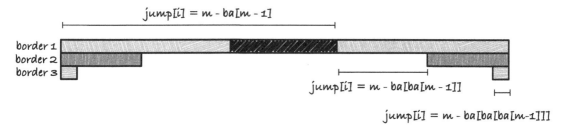

Figure 2-25. *Jump ranges for jump rule two*

We include the border of size zero in this preprocessing. It will guarantee us that if we have matched a string that cannot be matched anywhere else in the pattern, then we skip the entire string past the current attempted match.

Computing this jump table, once we have the border array, is straightforward.

```
uint32_t ba[m];
compute_border_array(iter->pattern, m, ba);
uint32_t jump2[m];
uint32_t b - ba[m - 1];
uint32_t jump = m - b;
for (uint32_t i = 0; i < m; i++) {
    if (i > b) {
        b = ba[b];
        jump = m - b;
    }
    jump2[i] = jump;
}
```

Combining the jump rules

We cannot take the maximum jump of the two jump tables here, unlike in the BMH algorithm where we can jump the maximum number of characters given by the two rules. We should not move to a border of the full string if there is an internal string that matches. This means that we should only use the second rule if we cannot use the first, that is, we use jump table two when jump table one is zero. We can combine the two jump tables, and only use the second if the first is zero, in this way:

```
// Combine the jump tables
iter->jump = malloc(m * sizeof(uint32_t));
for (uint32_t i = 0; i < m; ++i) {
    iter->jump[i] = jump1[i] ? jump1[i] : jump2[i];
}
```

With all these jump tables, the Boyer-Moore algorithm is more complicated than the previous algorithms. Still, if we put the border and Z array functionality in separate functions, then the BM iterator is not overly complex to initialize and use.

Let us combine everything we have seen. We add a jump table to the iterator:

```
struct bm_match_iter {
    const uint8_t *x; uint32_t n;
    const uint8_t *p; uint32_t m;
    int32_t rightmost[256];
    struct index_linked_list *rightmost_table[256];
    uint32_t *jump;
    uint32_t j;
};
```

When we initialize the iterator, we compute the two tables from the BMH algorithm; then we compute the two jump tables, using a reversed Z array and a reversed border array, respectively; and finally we combine the two tables.

```
void init_bm_match_iter(
    struct bm_match_iter *iter,
    const uint8_t *x, uint32_t n,
    const uint8_t *p, uint32_t m
) {
```

```
    iter->j = 0;
    iter->x = x; iter->n = n;
    iter->p = p; iter->m = m;
    for (uint32_t k = 0; k < 256; k++) {
        iter->rightmost[k] = -1;
        iter->rightmost_table[k] = 0;
    }
    for (uint32_t k = 0; k < m - 1; k++) {
        iter->rightmost[p[k]] = k;
        iter->rightmost_table[p[k]] =
            new_index_link(k,
                iter->rightmost_table[p[k]]);
    }

    uint32_t jump1[m];
    uint32_t jump2[m];

    for (uint32_t i = 0; i < m; i++) {
        jump1[i] = 0;
    }
    uint32_t rZ[m];
    compute_reverse_z_array(iter->p, m, rZ);
    for (uint32_t i = 0; i < m; i++) {
        // We don't have to check if rZ[i] - 0.
        // There, we will always write into n-0-1,
        // i.e., the last character in the string.
        // For the last index we set this to n - i - 1
        // which is zero. When this jump is zero,
        // one of the other rules will be used.
        jump1[m - rZ[i] - 1] = m - i - 1;
    }
    for (uint32_t i = 0; i < m; i++) {
        jump2[i] = 0;
    }
    uint32_t ba[m];
    compute_border_array(iter->p, m, ba);
```

```
    // Combine the jump tables
    iter->jump = malloc(m * sizeof(uint32_t));
    for (uint32_t i = 0; i < m; ++i) {
        iter->jump[i] = jump1[i] ? jump1[i] : jump2[i];
    }
}
```

We use a macro for jumping; in this case, we want the maximum of the jump table increment and the increment we get from the BMH tables. The function that increments the iterator should use this macro instead of BMH_JUMP(), but otherwise there are no changes.

```
#define BM_JUMP() MAX(iter->jump[i], BMH_JUMP())
```

This is the only change we need to make to the next_bmh_match() function to get next_bm_match():

```
bool next_bm_match(
    struct bm_match_iter *iter,
    struct match *match
) {
    // Aliasing to make the code easier to read...
    const uint8_t *x = iter->x;
    const uint8_t *p = iter->p;
    uint32_t n = iter->n;
    uint32_t m = iter->m;

    if (m > n) return false;
    if (m == 0) return false;

    // We need to handle negative numbers, and we have already
    // assumed that indices into the pattern can fit into
    // this type.
    int32_t i = m - 1;
    for (uint32_t j = iter->j; j < n - m + 1; j += BM_JUMP()) {

        i = m - 1;
        while (i > 0 && p[i] == x[j + i]) {
            i--;
        }
```

```
        if (i == 0 && p[0] == x[j]) {
            match->pos = j;
            iter->j = j + BM_JUMP();
            return true;
        }
    }
    return false;
}
```

Since we allocate the jump table in the initialize, we need to free it in the deallocation function.

```
void dealloc_bm_match_iter(
    struct bm_match_iter *iter
) {
    for (uint32_t k = 0; k < 256; k++) {
        free_index_list(iter->rightmost_table[k]);
    }
    free(iter->jump);
}
```

Aho-Corasick

The Aho-Corasick algorithm differs from the previous algorithms in that it does not only search for a single pattern but search simultaneously for a set of patterns. The algorithm uses a data structure, a *trie* (short for re*trie*val), that can store a set of strings and provide efficient lookups to determine if a given string is in the set.

Tries

A trie, also known as a prefix tree, is a tree where each edge holds a letter and where no child has more than one out edge with the same letter. Going from the root and down, you can read off all prefixes of one or more of the strings in the set, and when you have seen a full string from the set, you reach a node that is tagged with the string label from the set; see Figure 2-26.

If you want all your strings to sit in leaves—something that can be useful in certain algorithms—then you can add a sentinel to the strings; see Figure 2-27. This will place all strings in leaves, and if the strings are unique, you will get a one-to-one mapping between the leaves of the tree and the strings it contains. If you have duplicated strings, they will still end up in leaves, but there will no longer be a one-to-one mapping. No amount of trickery will prevent identical strings from ending up in the same node, so some leaves will correspond to multiple strings.

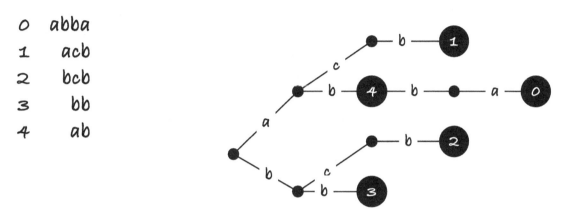

Figure 2-26. *The trie data structure*

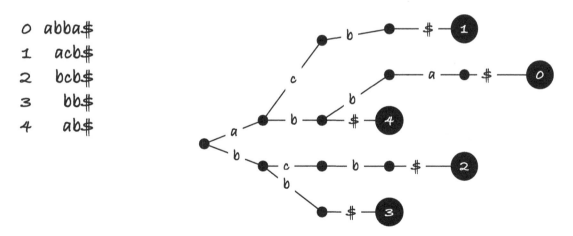

Figure 2-27. *A trie with sentinel strings*

One way to represent a trie is to have nodes that store the letter on their incoming edges, a string label if the node corresponds to a string in the set, a pointer to its parent, and pointers to its siblings and its children.

```
struct trie {
    uint8_t in_edge_label;
    int string_label;
    struct trie *parent;
    struct trie *sibling;
    struct trie *children;
};
```

The parent pointer isn't needed in many algorithms, but we need it in the Aho-Corasick algorithm, so I have included it here. As an example, Figure 2-28 is the representation of the trie in Figure 2-26. Notice that the child pointer points to tries. This is because all sub-tries are also tries themselves.

When we initialize a trie, we set the edge label to zero—we will change it to the correct label later—and we set the string label to minus one, the default number that indicates that the path to the node is not a string in the set the trie stores. The three pointers are set to default values: null.

```
void init_trie(
    struct trie *trie
) {
    trie->in_edge_label = '\0';
    trie->string_label = -1;
    trie->parent = 0;
    trie->sibling = 0;
    trie->children = 0;
}

struct trie *alloc_trie(void)
{
    struct trie *trie =
        malloc(sizeof(struct trie));
    init_trie(trie);
    return trie;
}
```

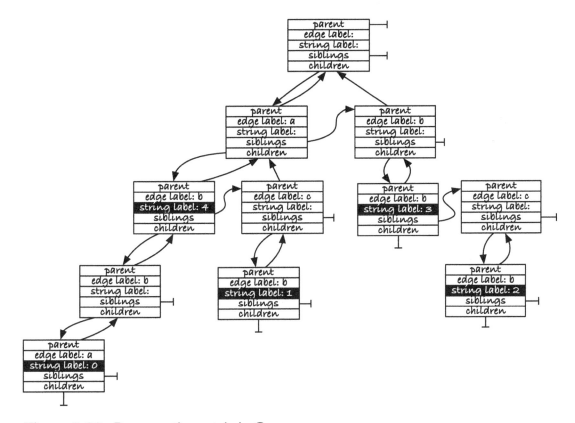

Figure 2-28. *Representing a trie in C*

I have written two functions for initializing tries, one that assumes that you have already allocated a root `struct trie` structure and one that does it for you. When you want a new trie, you create its root using one of these functions. The root has no siblings, but it will have children once we add strings to it.

When we deallocate a trie, we recursively delete children and siblings. We free them because the construct algorithms—see the following function—heap allocate the subnodes.

```
void dealloc_trie(
    struct trie *trie
) {
    // Depth-first traversal freeing the trie.
    if (trie->children)
        free_trie(trie->children);
```

```
    if (trie->sibling)
        free_trie(trie->sibling);
}

void free_trie(
    struct trie *trie
) {
    dealloc_trie(trie);
    free(trie);
}
```

To construct a trie, we insert the input set string by string. When we add the string p_i, we search down the trie, T, and either find an existing node at the end of p_i, or we find that we cannot continue searching beyond some point k, that is, $p_i[0, k]$ matches, but there is no edge with character label $p_i[k]$. In the first case, we set the node's `string_label` to i, and in the second case, we must insert the string $p_i[k, m]$ in the node we reached before we couldn't go any longer. So the straightforward approach is to find out where the string sits or where it branches off the trie and insert it there.

Whenever we need to add a substring to a node, the trie we add is a string of nodes with no branching. We can build such a trie using the following function:

```
static struct trie *
string_to_trie(
    const uint8_t *str,
    int string_label
) {
    const uint8_t *s = str;
    while (*s) s++;

    struct trie *trie = 0;
    do {
        s--;
        struct trie *new_node = alloc_trie();
        new_node->in_edge_label = *s;
        new_node->string_label = string_label;
        new_node->children = trie;
```

```
    if (trie) trie->parent = new_node;
    trie = new_node;

    string_label = -1; // so we only label the leaf...

} while (s != str);

    return trie;
}
```

It starts from the end of the string and iteratively constructs a node for each letter, and sets that node's child to the previous node we created. It sets the string label in the root and then updates the `string_label` variable, so the remaining nodes will be set to -1 indicating that they are not representing a string.

Constructing a trie from a string is useful when we build a trie from a single sequence or when we need to add the suffix of a string to an existing node. To search, we need to find which edge to follow for each node in the trie. The following function does that by iterationg through all children w. The w variable is set to the child of the node, and we iterate through the children via their sibling pointers.

```
struct trie *out_link(
    struct trie *v,
    uint8_t label
) {
    for (struct trie *w = v->children;
         w; w = w->sibling) {
        if (w->in_edge_label == label)
            return w;
    }
    return 0;
}
```

With these two helper functions, we can write a function for adding a string to a trie. It will first check if the trie has any children. If not, we build a trie for the string and insert it as the child of the original node. If there are children, we start the search. For each letter in the string, we get the out edge of the current node and update the current node to be the output child. We abort the loop if we find a mismatch or reach the end of our string. If we reach the end of the string—this happens when *str == 0—then we set the string label. If we do not reach the end of the string, we have found a node that doesn't have the next character as an edge label. We can take the suffix of the pattern after the mismatch and build a (single string) trie from it and then add it to the children of the node where we got the mismatch.

```c
void add_string_to_trie(
    struct trie *trie,
    const uint8_t *str,
    int string_label
) {
    if (!trie->children) { // first string is a special case
        trie->children = string_to_trie(str, string_label);
        trie->children->parent = trie;
        return;
    }

    while (*str) {
        struct trie *child = out_link(trie, *str);
        if (!child) {
            break;
        } else {
            trie = child;
            str++;
        }
    }

    if (*str == '\0') {
        // The string was already in the trie --
        // update with label.
        // We only allow this when the
        // string wasn't already inserted!
        assert(trie->string_label < 0);
        trie->string_label = string_label;

    } else {
        // Insert new suffix as a child of parent
        struct trie *new_suffix =
```

```
            string_to_trie(str, string_label);
        new_suffix->sibling = trie->children;
        trie->children = new_suffix;
        new_suffix->parent = trie;
    }
}
```

If you want to know if a string is in the trie, then you can search down in it. If there is a node where you cannot continue, the string is not in the trie. On the other hand, if you reach the end of the string, you are in a node. If this node has a string label, then the string is in the trie; otherwise, it is not. The following two functions implement this idea:

```
struct trie *get_trie_node(
    struct trie *trie,
    const uint8_t *str
) {
    if (!trie->children) return 0;

    while (*str) {
        struct trie *child = out_link(trie, *str);
        if (!child) {
            return 0; // we can't find the string
        } else {
            trie = child;
            str++;
        }
    }
    return trie;
}

bool string_in_trie(
    struct trie *trie,
    const uint8_t *str
) {
    struct trie *t  = get_trie_node(trie, str);
    return t && (t->string_label >= 0);
}
```

I split them into two functions because you sometimes want to get the node where a string is so you can do something with it. You cannot use `get_trie_node()` directly as a test. It returns a node or null, so you can test if there is a node on the path given by the string, but to test if it is in the trie's set of strings, you must also check the string label. The `string_in_trie()` function does that.

First, assume that we can always find the out edge with a given symbol in constant time. We use linked lists for this, so on the surface this doesn't seem to be the case, but we will always assume that the alphabet is of constant size, making a list search a constant time operation. When we insert pattern p_i of length m_i, we will in worst case search down m_i steps down the trie, so if $m = \sum_i m_i$, then the running time for constructing a trie is $O(m)$.

The Aho-Corasick (AC) algorithm works similarly to the KMP algorithm. It scans along the string x (using an index j) and searches down the trie at the same time. We increment the index j every time we see a match in the trie—and never decrement it— and we move the trie along x every time we have a mismatch in the trie; see Figure 2-29.

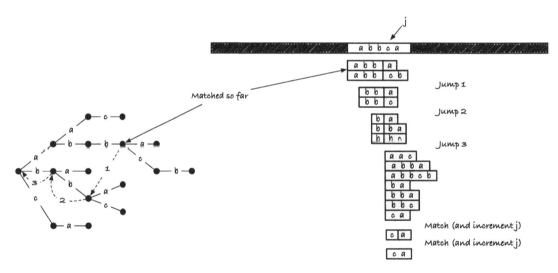

Figure 2-29. *Matching and mismatching in Aho-Corasick*

When we match along x, we move down the trie, matching character by character. All strings below the current position in the trie can potentially match x. If we have a mismatch, we need to move the trie to the right to the next position where we can potentially match. Consider any string you can read by concatenating the edge labels from the root and down the trie. That is, consider any string in the trie but not necessarily one labelled with the strings the trie contains. For such a string, p, let $f(p)$ denote the longest proper suffix of p that you can also find in the trie. We call this mapping from p to $f(p)$ the *failure link* of p because we will use it when we fail at matching deeper into the trie than p.

This definition of failure links sounds more complicated than the function really is. It matches the borders we used in the algorithms earlier, except that it uses a trie form of borders. When we have a mismatch, we want to move the trie to the right such that we have a match between the prefix of some of the strings in the trie and the part of x we are matching against. If you take p and all its suffixes, $p[1, m], p[2, m], p[3, m], ..., p[m, m]$, then $f(p)$ is the longest that you can find in the trie, that is, the longest of the suffixes such that if you search down the trie, you will reach the end of the string before you see a mismatch. For each node in the trie, v, we have a mapping from the string it represents and that string's failure link. In the following, I have listed failure links for the leaves in the trie in Figure 2-29, and for the inner nodes, we jump from when we mismatch.

p	$f(p)$
aac	ϵ
abbcb	b
ba	a
bba	ba
bbc	c
ca	a
abb	bb
bb	b
B	ϵ
abba	bba

Recall that ϵ denotes the empty string.

In the Aho-Corasick algorithm, we will represent failure links as pointers from each node to its failure link node. For nodes where the failure link is empty, we will set the pointer to point at the root of the trie. We will compute the failure nodes in a preprocessing step. Whenever we have a mismatch in the algorithm, we will move from the current node to its failure link—conceptually moving the trie further along x.

A version of the algorithm could look like this:

```c
void aho_corasick_match(
    const char *x,
    uint32_t n,
    struct trie *patterns
) {
    uint32_t j = 0;
    struct trie *v = patterns;

    while (j < n) {
        struct trie *w = out_link(v, x[j]);
        while (w) {
            // The matching part
            if (w->string_label >= 0) {
                // String hits->string_label ends in
                // index j. If we know the length
                // of hits->string_label, we could
                // report the beginning.
                // We will do so in the iterator
                // code.
                REPORT(w->string_label, j);
            }

            v = w;
            j++;
            w = out_link(v, x[j]);
        }

        // When we get here, we do not match
        // any longer
        if (is_trie_root(v)) {
            j++;
```

```
        } else {
            v = v->failure_link;
        }
    }
}
```

We search down the trie by, at each step, getting the out edge that matches the $x[j]$ we are looking at. The function we use is this:

```
struct trie *out_link(
    struct trie *v,
    uint8_t label
) {
    for (struct trie *w = v->children; w; w = w->sibling) {
        if (w->in_edge_label == label)
            return w;
    }
    return 0;
}
```

When we see a match to one of the strings in the trie, that is, a node with a nonnegative string label, we report a match. When it happens, j points to the *end* of the match and that is what we report (we will change that at the end of the chapter). When we have a mismatch, that is, we cannot find a node with the out label we want, then the matching phase ends and we need to move the matching trie. We have a special case if we are at the root. There, the failure link goes back to the root again, and we would not move if we used it. So if we are at the root, we increase j instead of jumping in the trie. We test if we are at the root by testing whether the trie has a parent:

```
static inline bool is_trie_root(
    struct trie *trie
) {
    return trie->parent == 0;
}
```

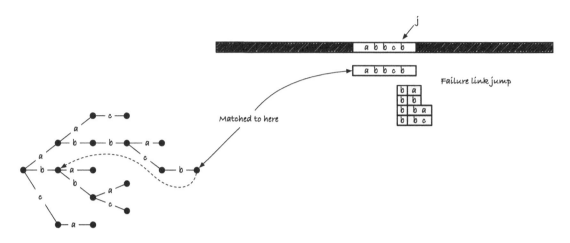

Figure 2-30. *Problem with missing matches when one string is a substring of another*

If there are no strings that are substrings of others, this algorithm works. However, when one string is a substring of another, the algorithm can skip the string completely. Consider Figure 2-30. We have matched *abbcb*, and we will then have a mismatch (because we cannot go any further from that node in the trie). The mismatch means we jump to the failure link, which is the string *b*. It is from here we will continue our search. We are now in the sub-trie with the root *b*. Not all nodes in the trie will have a string label but assume for the example that *bb* has. That means that we should report occurrences of it, and if the next character is *b* we will do so. However, we have already encountered it in the string we have scanned, but we never reported it there because we were elsewhere in the trie when we encountered it, specifically in the node *abb*. With the shift from the failure link, we have moved past that position entirely, and we are not coming back. Substrings are a problem.

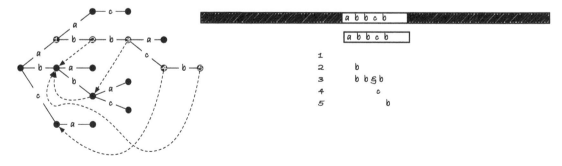

Figure 2-31. *Output lists and matches*

What we want to do is output all strings that match at a position, and all such strings can be found by traversing the failure links of the nodes; see Figure 2-31. All strings that match from a node we have reached in the trie must be suffixes of the current string in the trie, and we can get all of them by running through the failure link.

When we match the first character in *abbcb*, we do not match any additional string in the trie, but when we match *ab*, we also have a match of *b* that ends in this position. We can get that from following the failure link. When we match *abb*, we should also report a match of *bb* and *b*, and we can get those by following the failure link twice, first for *bb* and then for *b*. When we match *c*, we should report *c*, and again we can see this using the failure link. Finally, when we match the last *b* in the string, we should report *b* as well as the full string. Unlike in this example, we do not want to output all nodes we can find from the failure links but only those with a nonnegative string label. So we skip those that do not by pointing to the next that does. The list we get from doing this is what we call the *output list*.

For each string v in the tree, you can go through the failure links $v, f(v), f^2(v), ..., f^n(v)$ from the node up to the root. Each link, by definition, is closer to the root than the previous, so we will eventually get there. From the nodes you see on this path, extract those with a nonnegative string label. That is the output list.

To see that we output all matches that end at index j when we run through the output list, observe that when we move through the failure links, we get all the strings that match a suffix of the string we are looking at. To see that we do not miss any strings we should emit a match for, observe that every time we jump a failure link, we get the longest possible match, and therefore we cannot jump over another match.

Adding the output lists to the search algorithm, we get this:

```c
void aho_corasick_match(
    const uint8_t *x,
    uint32_t n,
    struct trie *patterns
) {
    uint32_t j = 0;
    struct trie *v = patterns;

    while (j < n) {
        struct trie *w = out_link(v, x[j]);
```

```
    while (w) {
        for (struct output_list *hits = w->output;
            hits != 0;
            hits = hits->next) {
            // hits->string_label ends in j
            REPORT(hits->string_label, j);
        }

        v = w;
        j++;
        w = out_link(v, x[j]);
    }

    if (is_trie_root(v)) {
        j++;
    } else {
        v = v->failure_link;
    }
}
}
```

This time we do the traversal as before, but in each node, we run through the output list before we do anything else. We do not check the string label except for reporting the output; we know that we only have hits in the output list. Except for the loop through the output list, there is nothing new in the function.

Preprocessing

Before we see the final version of the algorithm, we will see how to add the failure link and the output list to the trie data structure. First, of course, we need to add them to the trie structure:

```
struct output_list {
    int string_label;
    struct output_list *next;
};
```

```
struct trie {
    uint8_t in_edge_label;
    int string_label;
    struct trie *parent;
    struct trie *sibling;
    struct trie *children;

    // For Aho-Corasick
    struct trie *failure_link;
    struct output_list *output;
};
```

We initialize them with null pointers:

```
void init_trie(struct trie *trie)
{
    trie->in_edge_label = '\0';
    trie->string_label = -1;
    trie->parent = 0;
    trie->sibling = 0;
    trie->children = 0;

    // For Aho-Corasick
    trie->failure_link = 0;
    trie->output = 0;
}
```

To set all failure links and the output lists, we will traverse the trie in a breadth-first manner. In that way, whenever we see a node in the trie, its parent and all the nodes closer to the root will already have their failure link and output list set.

Consider a node, v, and let $p(v)$ be its parent and $f(p(v))$ be the failure link of v's parent. Node v is the string $p(v)$ followed by some letter a (see Figure 2-32 a). The failure link of v must be a suffix of $p(v)$ followed by a. It cannot be a longer string since this would contradict that $f(p(v))$ is the longest suffix of $p(v)$ that is in the trie; we would be able to get a longer one by adding the first part of the failure link of v (see Figure 2-32 b).

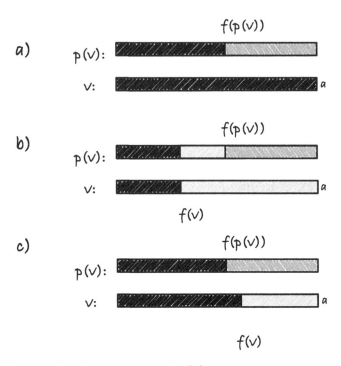

Figure 2-32. *Relationship between v and p(v)*

Therefore, $f(v)$ must start with a suffix of $p(v)$ (Figure 2-32 c). It might not be the longest suffix of $p(v)$ with an a concatenated—there might not be an out edge of $f(p(v))$ with label a, but it will be some suffix, and we can get all suffixes of $p(v)$ following failure links, and we want to pick the longest one.

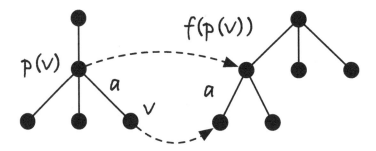

Figure 2-33. *Jumping the failure link of a parent to get the failure link of a child*

To set the failure link for node v, we first exploit that the parent of the node will have a failure link, so we can jump to the node it points to, $f(p(v))$. If we can find an out edge there that matches a, then the node at the end of the out edge will be v's failure link. We have the longest suffix of $p(v)$ that is in the trie, and we must have a suffix of $p(v)$ as the initial sequence to the failure link of v, $f(v)$. If we can extend it with a, we have the longest suffix of $p(v)$ plus a so the longest suffix of v in the trie; see Figure 2-33. If we cannot extend $f(p(v))$, then we take the next longest suffix of $p(v)$ in the trie, $f(f(p(v)))$, and try there, and we continue following failure links until we find one that we can extend. If we handle nodes in a breadth-first manner, we are guaranteed that all nodes closer to the root than v will have their failure link set, so we have $f(p(v))$ and all $f^n(p(v))$ set since these will be higher in the trie; they are suffixes of $p(v)$ and must, therefore, be shorter strings and thus higher in the trie. If there are no places we can extend, then the only option we have is to set the failure link to the root.

To implement a breadth-first traversal of the trie, we need a queue structure. The `pointer_queue` data structure can be found in the Appendix; the operations you can do on it are what you would expect of a queue, that is, it is a first-in, first-out data structure, `enqueue_pointer()` adds a link to a pointer to the back of the queue, `pointer_queue_front()` gives you the front element of the queue, and `dequeue_pointer()` removes the first element from the queue. When we need to do a breadth-first traversal of the trie, we need to add all siblings of a node when we reach a new node, and for that, we use a function, `enqueue_siblings()`:

```c
void enqueue_siblings(
    struct pointer_queue *queue,
    struct trie *siblings
) {
    for (struct trie *s = siblings; s; s = s->sibling)
        enqueue_pointer(queue, (void*)s);
}
```

To insert all children of a node, you can call `enqueue_siblings()` on its first child.

We use it in the function `compute_failure_link_for_node()` that handles the breadth-first traversal. It creates and later frees the queue, inserts the children of the root to start the traversal with, and then continues to handle nodes as long as there are nodes in the queue.

```c
void compute_failure_links(
    struct trie *trie
) {
```

```
    // We don't want to recompute them if we
    // already have set up the failure links.
    if (trie->failure_link) return;

    // Make the root its own failure link.
    trie->failure_link = trie;

    struct pointer_queue *nodes = alloc_pointer_queue();
    enqueue_siblings(nodes, trie->children);
    while (!is_pointer_queue_empty(nodes)) {
        struct trie *v =
            (struct trie *)pointer_queue_front(nodes);
        dequeue_pointer(nodes);
        compute_failure_link_for_node(v, trie, nodes);
    }

    free_pointer_queue(nodes);
}
```

It is in the compute_failure_link_node() we do the real work—setting the failure link and output list for a specific node. This is where we search the failure links of the parent to find one we can extend and also where we will set the output list.

```
void compute_failure_link_for_node(
    struct trie *v,
    struct trie *root,
    struct pointer_queue *queue
) {
     // Breadth-first traversal...
    enqueue_siblings(queue, v->children);

    if (is_trie_root(v->parent)) {
        // Special case: immediate children of the
        // root should have the root as parent.
        v->failure_link = v->parent;

    } else {
```

```c
        uint8_t label = v->in_edge_label;
        struct trie *w = v->parent->failure_link;
        struct trie *out = out_link(w, label);
        while (!out && !is_trie_root(w)) {
            w = w->failure_link;
            out = out_link(w, label);
        }

        if (out) {
            v->failure_link = out;
        } else {
            v->failure_link = root;
        }
    }

    // Compute output list
    if (v->string_label >= 0) {
        v->output = new_output_link(v->string_label,
                                    v->failure_link->output);
    } else {
        v->output = v->failure_link->output;
    }
}
```

For the output list, observe that we will have to output all the strings in the output link of the failure link of v—those are the strings that are suffixes of v with a string label. If v has a string label we must also output it, so in that case we prepend v's label to the list; otherwise, we take the output of $f(v)$.

In the traversal, we use two helper functions: is_trie_root() and new_output_link(). We have seen is_trie_root() before but not new_output_link(). It looks like this:

```c
struct output_list *
new_output_link(
    int label,
    struct output_list *next
) {
```

```
    struct output_list *link =
        malloc(sizeof(struct output_list));
    link->string_label = label;
    link->next = next;
    return link;
}
```

When deallocating a trie, we need to handle the outlink as well as children and siblings. We do not need to scan through the list nodes, however. The output list is a linked list, but there is at most one link per string label, and that is associated with the trie node with that label. We don't need to handle the rest of the output list since those will be handled when their corresponding trie nodes are deleted.

```
void dealloc_trie(
    struct trie *trie
) {
    // Depth-first traversal freeing the trie.
    if (trie->children) free_trie(trie->children);
    if (trie->sibling) free_trie(trie->sibling);

    if (trie->output && trie->string_label >= 0) {
        free(trie->output);
    }
}
```

When we examine the running time for the preprocessing, we will assume that the trie is already built; if you want to include it, just add the construction to this running time. Building the trie can be done in time equal to the total sum of the lengths of strings in it, $O(m)$. Constructing the failure links can be done in the same time.

It isn't obvious that we can construct the failure links in linear time. For each node v at depth $d(v)$, we can in principle follow $d(v)$ failure links, giving us a running time of the square of the number of nodes in the trie. This, however, is not a tight bound. To see this, consider a node v and the path down to it. When we compute the failure links, we do it breadth-first, but for now consider what amounts to a depth-first traversal. If the failure link is set for v and we need to compute it for a child of v, w, then the node depth of $f(w)$ can at most be one more than the node depth of $f(v)$. When we compute $f(w)$, we might decrease the failure depth by a number of steps but we can only increase it by one. As we move down a depth-first path, we can increase the failure link depth by one at each step, but we cannot decrease it more than we have increased it so far. So the total search for suffix links on such a path is bounded by the depth of the path.

The algorithm with iterators

If we have a global REPORT() function (which we will avoid later), then the search algorithm can look like this:

```
void aho_corasick_match(
    const uint8_t *x,
    uint32_t n,
    struct trie *patterns
) {
    uint32_t j = 0;
    struct trie *v = patterns;

    while (j < n) {
        struct trie *w = out_link(v, x[j]);
        while (w) {
            for (struct output_list *hits = w->output;
                 hits != 0;
                 hits = hits->next) {
                // String hits->string_label ends in
                // index j. If we know the length
                // of hits->string_label, we could
                // report the beginning.
                // We will do so in the iterator
                // code.
                REPORT(hits->string_label, j);
            }

            v = w;
            j++;
            w = out_link(v, x[j]);
        }
```

```
        if (is_trie_root(v)) {
            j++;
        } else {
            v = v->failure_link;
        }
    }
}
```

We do not want this type of global reporting function, of course, nor do we want a callback. They make it hard for others to use our code. Again we want an iterator. We will initialize the iterator with a trie that is already constructed, in case the user of the algorithm needs to use the trie on several strings or for other purposes and does not want to create the trie anew each time. We also want to know the pattern lengths so we can report the beginning of matches rather than the ends of patterns.

```
void init_ac_iter(
    struct ac_iter *iter,
    const uint8_t *x,
    uint32_t n,
    const uint32_t *pattern_lengths,
    struct trie *patterns_trie
) {
    assert(iter);
    iter->x = x; iter->n = n;

    iter->pattern_lengths = pattern_lengths;
    iter->patterns_trie = patterns_trie;

    iter->nested = true;
    iter->j = 0;
    iter->v = patterns_trie;
    iter->w = 0;
    iter->hits = 0;

    // We need these for this algorithm.
    compute_failure_links(patterns_trie);
}
```

The resources for the iterator are all handled outside of the iterator so we do not have to free any resources.

```
void dealloc_ac_iter(struct ac_iter *iter)
{
    // Nop
}
```

The function for incrementing the iterator is more involved. We have nested loops in the algorithm where we have an outer loop that runs through the string x, and then we have a nested loop that matches down the trie using failure links and then yet another nested loop that iterates through the output list. We need to leave the iterator in any of these loops and resume in the same loop when we increment the iterator. Therefore, the iterator has the variable hits that is nonnull if we are in the process of outputting hits. We check if it is null and return a match if it isn't. We use another variable in the iterator, nested, that is true if we are in the nested loop over failure links and matches, the while (w) look from the implementation earlier. If nested is true, we get the outlink form w, and if there is one, we update the various values in the iterator so we can return to the beginning of the loop. For restarting the loop, we call next_ac_match() recursively. If there isn't an outgoing edge with the right label, we should leave the nested loop instead, so here we set nested to false and continue to the next part of the function that handles the updates in the outer loop. After the updated variables, we continue the loop by a recursive call again. The recursive calls are likely to be tail-optimized by the compiler so we will not pay a runtime penalty and we do not need to worry about exceeding the stack space.

```
bool next_ac_match(
    struct ac_iter *iter,
    struct ac_match *match
) {
    if (iter->hits) {
        match->string_label = iter->hits->string_label;
        // We use the pattern length to output
        // the start of a match instead of the end.
        match->index = iter->j -
            iter->pattern_lengths[match->string_label];
        iter->hits = iter->hits->next;
```

```
        return true;
    }

    if (iter->nested) {
        iter->w = out_link(iter->v, iter->x[iter->j]);
        if (iter->w) {
            iter->hits = iter->w->output;
            iter->v = iter->w;
            iter->j++;
            iter->w = out_link(iter->v, iter->x[iter->j]);
            return next_ac_match(iter, match);
        } else {
            iter->nested = false;
        }
    }

    if (iter->j < iter->n) {
        if (is_trie_root(iter->v)) {
            iter->j++;
        } else {
            iter->v = iter->v->failure_link;
        }
        iter->nested = true;
        return next_ac_match(iter, match);
    }

    return false;
}
```

For the running time of the main algorithm, we can reason similarly to how we did for the KMP algorithm. We never decrease j, but we increase it for each match. We never move the trie to the left but move it to the right every time we have a mismatch. Both j and trie cannot move past the end of x, so the running time is (n) plus the total number of matches we output, z, which is not a constant, so the total time is $O(n + z)$.

Comparisons

Theoretical analysis of algorithms is one thing, and actual running times another— and more important property. I have simulated random strings with three different alphabets: EQUAL, all symbols are the same; DNA, an alphabet of size four (A, C, G, T); and a full 8-bit character set. If our analysis (and implementation) is correct, the naïve algorithms, BMH and BM, should have worst-case complexity on EQUAL, but when we consider random strings, the performance should get better the larger the alphabet. The other algorithms should run in linear time regardless of the alphabet. The relative performance of the two classes of algorithms depends on the complexity of the implementation. So consider Figure 2-34. In the figure, I have used $m = 200$. The lines are loess fitted to the time measurements. The behavior is as expected: The first three algorithms perform poorly with the EQUAL alphabet but comparable to the other algorithms on the DNA alphabet. The naïve algorithm is a little faster because it is much simpler. With random strings, the BMH and BM algorithms outcompete the others, with BM (the more complex of the two) the fastest. With the largest alphabet, the naïve algorithm, simple as it is, is faster than border and KMP, and the BMH and BM algorithms dramatically faster.

The algorithms also depend on m, and in Figure 2-35, you can see the running time of the linear-time algorithms for different m. In Figure 2-36 you can see the same for the worst-case quadratic time algorithms. Notice that the linear-time algorithms hardly depend on m. There is some dependency from the preprocessing step, but it is very minor. The worst-case quadratic time algorithms depend on both n and m. When we fix m, we always get a straight line for $O(nm)$ algorithms, but the growth depends on m as we see. They are all faster for smaller m and faster for larger alphabets (the y axes are not on the same scale so you can see the running time for the fastest cases).

You are unlikely to run into truly random strings, but genomic DNA data is close enough that the running time will be the same. Natural languages are hardly random, but BMH and BM are known to perform sublinear there as well. The best algorithm depends on your use case, but with reasonably large alphabets, BM and BMH are likely to be good choices.

You can find the code I used for the experiments on GitHub: `https://github.com/ mailund/stralg/blob/master/performance/match_search.c`.

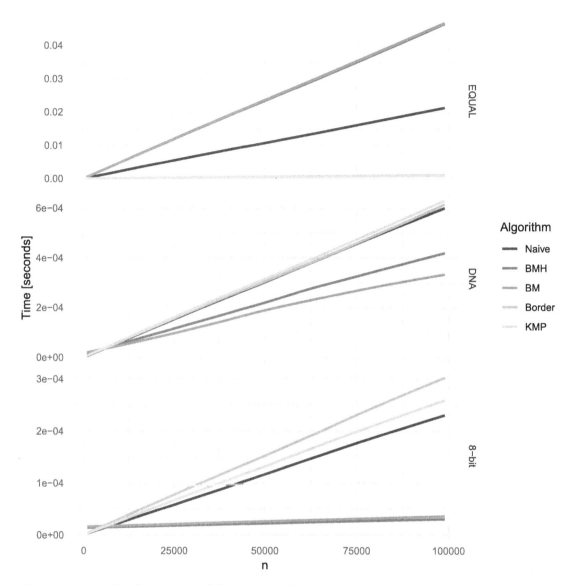

Figure 2-34. *Performance of the search algorithms*

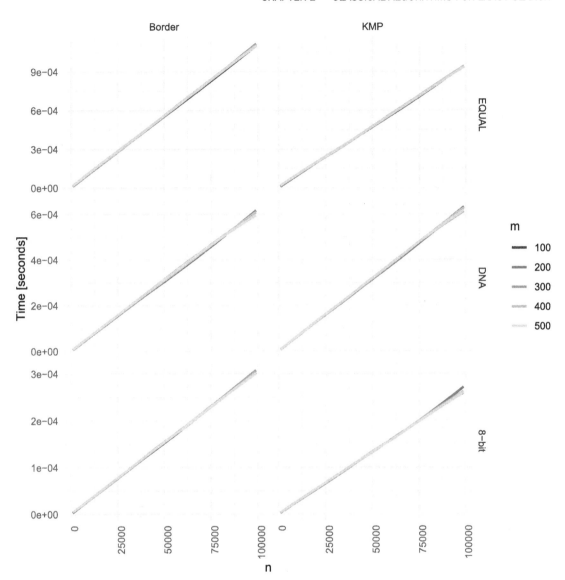

Figure 2-35. *Dependency on m for the linear algorithms*

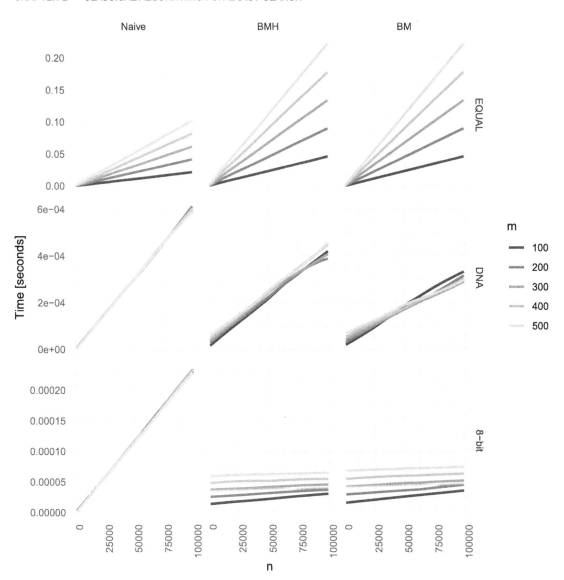

Figure 2-36. *Performance of the worst-case quadratic time algorithms for different m*

CHAPTER 3

Suffix trees

The *suffix tree* is a fundamental data structure when it comes to string algorithms. It captures the structure of a string via all the string's suffixes and uses this structure as the basis of many algorithms. We will only use it for searching, where it provides linear search for a pattern after a linear preprocessing of the string we search in.

Imagine that you have listed all the suffixes of a string $x\$$ with the sentinel $\$$ (which in C is usually, and always in this chapter, zero). The sentinel is important here and you must always include it in suffix trees. So, we have the suffixes $x\$[0, n + 1]$, $x\$[1, n]$, $x\$[2, n]$, ..., $x\$[n, n + 1]$, which obviously contain all the information that the string does (the first suffix is the entire string). If we want to search for a pattern p in x, then we can find the suffixes where p is a prefix, that is, suffixes $x[j, n]$ where $p = x[j, j + m]$. Iteratively matching p against all suffixes is not efficient, it would take time $O(nm)$, and if we explicitly list all suffixes, we would use $O(n^2)$ time and space on top of this. If, however, we construct a trie of all the suffixes, we can search in time $O(m)$. Consider the trie in Figure 3-1. It contains all the suffixes of the string *mississippi*$\$$. The sentinel guarantees us that there is a one-to-one mapping between leaves and suffixes. To search for a pattern, move down the trie until there is a mismatch or we reach the end of the pattern. If we reach the end of the pattern, then the leaves below that point are the positions where the pattern can be found in the string. If we, for example, search for the string "ss" from the root, we get to the white node in Figure 3-1. The leaves below this node in the tree, two and five, are the indices where "ss" occur in "*mississippi*$\$$", that is, indices 2 and 5.

© Thomas Mailund 2020
T. Mailund, *String Algorithms in C*, https://doi.org/10.1007/978-1-4842-5920-7_3

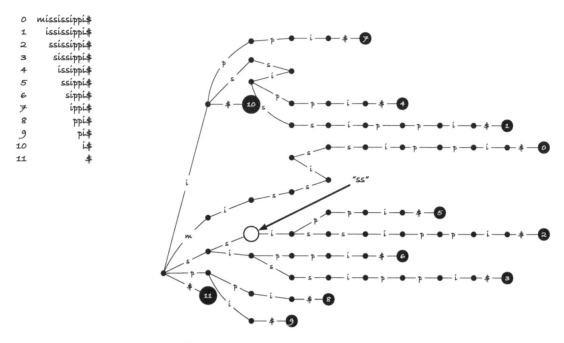

Figure 3-1. *Suffix trie for "mississippi"*

Constructing this "suffix trie" in the standard way—one string at a time—takes time proportional to the sum of the lengths of sequences we add to the trie, so building this suffix trie costs us $O(n^2)$ space and time usage for the preprocessing. A suffix tree is a tree containing all suffixes of a string but exploits the structure in a set of suffixes to reduce both space and time complexity to $O(n + m)$.

Compacted trie and suffix representation

A suffix tree is a trie containing all suffixes, but it is *compacted*. This means that we do not represent each character as an edge in the trie, but rather, we merge edges where nodes have out-degree one; see the left tree in Figure 3-2.[1] Since we have a single string, which all the edges are a subsequence of, we can represent the edge strings efficiently as indices or pointers into the string. The tree on the right in Figure 3-2 shows the actual representation of a suffix tree. The notation $[i, j]$ means from i to j with i included and j not included, that is, j is one past the last index.

---

[1]This is also called the PATRICIA tree, but compacted trie is easier to remember since it is a compact representation of a trie.

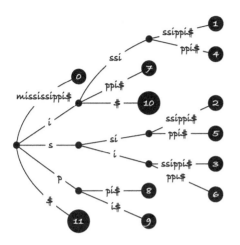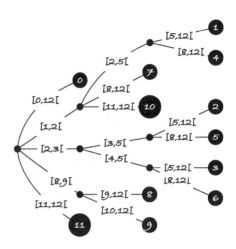

Figure 3-2. *Suffix tree, conceptual and actual*

The sentinel guarantees that there is a one-to-one correspondence between the string's suffixes and the suffix tree's leaves. Since each inner node has at least two children, the total number of nodes cannot exceed $2n - 1$ and neither can the number of edges, so the suffix tree can be stored in $O(n)$ space.

In the implementation, we will not use indices but pointers into the string. This is more convenient in many cases, and we can always get an index by subtracting the pointer by the string. We represent an edge with a `range` structure that we put in each node. The range in node v represents the edge label between v and its parent $p(v)$.

```
struct range {
    const uint8_t *from;
    const uint8_t *to;
};
static inline uint32_t range_length(struct range r) {
    return (uint32_t)(r.to - r.from);
}
```

The `range_length()` is a convenience function and shows how we can go from pointers to a length, and in this case, it will be an offset from the string pointed to by `r.to`.

In the simplest construction algorithm, we need a *range*, a *sibling list*, and a *child list* in each node, plus a *suffix label* if the node is a leaf. In the more advanced two algorithms, we also need a *parent pointer* and a *suffix link* pointer. What the parent pointer does should be self-evident, and the suffix link pointer will be explained when we get to McCreight's algorithm later in the chapter.

89

With all the information we need in a node, the structure looks like this:

```
struct suffix_tree_node {
    uint32_t leaf_label;
    struct range range;
    struct suffix_tree_node *parent;
    struct suffix_tree_node *sibling;
    struct suffix_tree_node *child;
    struct suffix_tree_node *suffix_link;
};

static inline uint32_t edge_length(
    struct suffix_tree_node *n
) {
    return range_length(n->range);
}
```

The edge_length() function is just another helper function we can use to, not surprisingly, get the length of the edge leading to the node.

We could use a root note as the type of a suffix tree—as we did for tries—but we will usually need access to the string that the tree is built from. We have pointers into the string on all edges, but in some of the algorithms in this chapter, we will need to consider them as indices, and that is easily done by subtracting the pointer to the string from the pointers on an edge. So we use a suffix_tree structure and store a pointer to the string in it.

```
struct suffix_tree {
    const uint8_t *string;
    uint32_t length;
    struct suffix_tree_node *root;
    struct suffix_tree_node_pool pool;
};
```

The pool variable is used to allocate nodes efficiently. We have an upper bound on the size of the number of nodes we can have, so we can preallocate a pool of nodes for the tree instead of using malloc() and free() for each node. This speeds up the construction and makes it easier to free the tree—we can free the pool and do not have to traverse the tree to free individual nodes.

```
struct suffix_tree_node_pool {
    struct suffix_tree_node *nodes;
    struct suffix_tree_node *next_node;
};
```

When we need a new node, we can get it from the pool. The new_node() function constructs a node from a suffix tree (where it can get the pool) and the two pointers that represent the edge label.

```
static struct suffix_tree_node *
new_node(
    struct suffix_tree *st,
    const uint8_t *from,
    const uint8_t *to
) {
    struct suffix_tree_node *v = st->pool.next_node++;

    v->leaf_label = 0;
    v->range.from = from;
    v->range.to = to;
    v->parent = 0;
    v->sibling = 0;
    v->child = 0;
    v->suffix_link = 0;

    return v;
}
```

This function should remain in the .c file and not be part of the public interface. We don't want the user to insert nodes willy-nilly. Suffix trees should be built using a construction algorithm.

To free a suffix tree, we first need to free the nodes. This is a trivial task because we have the nodes pool that we can deallocate with a single free() call.

```
void free_suffix_tree(struct suffix_tree *st)
{
    // Do not free string; we are not managing it.
    free(st->pool.nodes);
    free(st);
}
```

We should not free the string when we free the suffix tree. That is the responsibility of the user and part of the interface; the string is declared const, and we will use const strings for all our construction algorithms.

When allocating a new tree, we allocate the struct to set the string and length variables. Then we allocate the array we use as the node pool. Finally, we create a root node and set its parent to itself and its suffix link to itself (forget the suffix link for now, we get to it later). Adding a root to the tree when we construct it makes all other functions easier to write since they avoid handling special cases where a node is null.

```
static struct suffix_tree *
alloc_suffix_tree(
    const uint8_t *string
) {
    struct suffix_tree *st =
        malloc(sizeof(struct suffix_tree));
    st->string = string;
    uint32_t slen = (uint32_t)strlen((char *)string);
    st->length = slen + 1; // We are using '\0' as sentinel.

    // This is the max number of nodes in a tree where all
    // nodes have at least degree two. There is a special case
    // when the string is empty -- it should really only happen
    // in testing, but never the less.
    // In that case, there should be
    // two and not one node (the root and a single child).
    uint32_t pool_size = st->length == 1
                            ? 2 : (2 * st->length - 1);
    st->pool.nodes =
        malloc(pool_size * sizeof(struct suffix_tree_node));
```

```
st->pool.next_node = st->pool.nodes;

st->root = new_node(st, 0, 0);
st->root->parent = st->root;
st->root->suffix_link = st->root;

return st;
}
```

Naïve construction algorithm

The simplest way to build a suffix tree is to consider it a trie and insert one string at the time, starting with the first suffix. We cannot *quite* consider it a trie since it is compacted, but we can look at one character at a time as we scan along edges in effect doing the same work as we would for building a trie. This naïve approach is implemented in the naive_suffix_tree() function:

```
struct suffix_tree *naive_suffix_tree(
    const uint8_t *string
) {
    struct suffix_tree *st = alloc_suffix_tree(string);

    // We insert the first suffix manually to
    // ensure that all inner nodes have at least one child.
    // The root will be a special case
    // for the first suffix otherwise,
    // and we do not want to deal with that
    // in the rest of the code.
    struct suffix_tree_node *first =
        new_node(st, st->string, st->string + st->length);
    st->root->child = first;
    first->parent = st->root;
```

```
const uint8_t *xend = st->string + st->length;
for (uint32_t i = 1; i < st->length; ++i) {
    struct suffix_tree_node *leaf =
        naive_insert(st, st->root, string + i, xend);
    leaf->leaf_label = i;
}

return st;
}
```

First, we ensure that there is at least one edge out of the root—otherwise, we would need to handle the case where, and there isn't a special case in all the other functions we will write. After setting the first suffix as the first child of the root (and setting the parent pointer of it to the root), we iterate through all the remaining suffixes and insert them using the following `naive_insert()` function. This function will return the new leaf representing the suffix, and we set its label accordingly.

The `naive_insert()` function takes the suffix tree, a node to search out from (the root in `naive_suffix_tree()`), and a string given by a start pointer ($x + i$ for the start of suffix i) and an end pointer (the end of the string in `naive_suffix_tree()`.

First, `naive_insert()` checks if there is an out edge from the node it should search from, v. If there isn't, then this is where we should add the string, so we create a new node and insert it as a child of v using `insert_child()` (listed in following code). If there is an out edge, we scan along it. We get a pointer to the start of the interval of the edge, s, and we have the pointer x pointing to the beginning of the string we want to insert. We scan along the edge as long as s and x point to the same character; see Figure 3-3 for an illustration of how scanning an edge maps to scanning an interval in the suffix tree's string. In the figure, variables `from` and `to` define the interval of the edge we scan, `s` the point in the edge we have scanned to, `x` the position in the string we insert that we have scanned so far, and `xend` the end of the string we are inserting.

If we find a mismatch, we need to break the edge in two and add an edge to the leaf. We do that using the function `split_edge()` described later in this section. If we reach the end of the edge's interval, we must continue from the node w at the end of the edge. We do this by a recursive call.

```c
static struct suffix_tree_node *
naive_insert(
    struct suffix_tree *st,
    struct suffix_tree_node *v,
    const uint8_t *x,
    const uint8_t *xend
) {
    // Find child that matches *x.
    struct suffix_tree_node *w = find_outgoing_edge(v, x);

    if (!w) {
        // There is no outgoing edge that matches
        // so we must insert here.
        struct suffix_tree_node *leaf = new_node(st, x, xend);
        insert_child(v, leaf);
        return leaf;

    } else {

        // We have an edge to follow!
        const uint8_t *s = w->range.from;
        for (; s != w->range.to; ++s, ++x) {
            if (*s != *x) {
                struct suffix_tree_node *u =
                    split_edge(st, w, s);
                struct suffix_tree_node *leaf =
                    new_node(st, x, xend);
                insert_child(u, leaf);
                return leaf;
            }
        }
        // We made it through the edge, so continue
        // from the next node.
        // The call is tail-recursive, so the compiler
        // will usually optimize it to a loop.
        return naive_insert(st, w, x, xend);
    }
}
```

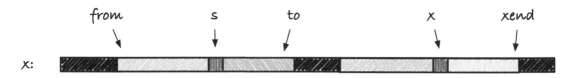

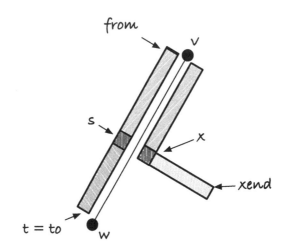

Figure 3-3. *Scanning along an edge by scanning in the string*

The find_outgoing_edge() function does what you would expect. It scans through the children of a node, tests each edge for whether it matches the character we are looking for, and returns the node if it finds one. If it gets all the way through the children, that is, to a node where the sibling pointer is null, then it returns null.

```
static struct suffix_tree_node *
find_outgoing_edge(
    struct suffix_tree_node *v,
    const uint8_t *x
) {
    struct suffix_tree_node *w = v->child;
    while (w) {
        if (*(w->range.from) == *x) break;
        w = w->sibling;
    }
    return w;
}
```

The simplest way to add a child to a node is to prepend it to the linked list structure. This, however, will leave the children list reversely sorted according to when we insert edges, which for all intents and purposes means randomly sorted. There are algorithms where we need to traverse the tree such that we see the suffixes in lexicographical order. If we keep the children sorted according to their start symbol, this will simply be a depth-first traversal where, for each node, we iterate through the nodes in the order they have in the children's list. It requires a little more work to insert a child at its correct position, but it is mostly straightforward except for one special case. If the new child's symbol is less than the first node's, we prepend the child. Otherwise, we scan through the existing children until we find a letter that is larger than the new child's symbol, and we insert the child there. If we reach the last node, recognizable by it having null for a sibling, we prepend the new child. After inserting the child, we must remember to set its parent to the node we added it to.

```c
static void insert_child(
    struct suffix_tree_node *parent,
    struct suffix_tree_node *child
) {
    // We need this when we split edges.
    if (!parent->child) {
        parent->child = child;
        return;
    }

    const char x = *child->range.from;
    struct suffix_tree_node *w = parent->child;
    if (x < out_letter(w)) {
        // Special case for the first child.
        child->sibling = parent->child;
        parent->child = child;
    } else {
        // Find w such that it is the first chain
        // with an outgoing edge that is larger
        // than the new.
        while (w->sibling && x > out_letter(w->sibling))
            w = w->sibling;
```

```
        child->sibling = w->sibling;
        w->sibling = child;
    }
    child->parent = parent;
}
```

The out_letter() gives us the first symbol of an edge:

```
inline static char out_letter(
    struct suffix_tree_node *v
) {
    return *(v->range.from);
}
```

Finally, we come to the function for splitting an edge on a mismatch. Consider Figure 3-4 where on the left we have the edge we have scanned down and the position of the mismatch. We have to split the edge at the mismatch position, which is where the variable s points. The edge going down to the new node must, therefore, go from the pointer from to s and the edge below the new node must go from s to the pointer to. We will insert a new leaf as the second edge out of the new node, and this must go from the pointer x to xend in the calling function but we only break the edge with the new node, *u*, in this function. We add the other edge outside of this function. In the implementation of the function split_edge(), the node *w* is an argument as is *s*. We get the node *v* from *w*'s parent pointer, we create node *u*, and we set the start of its edge to be the from of the edge to *w* and the end to be s. Now *u*'s parent should be *v* and its (so far only) child should be *w*. We update *w*'s start position to be *s* (it already has the right endpoint) and update the child and parent pointers for the nodes. We have to remove *w* from *v*'s children—it is now a child of *u* instead—and we insert *u* as a new child of *v*. We return the new node so the caller can insert the leaf as a child of it.

```
static struct suffix_tree_node *
split_edge(
    struct suffix_tree *st,
    struct suffix_tree_node *w,
    const uint8_t *s
) {
    struct suffix_tree_node *v = w->parent;
    struct suffix_tree_node *u =
```

```
      new_node(st, w->range.from, s);
   u->parent = v;
   u->child = w;
   w->range.from = s;
   w->parent = u;

   remove_child(v, w);
   insert_child(v, u);

   return u;
}
```

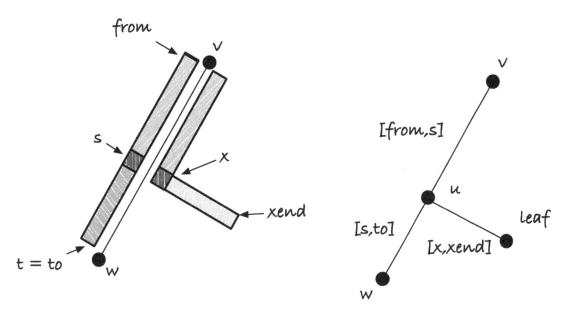

Figure 3-4. *Splitting an edge*

The return value of split_edge() is the new node and we use that to add the new leaf. We only need the *s* pointer when we split the edge if we do this. We cannot create the edge to the leaf with a range x to xend from the *w* edge and the pointer *s*, so if we wanted split edge to insert the leaf as well, we would need more arguments to the function. In naive_insert() we already know x and xend so we create the leaf there and insert it as the second child of our new node. This is done with the following code:

```
struct suffix_tree_node *u = split_edge(st, w, s);
struct suffix_tree_node *leaf = new_node(st, x, xend);
insert_child(u, leaf);
```

99

The remaining function we need to implement to complete the algorithm is the one for removing a child from a node's child list. We have three cases: If the list is empty—in which case, we do nothing. If it is the first child—in which case, we change the children list to the first sibling, which will also remove the child. In the final case, the node is somewhere in the middle of the list, so we scan through the list and if we find the node we unlink it.

```c
static void remove_child(
    struct suffix_tree_node *v,
    struct suffix_tree_node *w
) {
    if (!v->child) return;
    if (v->child == w) {
        v->child = w->sibling;
        w->sibling = 0;
    } else {
        struct suffix_tree_node *u = v->child;
        while (u->sibling) {
            if (u->sibling == w) {
                u->sibling = w->sibling;
                w->sibling = 0;
                return;
            }
            u = u->sibling;
        }
    }
}
```

Suffixes:	Sorted	SA	LCP
mississippi$ (0)	$	(11)	0
ississippi$ (1)	i$	(10)	0
ssissippi$ (2)	ippi$	(7)	1
sissippi$ (3)	issippi$	(4)	1
issippi$ (4)	ississippi$	(1)	4
ssippi$ (5)	mississippi$	(0)	0
sippi$ (6)	pi$	(9)	0
ippi$ (7)	ppi$	(8)	1
ppi$ (8)	sippi$	(6)	0
pi$ (9)	sissippi$	(3)	2
i$ (10)	ssippi$	(5)	1
$ (11)	ssissippi$	(2)	3

Figure 3-5. *Suffix array and longest common prefix array*

Suffix trees and the SA and LCP arrays

In this section, we briefly cover the close relationship between two special arrays and a suffix tree. These arrays are the topic of the entire next chapter, but in this section, we only consider how we can use them to build a suffix tree. If you take a list of all the suffixes of a string and then sort them (see Figure 3-5), the *suffix array* (SA) is the suffix indices in this sorted order. The *longest common prefix* (LCP) array is the longest prefix of a suffix and the suffix above it in the sorted order—the underlined prefixes in Figure 3-5. In this section, we shall see that we can construct the arrays from a suffix tree in linear time and that we can construct the suffix tree from the two arrays in linear time.

Constructing the SA and LCP arrays

If we depth-first traverse a suffix tree with children sorted alphabetically, we will see all leaves in sorted order, an observation that should be immediately obvious. Thus, if we keep a counter of how many leaves we have seen so far and use it to index into the suffix array, we can build the suffix array simply by putting leaf nodes at the index of the counter as we traverse the tree.

Getting the LCP array is only slightly more involved. If we let *branch length* be the total length of the string, we read from the root down to a node *v*. All children of *v* will share a prefix of exactly this length, so if we iterate through *all but the first* child, we will have at least this longest common prefix. Children of the children will share longer prefixes, but we can handle that by recursion. The problem with the first child is that though it shares the prefix with the other children, it does not share it with the previous string in the suffix array.

Consider Figure 3-6. The letters represent branch lengths and the numbers the leaves in the tree. Notice how the leftmost node in any of the subtrees has a lower LCP than its siblings. If we traverse the tree and keep track of how much we share to the left, we can output that number for each leaf. For the first child of a node, we send this left-shared number unchanged down the tree, while at the remaining trees, we update the value by adding the edge length of the children's parent node.

Onto the implementation of the algorithm, we use this structure to reference the two arrays and to keep track of which index we need to update in the array next time we see a leaf.

```
struct sa_lcp_data {
    uint32_t *sa;
    uint32_t *lcp;
    uint32_t idx;
};
```

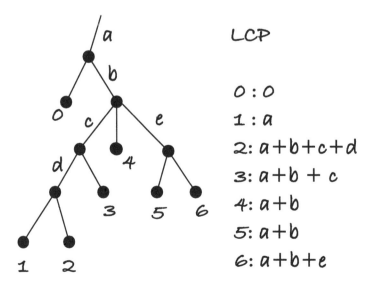

Figure 3-6. *Branch lengths and LCP array*

In the function st_compute_sa_and_lcp(), we create and initialize an instance of the structure and call a recursive function, lcp_traverse(), with the root as the node and both the left-shared branch length and the node's branch length as its input.[2]

```
void st_compute_sa_and_lcp(
    struct suffix_tree *st,
    uint32_t *sa,
    uint32_t *lcp
) {
    struct sa_lcp_data data; // type defined earlier
    data.sa = sa; data.lcp = lcp; data.idx = 0;
    uint32_t shared_depth = 0;
    uint32_t branch_depth = 0;
    lcp_traverse(st->root, &data,
                 shared_depth, branch_depth);
}
```

In the traversal, we update the SA and LCP array each time we see a leaf; we propagate the shared left-depth to the first node and use the current node's depth as both the left and the node depth in the recursive calls.

```
static void lcp_traverse(
    struct suffix_tree_node *v,
    struct sa_lcp_data *data,
    uint32_t left_depth,
    uint32_t node_depth
) {
    if (!v->child) {
        // Leaf
        data->sa[data->idx] = v->leaf_label;
        data->lcp[data->idx] = left_depth;
        data->idx++;
    } else {
```

---

[2]The traversal is easier to follow with a recursive function, but for large trees, it will hit the stack limit and crash the program. Using an explicit heap-allocated stack solves the problem. I do not show that implementation here, but you can find it at https://github.com/mailund/stralg.

```
        // Inner node
        // The first child should be treated differently than
        // the rest; it has a different branch depth because
        // the LCP is relative to the last node in the previous
        // leaf in v's previous sibling.
        struct suffix_tree_node *child = v->child;
        uint32_t this_depth
            = node_depth + edge_length(v);
        lcp_traverse(child, data,
                     left_depth, this_depth);
        for (child = child->sibling;
             child;
             child = child->sibling) {
            // Handle the remaining children
            lcp_traverse(child, data,
                         this_depth, this_depth);
        }
    }
}
```

Since the entire algorithm is a depth-first traversal where we do constant time work at each node, the running time is the same as the size of the tree, so $O(n)$.

Constructing the suffix tree from the SA and LCP arrays

We can construct a suffix tree from the SA and LCP arrays by, conceptually, doing a depth-first traversal of the tree while constructing it at the same time. We insert the suffixes in a different order than for the naïve approach; we insert them according to the suffix array, so we first insert sa[0], then sa[1], and so on. When inserting the first suffix, we add an edge from the root to a leaf labelled sa[0]. Then we split that edge to insert sa[1] and an edge to it. For sa[2] we start in sa[1] and figure out where we should break an edge and insert the new leaf. This can either be on the edge down to sa[1] or the edge above it (see Figure 3-7), but it cannot be on the edge down to sa[0] since sa[1] is lexicographically smaller than sa[2] which means it must be to the right or above the edge to sa[1]. We continue inserting this way by inserting sa[3], sa[4], and so on by first moving up the tree to find the place where they should be inserted and then inserting the new leaf. You can think of this as a depth-first traversal. When you insert a new leaf, you move down the recursion (very quickly, of course, since you only insert a single edge), and when you move up the tree to find an edge to split, you in effect return from the depth-first recursion.

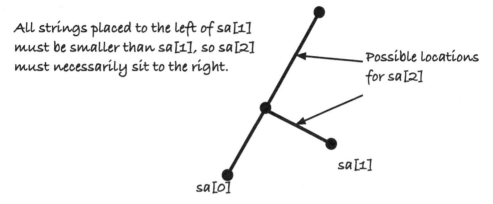

All strings placed to the left of sa[1] must be smaller than sa[1], so sa[2] must necessarily sit to the right.

Possible locations for sa[2]

sa[1]

sa[0]

Figure 3-7. *Possible placements of sa[2]*

The main function for the algorithm looks like this:

```
struct suffix_tree *
lcp_suffix_tree(
    const uint8_t *string,
    uint32_t *sa,
    uint32_t *lcp
) {
    struct suffix_tree *st = alloc_suffix_tree(string);

    uint32_t first_label = sa[0];
    struct suffix_tree_node *v =
        new_node(st, st->string + sa[0],
                    st->string + st->length);
    v->leaf_label = first_label;
    st->root->child = v;
    v->parent = st->root;
```

```
    for (uint32_t i = 1; i < st->length; ++i) {
        v = lcp_insert(st, i, sa, lcp, v);
    }

    return st;
}
```

We first add sa[0] to the tree and set the variable v to the new leaf. Then we iteratively add the remaining leaves with lcp_insert() that returns the new leaf inserted. This leaf is used by the function as the starting point for inserting the next leaf.

For the function doing the hard labor, lcp_insert(), consider Figure 3-8. If we are at the leaf for sa[i-1] and the longest prefix it shares with sa[i] is lcp[i], then the new leaf should be inserted lcp[i] symbols down the path from the root to sa[i-1], or n-sa[i-1]-lcp[i] up from the sa[i-1] leaf. We can search up that amount from sa[i-1] and break the edge there (or insert the new leaf in a node if we do not hit an edge).

The pointers we need to insert on the new edge to the leaf are lcp[i] into the suffix, that is, sa[i]+lcp[i], since this is what remains of the suffix after we have shared lcp[i]; see Figure 3-9. We don't know where the pointers on the edge we break are, they need not be anywhere sa[i-1], sa[i], or lcp[i], but we will know how far up the edge are we from how much we had left to search when we started climbing up the edge. If we call that amount length_up, then the break pointer is at to-length_up.

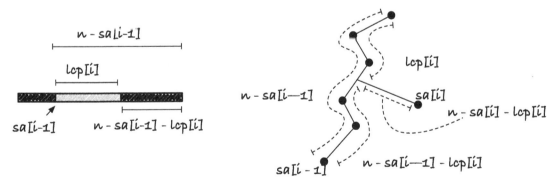

Figure 3-8. *Relationship between sa[i-1], lcp[i], and the suffix tree*

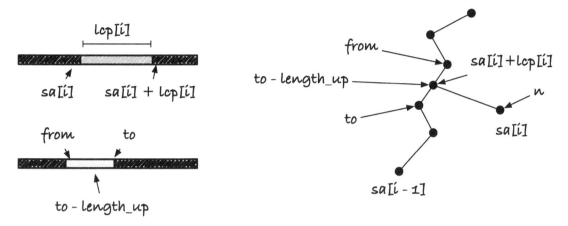

Figure 3-9. *Splitting the edge when inserting sa[i]*

With all the observations earlier, the actual implementation is straightforward. We get the length we have to move up from the calculations we just did, and then we get the length of the current edge we need to climb. Then we enter a loop that moves us up a number of edges until we have traversed all the way to our insertion point. In the loop, we each iteration subtract the edge length from the length we need to climb up—we have just moved up that amount, after all—we move to the parent node, and we get the length of the next edges. We do this until we hit an edge longer or equal to the next edge or until the new edge length is zero. In the first case, we have found the insertion point on an edge, and in the second case, we hit a node and need to insert the new leaf as a child of that node.

```
static struct suffix_tree_node *
lcp_insert(
    struct suffix_tree *st,
    uint32_t i,
    uint32_t *sa,
    uint32_t *lcp,
    struct suffix_tree_node *v
) {
    struct suffix_tree_node *new_leaf =
        new_node(st,
                 st->string + sa[i] + lcp[i],
                 st->string + st->length);
```

```
    new_leaf->leaf_label = sa[i];
    uint32_t length_up = st->length - sa[i-1] - lcp[i];
    uint32_t v_edge_len = edge_length(v);

    while ((length_up >= v_edge_len)
            && (length_up != 0)) {
        length_up -= v_edge_len;
        v = v->parent;
        v_edge_len = edge_length(v);
    }

    if (length_up == 0) {
        append_child(v, new_leaf);
    } else {
        struct suffix_tree_node *u =
                split_edge(st, v, v->range.to - length_up);
        // Append leaf to the new node
        // (it has exactly one other child).
        u->child->sibling = new_leaf;
        new_leaf->parent = u;
    }

    return new_leaf;
}
```

There is one new function, append_child(). It adds a child to the children's list. It could be done with the insert_child() function as well, but it is simpler since we know the edge we are inserting should go to the back of the list.

```
static void append_child(
    struct suffix_tree_node *v,
    struct suffix_tree_node *w
) {
    struct suffix_tree_node *child = v->child;
    while (child->sibling) {
        child = child->sibling;
    }
```

```
    child->sibling = w;
    w->parent = v;
}
```

To see that the running time is linear, observe that we construct the tree in what is essentially a depth-first traversal. We do not traverse nodes going down the recursion—that only makes the running time faster—but each time we move up the tree, it corresponds to returning from the recursion in the traversal. If this is not clear, I encourage you to work out a few examples on a piece of paper until you see that this is the case.

An alternative argument for the running time uses an amortization argument, not unlike those we used for, for example, border arrays, KMP, and Aho-Corasick. Consider the depth of the leaf we start an iteration from, v with node depth $d(v)$. The node depth $d(v)$ is the number of nodes on the path from node v to the root. When we search upward, we decrease the depth, but we cannot decrease it more than $d(v)$. After we find the node or edge, we potentially increase the depth of all the nodes lexicographically smaller than the suffix we are inserting (when we split an edge), or we leave them alone (when we insert a child to node). However, we will never explore that part of the tree when we insert lexicographically larger suffixes. We will look at nodes and edges closer to the root than that point, but we will never return to that subtree since we will never insert a lexicographically smaller string in the algorithm. So we can ignore those increases in depth and only consider the increase when we insert a new leaf. That increase is at most one. The algorithm can at max increase the depth by one (for the relevant part of the tree) in each iteration, and we cannot decrease the depth more than we have increased it, so since there are $O(n)$ leaves in the tree, we have a linear running time.

If we use the SA and LCP arrays to build the suffix tree, and need a suffix tree to produce the arrays, we have a circular problem. We shall see in the next chapter, however, that we can build the arrays in linear time without using a suffix tree. We shall also see, in the next section, that we can build a suffix tree in linear time without the two arrays. A benefit of using the SA and LCP algorithm to construct suffix trees is that it will be easier to preprocess a string using a suffix tree and then serialize it to a file when you expect many searches in the same string over time. The two arrays are trivial to write to a string, while serializing the tree structure itself means saving a structure with pointers and reconstruct them when the tree is read from file.

McCreight's algorithm

McCreight's algorithm lets us construct suffix trees in linear time without any additional data structure beyond the string itself. It inserts suffixes in the order they appear in the string, $x[0, n]\$$, $x[1, n]\$$, ..., $\$$, just like the naïve algorithm, except that it inserts the next suffix faster than the naïve algorithm. It keeps track of the last leaf inserted, like the SA and LCP algorithm, but the two tricks it uses to achieve linear construction time are different. From the latest leaf that we insert, we use a pointer to jump to a subtree somewhere else in the tree, where the next leaf should be inserted. Then we search for the insertion point in that tree, first using a search method that is faster than the naïve one and then searching the last piece of the suffix using the slow scanning method from the naïve algorithm.

Before we start we need to get some terminology and notation defined: Any suffix $y = x[i, n]\$$ can be split into two, potentially empty, substrings $y = h(y)t(y)$ where $h(y)$ is the longest string that matches a prefix of a longer suffix $x[j, n]\$$, $j < i$. This is just another way to say that $h(y)$ is how far down the tree we go when inserting suffix i, that is, it is the point in the tree where we need to insert a new leaf for suffix i. We call the two strings the *head*, $h(y)$, and *tail*, $t(y)$, of suffix i. For convenience, we will use i for the strings for suffix $x[i, n]\$$, that is, if $y = x[i, n]\$$, then $h(i) = h(y)$ and $t(i) = t(y)$.

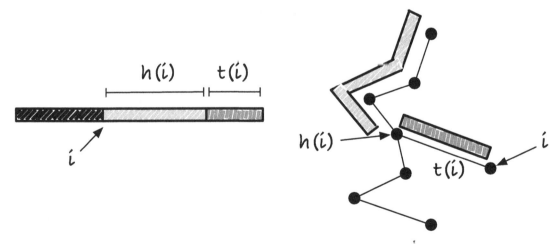

Figure 3-10. *Inserting suffix i by finding its head and appending its tail*

What we did in the naïve algorithm was searching one character by one character from the root to the point where suffix i would branch off the existing tree, that is, we searched for $h(i)$, and then we inserted a new leaf with label $t(i)$. We searched with the naïve search algorithm, one character at a time, and when we could not continue down the tree, we had found $h(i)$. We did not need to insert that string—by definition, it is already in the tree—but we needed a new leaf and the remaining part of the suffix, $t(i)$, on the edge to the leaf; see Figure 3-10. In McCreight's algorithm, we do essentially the same, but we exploit the structure of suffixes to search for $h(i)$ faster.

For a string ay let its *suffix link* $s(ay)$ be defined as the string with the first symbol removed, that is, $s(ay) = y$, with the special case $s(\varepsilon) = \varepsilon$ for the empty string. If v is a node in the tree where ay is the string we would read from the root to v, then $s(v)$ is the node where we would find y when reading from the root and down. We will see in the algorithm that all nodes in a tree have a suffix link that is a node so we can represent them as pointers from nodes to nodes. Jumping these pointers is the first trick to McCreight's algorithm.

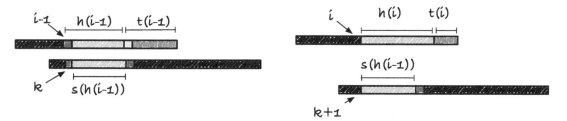

Figure 3-11. *The head of a suffix is longer to or equal to the previous suffix' suffix link*

First, observe that $s(h(i-1))$ is a prefix of $h(i)$. Consider $h(i-1)$. This string is how far down the tree we could scan before we found a mismatch when we inserted suffix $i-1$. Therefore there was a longer suffix, $k < i-1$, whose prefix matches $h(i-1)$ and then had a mismatch (there might be strings that match more of suffix $i-1$, but by definition, this was the longest at the time we inserted $i-1$). Now consider $h(i)$. This is the longest prefix matching a prefix of a string we already inserted in the string. If we look at suffix $k+1$, we can see that this will match s(h(i-1)); see Figure 3-11. Because we match at least suffix $k+1$ to this point, $s(h(i-1))$ must be a prefix of $h(i)$. If we only have suffix $k+1$ that matches to this point, then we would have exactly h(i)=s(h(i-1)), but there might be longer strings matching a prefix of suffix i; after all, this suffix starts with a different character, and there might be suffixes that do the same and matches longer prefixes. Regardless, we know that s(h(i-1)) is a prefix of $h(i)$.

If we have a pointer from $h(i-1)$ to $s(h(i-1))$, then we can jump it and skip past this prefix in the search for $h(i)$. Essentially, this is what we will do except that we do not have this suffix link when we need it. An invariant in the algorithm will be that we have suffix links for all nodes *except* possibly the parent of the last leaf we inserted. Not to worry, we can do something almost as good. While $h(i-1)$ might not have a suffix link pointer, its parent does $p(h(i-1)) \mapsto s(p(h(i-1)))$. This suffix link is also a prefix of $h(i)$. See Figure 3-12. The dashed arrow is a pointer we are guaranteed to have, while the dotted arrow is the pointer we wished we had but might not.

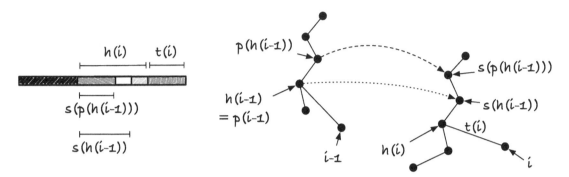

Figure 3-12. *Head and suffix links and their "jump pointers"*

The overall steps in the algorithm are this: We start by creating the first leaf and connecting it to the root. After that, we go through each suffix in order and get the parent of the last leaf we inserted ($h(i-1)$ in Figure 3-13 and the code). As an invariant of the algorithm, we will have that all nodes, *with the possible exception of $h(i-1)$*, will have a suffix link pointer. This is vacuously true after we have inserted the first leaf. For the root, though, it has a suffix link. We set the root's suffix link to the root itself in `alloc_suffix_tree()`, so although we need to set the suffix link when we increment i, to ensure the invariant, it is already satisfied at this point.

From the parent of leaf $i-1$, called v in the code and in Figure 3-13, we call a function, `suffix_search()`, that returns $s(h(i-1))$, called w in the code. This is the suffix link of v, so we set the pointer ensuring the invariant for the next iteration of the loop. The $h(i)$ string is somewhere in the subtree of $s(h(i-1))$ since $s(h(i-1))$ is a prefix of it. So we need to search a little more from node w. We do this in two steps. We jump to $s(p(h(i-1)))$ using the suffix link and then we search for w from there. In the search, called "scan 1" in the figure, we can move faster than the naïve search. We know that the string from $s(p(h(i-1)))$ to $s(h(i-1))$ is already in the tree which means that we can jump from node to node rather than scan along an edge. At each node we need to find which outgoing edge matches the current symbol in $s(h(i-1))$ to choose the right path in the suffix tree, but we do not need to compare characters when we move along an edge. We do not know how far down $h(i)$ is from $s(h(i-1))$, so in this part of the search, we need to use the naïve scan, called "scan 2" in the figure. The details of suffix_search() are described in the following texts.

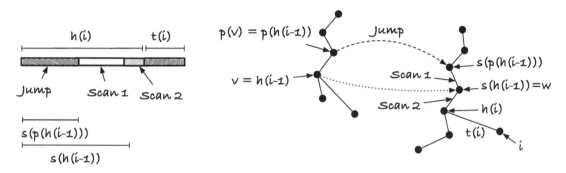

Figure 3-13. *Searching for the head of suffix i*

The implementation of the main function looks like this:

```
struct suffix_tree *
mccreight_suffix_tree(
    const uint8_t *x
) {
    struct suffix_tree *st = alloc_suffix_tree(x);
    uint32_t n = st->length;

    struct suffix_tree_node *leaf =
        new_node(st, x, x + st->length);
    leaf->parent = st->root; st->root->child = leaf;
    leaf->leaf_label = 0;

    for (uint32_t i = 1; i < st->length; ++i) {

        // Get the suffix of p(i-1) = h(i-1) = v
        struct suffix_tree_node *v = leaf->parent;
        struct suffix_tree_node *w = suffix_search(st, v);
        v->suffix_link = w;

        // Find head for the remaining suffix
        // using the naïve search.
```

```
    if (leaf->parent != st->root) {
        const uint8_t *y = leaf->range.from;
        const uint8_t *z = leaf->range.to;
        leaf = naive_insert(st, w, y, z);
    } else {
        // Search from the top for
        // the entire suffix.
        leaf = naive_insert(st, w, x + i, x + n);
    }

    // Move on to the next suffix.
    leaf->leaf_label = i;
}

    return st;
}
```

For the "naive search" and "scan 2" from Figure 3-13, there are two cases depending on whether we need to search from the root or not. The general case is when $h(i - 1)$ is nonempty (which also means that it is not the root). With `suffix_search()` we have searched for $h(i)$ to the point $s(h(i - 1))$. The string we have to continue our search with is $t(i - 1)$ (see Figure 3-14 A). We search for $t(i - 1)$ because it makes the code slightly easier and in any case is the same string we would search for if we searched $s(h(i - 1))$ toward the end of the string (see the figure). We will continue searching for $t(i - 1)$ until we get a mismatch, at which point we have found $h(i)$.

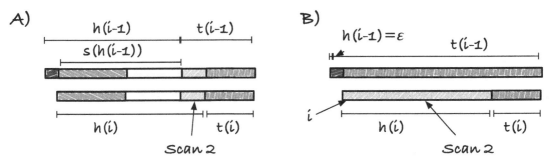

Figure 3-14. *Cases for scan 2*

If $h(i - 1)$ is empty (i.e., the root), we cannot search from $t(i - 1)$. The string $t(i - 1)$ is the entire suffix $x[i - 1, n]\$$ (see Figure 3-14 B). We need to scan for the entire suffix $x[i, n]\$$ to find $h(i)$.

114

Now, the `suffix_search()` function is responsible for finding $s(v) = w$ for node v; see Figure 3-13 and Figure 3-15. For this it uses two operations, it goes up to $p(v)$ and then jumps to $s(p(v))$, and then it searches from there to w in the "scan 1" step. If the edge label on the edge from $p(v)$ to v is the string from x to y (i.e., the pointers in the node representing v have the range from x to y), then it is this string we must search for once we have made the parent and suffix jumps.

There are four cases, depending on how v and $p(v)$ sit in the tree; see Figure 3-16. (A) It might be the case that v is the root. Since the suffix of the root is the root itself, we have that w is the root so our function can return that. (B) v might be a child of the root with a single symbol as its edge label. The suffix of a single symbol is the empty string which is the root, so again we can return the root. (C) It is also possible that the parent of v is the root but with a longer edge label, the string from pointer x to pointer y. In this case, we must search from the root for the string $x + 1$ to y where we add one to x for the same reason that we had to add one when searching with the naïve algorithm from the root (see earlier texts). Finally, (D), we have that $p(v)$ is not the root, so we can jump from v to $s(p(v))$ following the parent and suffix link pointer, respectively. From this point we must search for the string x to y since this is the missing string between $p(v)$ and v.

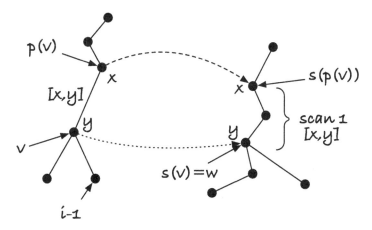

Figure 3-15. *General case of suffix search*

The code for handling the four cases can look like this:

```
static struct suffix_tree_node *
suffix_search(
    struct suffix_tree *st,
    struct suffix_tree_node *v
) {
```

```
    if (v == st->root) {
        // Case A
        return v;
    } else if (v->parent == st->root
                && range_length(v->range) == 1) {
        // Case B
        return st->root;

    } else if (v->parent == st->root) {
        // Case C
        const uint8_t *x = v->range.from + 1;
        const uint8_t *y = v->range.to;
        return fast_scan(st, st->root, x, y);

    } else {
        // The general case, case D
        const uint8_t *x = v->range.from;
        const uint8_t *y = v->range.to;
        struct suffix_tree_node *w =
                v->parent->suffix_link;
        return fast_scan(st, w, x, y);
    }
}
```

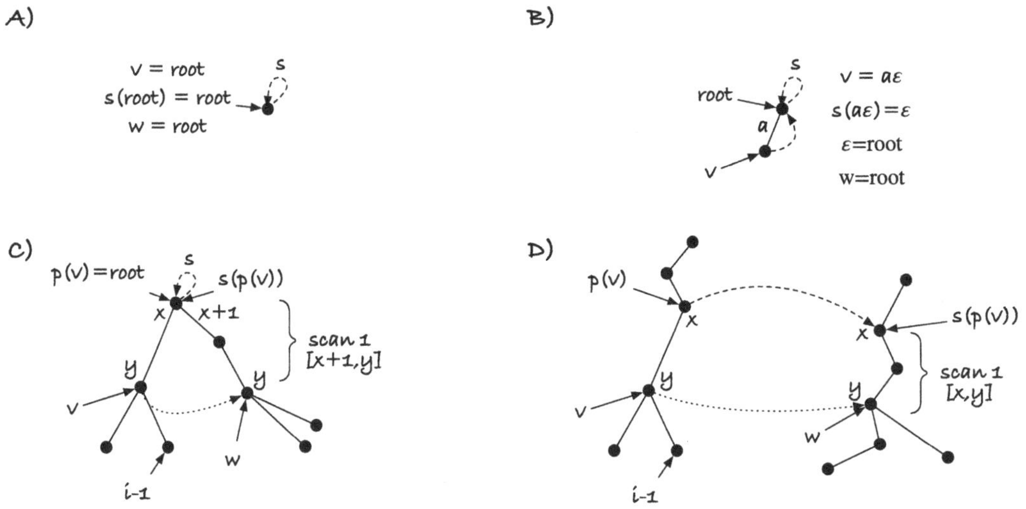

Figure 3-16. *Four cases for finding the suffix of node v*

116

The `fast_scan()` function handles the "scan 1" part of the algorithm, and as the name suggests, it is faster than the naïve search we use for "scan 2". We call it with a node and a string range. Call these v, x, and y. We want it to return the node w below v where the path label spells out the string from x to y or create such a node if it doesn't exist (so we always get a node from a call to the function). It is the same behavior as the naïve search in the tree has, but we will exploit that when we use `fast_scan()`, we call it with a string that we *know* is in the tree below node v. It is guaranteed by the observation that $s(h(i-1))$ is a prefix of $h(i)$. If we know that a string is in the tree, we do not need to compare every symbol down an edge against it. If we know which edge to follow, we can jump directly from one node to the next. This is what `fast_scan()` does.[3]

Let w be the node at the end of the edge where the first letter matches the first symbol we are searching for, and let s and t be the pointers that define the edge label from v to w. Let n be the length of the string, $n = t - s$, and let $z = x + n$, that is, z is the point we get to if we move x forward by the length of the v to w edge.

We have three cases for `fast_scan()`, depending on how the string s to t compares to the string from x to y; see Figure 3-17. (A) The two strings could match exactly. This means that we have found the string we are looking for so we can return w. (B) The string x to y might be shorter than then string from s to t—which we can recognize by $z < y$. In this case, we need to create a new node for where the x to y string ends and return the new node, node u in the figure. Finally, (C) the x to y string might be longer than the string from s to t. If this is the case, we need to search for the remainder of x to y, the string from z to y, starting in node w and we do this recursively.

The implementation can look like this:

```
static struct suffix_tree_node *
fast_scan(
    struct suffix_tree *st,
    struct suffix_tree_node *v,
    const uint8_t *x,
    const uint8_t *y
){
```

---

[3]By definition, we know that $h(i)$ is in the tree, so you might argue that we could use fast_scan( ) to find it. The reason that we cannot is that although we know the string is in the tree, we do not know what the string *is*. We don't know when we are done with the scan. For this reason, the naive search is necessary for "scan 2".

```
// Find child that matches *x.
struct suffix_tree_node * w = find_outgoing_edge(v, x);
assert(w); // must be here when we search for a suffix

// Jump down the edge.
uint32_t n = edge_length(w);
const uint8_t *z = x + n;

if (z == y) {
    // Found the node we should end in.
    return w; // We are done now.

} else if (z > y) {
    // We stop before we reach the end node, so we
    // need to split the edge.

    // We need to split at distance k from
    // s on the edge from v to w (with label [s,t])
    //
    //         |---n----|
    //     v o--------o w (s,t)
    //     x *---*----* z
    //           y
    //         |-k-|
    //
    uint32_t k = (uint32_t)(y - x);
    assert(k > 0);
    const uint8_t *s = w->range.from;
    const uint8_t *split_point = s + k;
    return split_edge(st, w, split_point);

} else {
    // We made it through the edge,
    // so continue from the next node.
    // The call is tail-recursive,
```

```
        /// so the compiler will optimize
        // it to a loop.
        return fast_scan(st, w, z, y);
    }
}
```

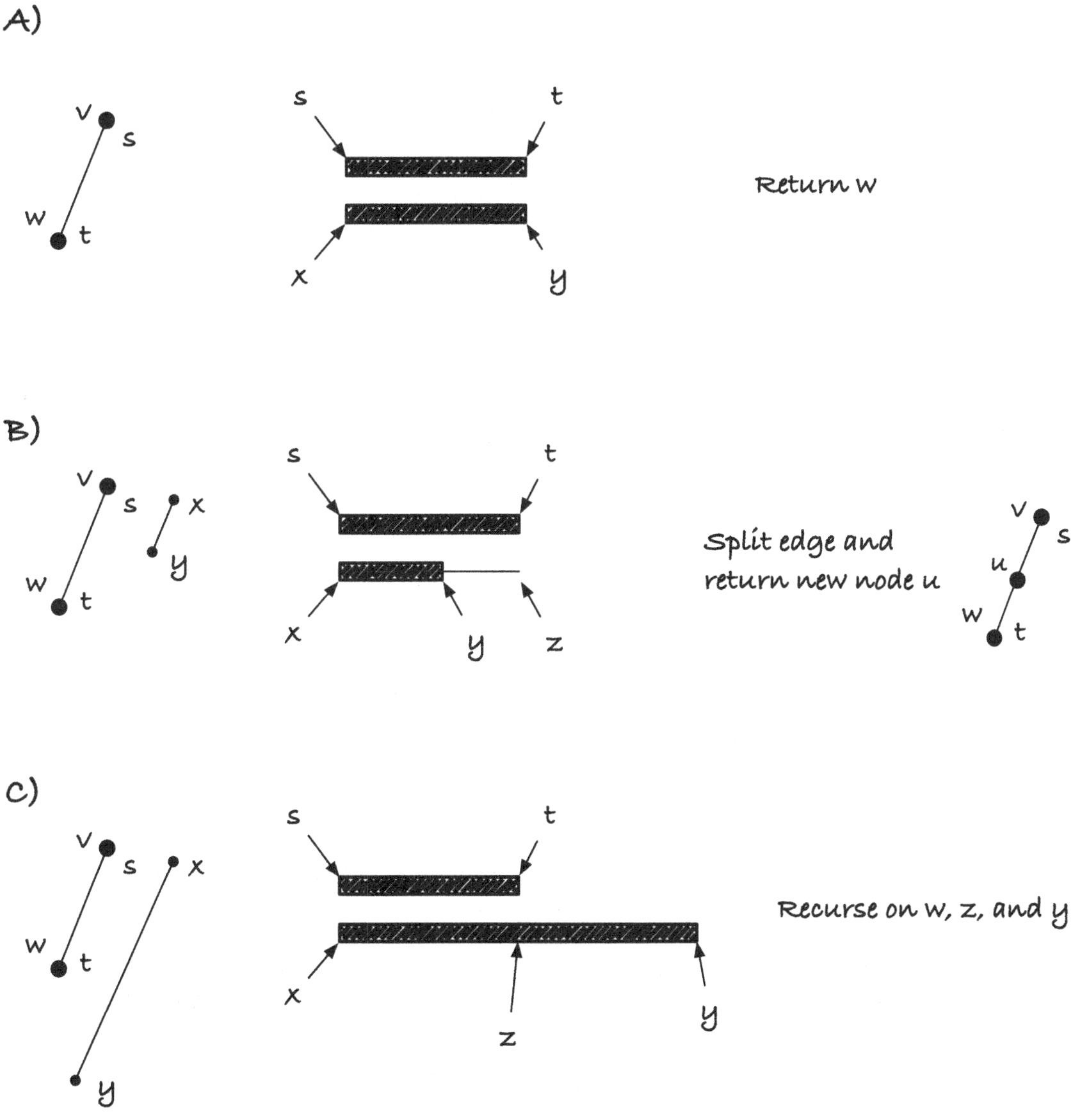
A)
v
s
w
t
s
t
x
y
Return w
B)
v
s
x
w
t
y
s
t
x
y
z
Split edge and
return new node u
v
s
u
w
t
C)
v
s
x
w
t
y
s
t
x
z
y
Recurse on w, z, and y

Figure 3-17. Fast scan cases

The second case in the fast scan, where we split an edge, leaves a node with a single child, violating an invariant of suffix trees. This should worry us, but it isn't a problem because we immediately after the fast scan search with a naïve insert. This naïve search will see a mismatch on the existing edge and insert $t(i)$ on an out edge of node u, returning us to a tree that satisfies the invariant.

To see that this is the case, see Figure 3-18. By definition, $h(i-1)$ is the longest prefix of suffix $i-1$ before we have a mismatch, so there must be some longer suffix, $k < i-1$, that shares prefix $h(i-1)$ and then mismatches. Let the symbol at the mismatch be a for suffix $i-1$ and b for suffix k. When we insert suffix i, suffix $k+1$ must have been inserted. Suffixes $k+1$ and i share the prefix $s(h(i-1))$ and the next character in $k+1$ after $s(h(i-1))$ is b, and since we broke a single edge, so there is only one symbol that continues from this point, we must conclude that the symbol after the point where we broke the edge must be b. Since $t(i-1)$—which is the string we will search for in after calling `fast_scan()`—begins with symbol a, we will get a mismatch immediately and conclude that $s(h(i-1))$ is indeed $h(i)$.

To analyze the running time of McCreight's algorithm, we split it into three parts: (1) The total work we do when jumping to parent and then the suffix of the parent, (2) the total work we do when using `fast_scan()` to handle "scan 1", and (3) the total work we do with `naive_insert()` to handle "scan 2".

Of the three, (1) is easy to handle. For each leaf we insert, of which there are n, we move along two pointers which take constant time, so (1) takes time $O(n)$.

For (2) we will use an amortization argument. Let $d(v)$ be the node depth of node v, that is, the number of nodes on the path from the root to v. Moving to the parent of v, $p(v)$, cannot decrease the depth more than one. If v is the root, which is its own parent, then $d(p(v)) = d(v)$ and otherwise $d(p(v)) = d(v) - 1$. Moving along a suffix pointer can also only decrease the depth by one. Consider Figure 3-19. For each path from the root down to v, we see a number of nodes, and each node has a suffix link (in the algorithm, node $h(i-1)$ might not have a suffix link, but we never jump from this node, so this has no consequence for the argument). In the following text, we shall argue that each of these suffix links is unique. In the general case, (A) in Figure 3-19, this means that $d(s(v)) = d(v)$. (B) An exception is when the first edge on the path has a single symbol as its label. In that case, the first node has the root as its suffix and $d(s(v)) = d(v) - 1$.

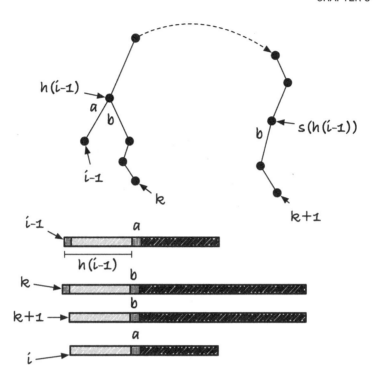

Figure 3-18. *Splitting an edge in fast scan*

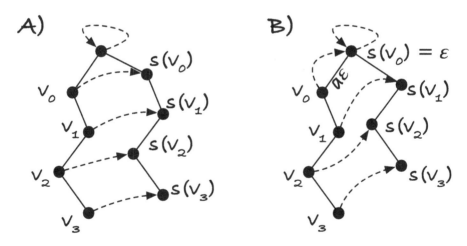

Figure 3-19. *Relationship between a path and the path of suffix links*

Now, to see that the suffix link nodes are unique, recall that all nodes in the tree correspond to a prefix of at least one suffix and that nodes on the same paths will have the node with the smallest depth be a prefix of the other. Let k be such a suffix for nodes v_i and $v_{i-1} = p(v_i)$; see Figure 3-20. Since v_{i-1} and v_i are different nodes, the edge label between them, y, is nonempty. If we now look at suffix $k + 1$, we get the suffix of v_{i-1} and v_i instead, and these are also separated by the nonempty string y; thus, they must be different nodes.

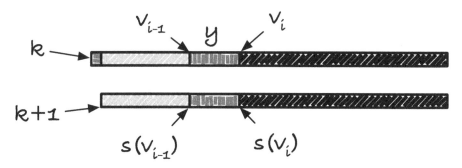

Figure 3-20. *Uniqueness of suffix links*

In each iteration of (2), the pointer jumps, thus decreasing the depth by at most two; after which "scan 1" (or fast scan) increases the depth by a number of nodes. It cannot, however, increase the depth by more than $O(n)$—there simply aren't paths long enough. In total, it can increase the depth by $O(n)$ plus the number of decreases in the algorithm which is bounded by $O(n)$. In total, the time we spend on (B) is linear.

Finally, for (C) consider the search for $h(i)$ from $h(i - 1)$. First we make a jump to $s(p(h(i - 1)))$, then a fast scan down to $s(h(i - 1))$, and then a slow scan down to $h(i)$. When we insert $h(i + 1)$, we jump and fast scan down to $s(h(i))$. If you consider these indices in the string we build our suffix over, rather than nodes in the tree, you will see that we always use a slow scan from one head to the other, that is, we slow scan from $h(i - 1)$ to $h(i)$ when inserting $h(i)$, from $h(i)$ to $h(i + 1)$ when inserting $h(i + 1)$, and so on; see Figure 3-21. These intervals do not overlap, and in each iteration, we move the pointer where a slow scan will start to the right. The total time we can spend in "scan 2" is thus $O(n)$.

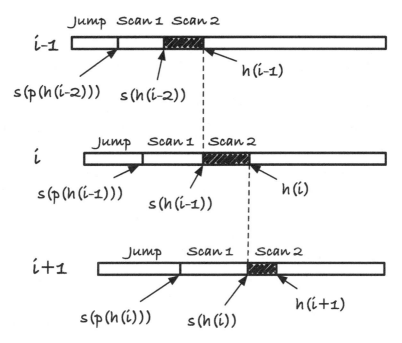

Figure 3-21. *Slow scan (scan 2) time usage*

Searching with suffix trees

To search for a pattern *p* in a suffix tree of a string *x*, we use the strategy from the naïve insert we have seen before. We scan down edges in the tree until we either find the pattern or find a mismatch. If the first is the case, then the leaf of the subtree under the edge or the node where we had the hit will be the positions in *x* where *p* occurs. The function below implements it. Here the pattern is null-terminated, as C strings are, but do not confuse this null with the sentinel in *x*$. If we reach the end of the string, we have a null character, and that is how it is used. The function doesn't directly give us the positions where the pattern matches. It gives us the smallest subtree where the pattern matches the path label to it. All leaves in this subtree are positions where the pattern can be found in *x*.

The function searches for *p* from the node *v*. If *p* is empty, then we have a match at node *v*, and we return it. Otherwise, we find the out edge (the edge to a node *w*) where the first symbol matches the first symbol of *p*—it is along this edge and its subtree that *p* might be found. If we do not have a matching out edge, we cannot have a match, and we return a null pointer to indicate that. Assume that we do have an edge to scan along. Then we set *s* to its beginning and *t* to its end. The way we scan down the edge is by incrementing *s* and *p* and comparing what they point to. This means that *p* is not the

123

original pattern we are searching for when we run the algorithm, rather it is a pointer to how far into the pattern we have matched so far. Similarly, *s* is a pointer into how far along the edge we have matched; see Figure 3-22. If we reach the end of the pattern, that is, *p* points to the null symbol that terminates the string, then we have a match. Although Figure 3-22 shows a single substring of *x* where the pattern matches, the substring that is the edge label, the pattern will also match at all other leaves in the subtree rooted in *w*, so we return this node. If we see a mismatch between *s* and *p*, we do not have a match in the string, and we return a null pointer. It is important that we test for the end of string *p* before we check for a mismatch between the characters at *s* and *p*. If *p* points to the termination symbol and *s* does not, we will have a mismatch in a comparison between the strings, but we want this to be a complete match. If we get to the end of the edge without exhausting the pattern, we continue searching recursively from *w*. The pattern pointer is already incremented to the point in the pattern where we should continue our search, and the recursion continues the search. The tail recursion will be translated into a loop by most compilers, so the runtime penalty of recursion is minimal.

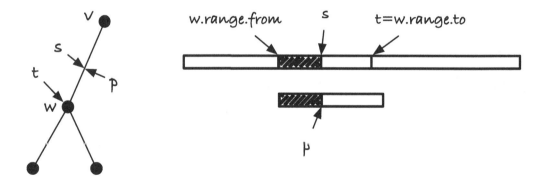

Figure 3-22. *Scanning along an edge when searching for a pattern*

```
static struct suffix_tree_node *
st_search_internal(
    struct suffix_tree *st,
    struct suffix_tree_node *v,
    const uint8_t *p
) {
    if (*p == '\0')
        // We are searching from an empty string,
        // so we must already be at the right node.
        return v;
```

```
    // Find child that matches *x.
    struct suffix_tree_node *w = v->child;
    while (w) {
        if (*(w->range.from) == *p) break;
        w = w->sibling;
    }
    if (!w) return 0; // The pattern is not here.

    // We have an edge to follow!
    const uint8_t *s = w->range.from;
    const uint8_t *t = w->range.to;
    for (; s != t; ++s, ++p) {
        if (*p == '\0') return w; // End of the pattern
        if (*s != *p)   return 0; // Mismatch
    }

    // We made it through the edge,
    // so continue from the next node.
    return st_search_internal(st, w, p);
}
```

To search in the entire tree, we need to search from the root which is what st_search() does:

```
struct suffix_tree_node *
st_search(
    struct suffix_tree *st,
    const uint8_t *p
) {
    return st_search_internal(st, st->root, p);
}
```

Leaf iterators

It is not hard to implement a depth-first traversal of a tree to extract the indices where we have matches, but for a user, iterators are easier to use, which was also our rationale for using them in the matching algorithms in the last chapter. Iterators can be hard to implement, but it is worth it to make the code more usable. An iterator for a depth-first

125

traversal is more complex than the ones we saw in the last chapter, however, because a depth-first traversal is recursive in nature which means that we need a stack, and for an iterator, we need an explicit stack. An explicit stack also solves another problem. A recursive traversal of the tree can have a deep recursion stack and might exceed the available stack space.

A simple way to implement a stack is to use a linked list where we push frames to the front of the list and pop them from the front as well (naturally). Our recursion is over nodes so that is what we put in our stack frames.

```c
struct st_leaf_iter_frame {
    struct st_leaf_iter_frame *next;
    struct suffix_tree_node *node;
};
static struct st_leaf_iter_frame *
new_frame(struct suffix_tree_node *node)
{
    struct st_leaf_iter_frame *frame =
        malloc(sizeof(struct st_leaf_iter_frame));
    frame->node = node;
    frame->next = 0;
    return frame;
}
```

An iterator contains a stack and the results of iterations are leaf nodes.

```c
struct st_leaf_iter {
    struct st_leaf_iter_frame *stack;
};
struct st_leaf_iter_result {
    struct suffix_tree_node *leaf;
};
```

When we initialize a new iterator from a node—the root in the tree that we wish to iterate over—we put the node in a frame and make that frame the list. There is a special case when the node is null, that is, the tree is empty. There we leave the stack empty. This way, we do not need to worry about frames with null nodes and the empty stack is the obvious indicator that we are done with the iteration.

```
void init_st_leaf_iter(
    struct st_leaf_iter *iter,
    struct suffix_tree *st,
    struct suffix_tree_node *node
) {
    if (node) iter->stack = new_frame(node);
    else iter->stack = 0;
}
```

If the stack were always empty when we deallocate an iterator, we wouldn't need to do anything, but it might not be. In that case we need to free all the frames in the stack.

```
void dealloc_st_leaf_iter(
    struct st_leaf_iter *iter
) {
    struct st_leaf_iter_frame *frame = iter->stack;
    while (frame) {
        struct st_leaf_iter_frame *next = frame->next;
        free(frame);
        frame = next;
    }
}
```

It is, not surprisingly, in next_st_leaf() the real work is done. Here we follow the steps a recursion would take. We get the next frame from the stack if there are any. If the node in the frame has children, it is not a leaf, so we push its children onto the stack (we get to reverse_push() and why we want it below). If it is a leaf, we free the frame and return it. If it wasn't a leaf, we also free the frame—just a few lines later in the function—and pop the next frame in the stack.

```
bool next_st_leaf(
    struct st_leaf_iter *iter,
    struct st_leaf_iter_result *res
) {
    struct st_leaf_iter_frame *frame = iter->stack;
    while (frame) {
        // Pop the frame.
```

```
        iter->stack = frame->next;
        struct suffix_tree_node *node = frame->node;

        if (node->child) {
            // We have to push in reverse order to get
            // an in-order depth-first traversal.
            reverse_push(iter, node->child);

        } else {
            // Leaf
            // clean up and return result
            free(frame);
            res->leaf = node;
            return true;
        }

        // Get rid of the frame and pop the next.
        free(frame);
        frame = iter->stack;
    }
    return false;
}
```

The order in which we see a node's children in the recursion depends on the order in which we add them to the stack. In a standard recursive implementation, we can call the function on each child in turn, but with the explicit stack, we need to push all of them to the stack before we pop the first again. If we push the children from the first child and follow its sibling pointers to the last, then the first child will be below the second that is below the third and so forth; see Figure 3-23. If we push the last child first, then the second last, and so on, then we have a stack that, when we pop off and process nodes, will give us the same traversal order as a direct depth-first traversal. If you do not care about which order you traverse the tree, you can use either, but the reverse_push() function is not substantially more complicated than the direct approach:

```
static void reverse_push(
    struct st_leaf_iter *iter,
    struct suffix_tree_node *child
) {
```

```
if (child->sibling)
    reverse_push(iter, child->sibling);
struct st_leaf_iter_frame *child_frame =
    new_frame(child);
child_frame->next = iter->stack;
iter->stack = child_frame;
}
```

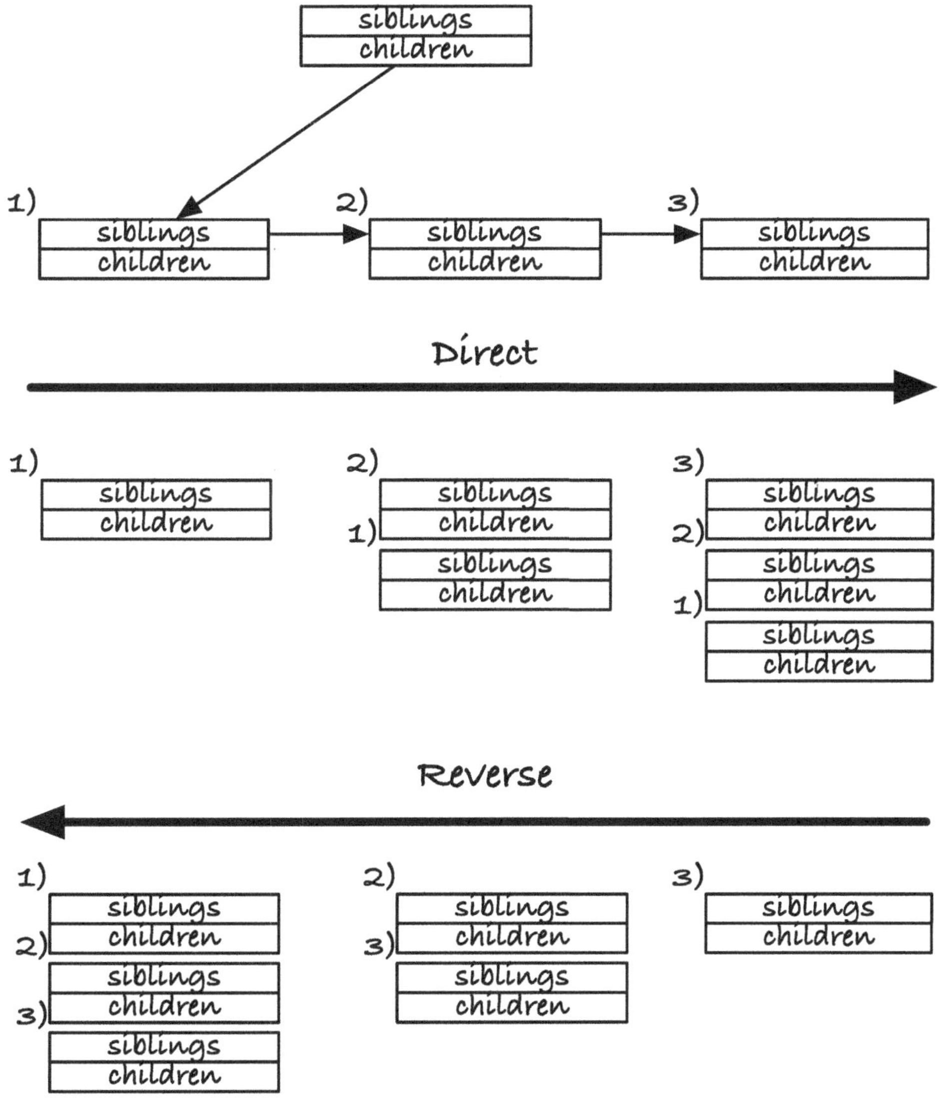

Figure 3-23. *Pushing children, direct or reversed*

If we want an iterator through the positions where the pattern match, we can wrap the leaf iterator in another iterator for that. The implementation is quite simple. We iterate through leaves—using the iterator earlier—and for each, we set the position and return true. When there are no more leaves, there are no more matches either.

```c
struct st_search_iter {
    struct st_leaf_iter leaf_iter;
};
struct st_search_match {
    uint32_t pos;
};
void init_st_search_iter(
    struct st_search_iter *iter,
    struct suffix_tree *st,
    const uint8_t *p
) {
    struct suffix_tree_node *match = st_search(st, p);
    init_st_leaf_iter(&iter->leaf_iter, st, match);
}

bool next_st_match(
    struct st_search_iter *iter,
    struct st_search_match *match
) {
    struct st_leaf_iter_result res;
    if (!next_st_leaf(&iter->leaf_iter, &res))
        return false;
    match->pos = res.leaf->leaf_label;
    return true;
}

void dealloc_st_search_iter(
    struct st_search_iter *iter
) {
    dealloc_st_leaf_iter(&iter->leaf_iter);
}
```

Comparisons

The naïve implementation runs in worst-case $O(n^2)$, while the other two algorithms run in $O(n)$, but how do they compare in practice? The worst input for the naïve algorithm is input where it has to search completely through every suffix to insert it, but for random strings, we expect mismatches early in the suffixes, so here we should get a better running time. It is harder to reason about best- and worst-case data for the other algorithms. For the McCreight's algorithm, one could argue that it will also benefit from early mismatches since it has a naïve search algorithm as the final step in each iteration. The LCP algorithm doesn't scan in any way but depends on the SA and LCP arrays (which in turn depends on the string underlying the suffix tree, of course). The algorithm corresponds closely to a depth-first traversal of the suffix tree, so we would expect it to be faster when there are fewer nodes, that is, when the branch-out of the inner nodes is high. We can experiment to see if these intuitive analyses are correct—it turns out that the fan-out of nodes is a key factor and the larger it is, the *slower* the algorithms get.

In Figure 3-24 you can see the running time of the three algorithms with three types of strings: Equal, strings consisting only on a single symbol; DNA, random[4] sequences over four symbols (A,C,G,T); and 8-bit characters. Figure 3-25 zooms in on the smaller string sizes and leaves out the time measurements for the naïve algorithm on the Equal alphabet.

Some of the results are as we would expect. The naïve algorithm performs very poorly on single-symbol strings but better on random strings. It is still slower than the other two algorithms on random DNA sequences. With the 8-bit alphabet, the naïve and McCreight's algorithm run equally fast—because mismatches occur faster with a larger alphabet—but notice two things: McCreight's algorithm is not running in linear time as it should be, and while the two algorithms run in the same time, they are both *slower* than when we use the two smaller alphabets.

The culprit is the linked lists we use for node's children. We have assumed that the alphabet is of a constant size—and generally, it is—but we are comparing running times for different alphabet sizes. The larger the alphabet, the longer it takes to insert nodes and to search for children. Profiling the algorithms reveals that most of the time is spent exactly on traversing these lists, and the larger the alphabet, the larger fraction of time this is. With the single-letter alphabet, Equal, we have the smallest fan-out of nodes—all inner node has two children (the letter and the sentinel). This is the optimal situation,

---

[4]Real DNA sequences are not random, but in my simulated data they are, and it is not *that* far from real DNA.

with respect to children list traversal, for McCreight and LCP (but still the worst case for the naïve algorithm where the search time dominates). McCreight does run in linear time for the smallest alphabet, but it will not run in linear time for the larger alphabets until all nodes have most of the alphabet as out edges. The time depends on the degrees of the nodes the algorithms search through, which affects all through algorithms. The time it takes to reach a fan-out close to the maximal, a degree equal to the alphabet size, depends on the length of the string. For those shown in the figures, we are still seeing this effect.

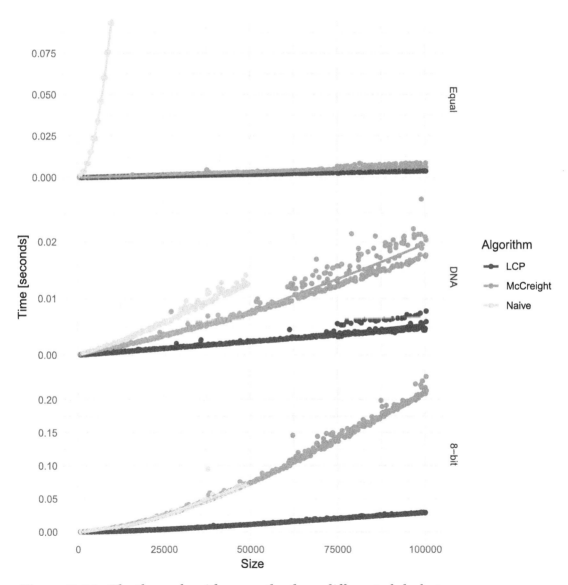

Figure 3-24. *The three algorithms on the three different alphabets*

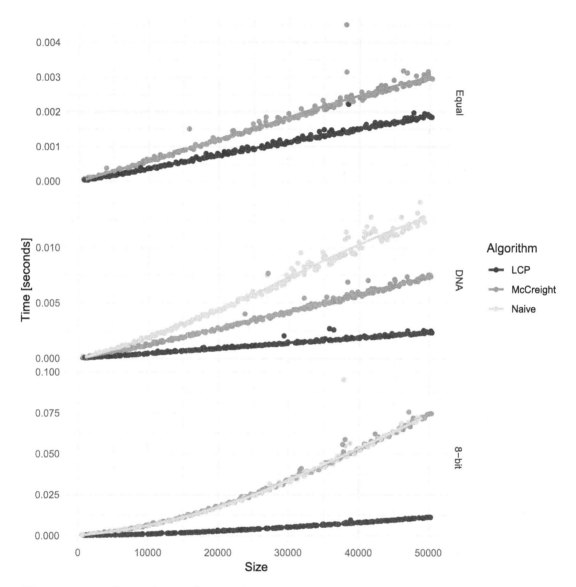

Figure 3-25. *Zoom in on short strings*

If the linked lists slow down our algorithm, we can consider an alternative.[5] We can use an array for the children, indexed by the alphabet symbols. With this, we can look up the edge for any symbol in constant time. I have shown the running times of the array-based and linked list–based algorithms in Figure 3-26. The array-based algorithms run

---

[5]I have not listed the implementation in this book since it closely resembles the linked list suffix trees. You can find the implementation at https://github.com/mailund/stralg.

in linear time and are not affected by the growing linked lists, but they *are* still affected by the alphabet size. The larger the alphabet, the larger arrays we need to store in each node, and the poorer IO efficiency we will see.

The fastest construction algorithm appears to be the LCP algorithm, linked list or array-based. We can examine their running time in Figure 3-27. The list-based is slightly faster for the smaller alphabets, and for the 8-bit alphabet, it is faster up to around string length 90,000, where the extra memory usage of the array-based implementation pays off. For smaller alphabets, it seems that the LCP algorithm with linked lists is the way to go.

The LCP algorithm gets its speed from not doing any searches. It does not build the suffix tree using only a string, however, but it needs the suffix array, SA, and the longest common prefix array, LCP. When we measure the running time of the algorithms, we should take into account that we need to *compute* these arrays before we can use the LCP algorithms. In this chapter, we have seen how to compute the SA and LCP arrays from a suffix tree, but of course, we do not want to include this construction on top of the LCP construction algorithm. We would never build a suffix tree so we could rebuild it with another algorithm. In the next chapter, we will see how to build the two arrays directly from a string, and in Figure 3-28, I have shown how LCP and LCP with the array construction compare to McCreight. The suffix array construction is potentially expensive, and its time usage depends on the alphabet size. The larger the alphabet, the faster it is, maybe counterintuitive but true. In the next chapter, I show several algorithms for computing the suffix array, two of them have this property, and it is one of those I have used for the experiments in this chapter. If we include the array construction, we need a large alphabet for the LCP algorithm to outcompete McCreight's algorithm. For the DNA alphabet, the two algorithms are equally effective, and for the single-symbol alphabet—the worst case for the array construction algorithm—McCreight's algorithm is much faster.

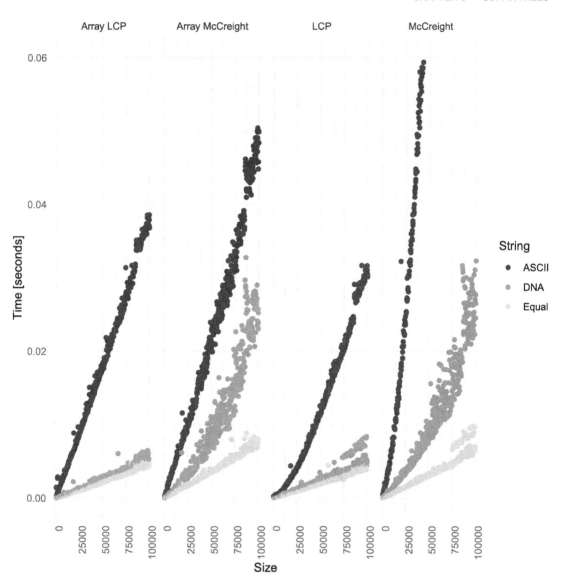

Figure 3-26. *Array-based children*

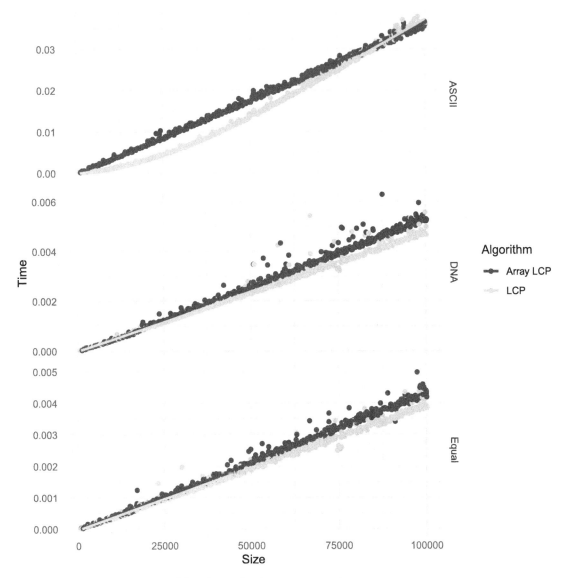

Figure 3-27. *Array- and list-based LCP constructions*

There is a scenario where we would always use the LCP construction algorithm based on the experimental results here. It is not uncommon to preprocess a string we will use for many queries. In bioinformatics, for example, we have strings that are millions of characters long, and we query them with millions of short patterns. In such scenarios, we build a search structure like a suffix array and save it to a file, so it is available every time we have new patterns to search for. It is hard to serialize a suffix tree but trivial to write two arrays to a file and read them in again. If we can read the arrays from a file, we can use the fast LCP algorithm to construct a suffix tree from them.

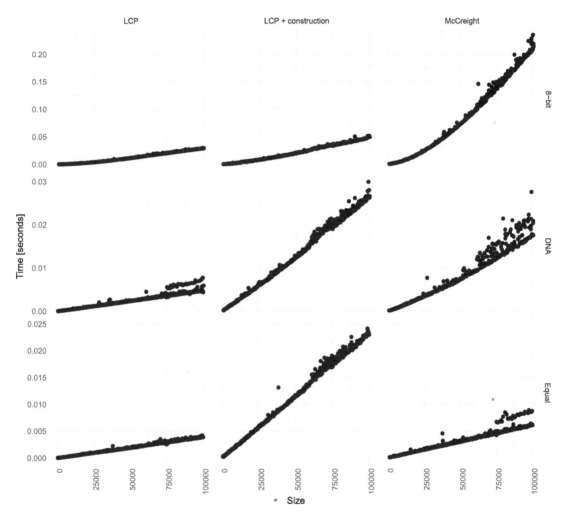

Figure 3-28. *Adding the array computations to LCP*

If we do not have the arrays precomputed, then McCreight's algorithm or even the naïve algorithm is competitive. The naïve algorithm is, obviously, only worth considering with a large alphabet, but its simplicity and a running time compatible with McCreight might make it a good choice. Further, if memory is a problem, and each word counts, you can implement it without the parent and suffix link pointer; McCreight needs both (and LCP needs the parent pointer but not the suffix link).

You can find the code I used for the measurements on GitHub: `https://github.com/mailund/stralg/blob/master/performance/suffix_tree_construction.c`.

CHAPTER 4

Suffix arrays

The *suffix array* data structure is closely tied to the suffix tree, and we have already seen in the previous chapter. The suffix array gives you the lexicographically (alphabetically) sorted order of the suffixes, where each suffix is represented by its index into the string x; see Figure 4-1.

The appeal of the suffix array over suffix trees is its space-efficient and straightforward representation. You can do many of the things you can do with a suffix tree, and with a little extra data and (unfortunately) added complexity, you can simulate suffix trees with suffix arrays. The memory efficiency is a crucial reason to prefer suffix arrays. Suffix trees are rather memory hungry. If you have a string of length n, you can have $O(n)$ nodes in your suffix tree.[1] If you build the suffix tree using the naïve algorithm—so you do not need the parent and suffix link pointers—each node takes up five computer words ($5w$).[2] You add one, the parent pointer, if you use the LCP algorithm ($6w$), and you add yet another for McCreight ($7w$). Those are the costs per node in the tree, and there can be twice as many nodes as characters in the string, so per character, we have $10w$, $12w$, and $14w$, respectively. In contrast, the suffix array is one computer word per suffix, that is, one computer word per character, (w).

---

[1] With my implementation. It is possible to compress it further, but the best representations in the literature are still not as memory efficient as a suffix array.

[2] A note on terminology, I will use "word" to mean the size of memory you use to store an integer. It will typically be the same as a computer word, that is, the size of its registers. On most computers today, that is 64 bits. In my implementation, however, I use 32-bit integers, so that is the word size here. I also use pointers, though, and those will be full words. I use the term "word" to avoid focusing on a specific number of bytes, since you can always change your integer type to something smaller, to save space, or something larger so you can index into longer strings. And I also don't want to distinguish between integers and pointers, although they have a different size in my implementation. Making the distinction will make the analysis and comparison between algorithms more complicated. Every time you see "word," just think the size of integers and pointers.

T. Mailund, *String Algorithms in C*, https://doi.org/10.1007/978-1-4842-5920-7_4

Suffixes: Sorted   Suffix array

Suffixes		Sorted	Suffix array
mississippi$	(0)	$	11
ississippi$	(1)	i$	10
ssissippi$	(2)	ippi$	7
sissippi$	(3)	issippi$	4
issippi$	(4)	ississippi$	1
ssippi$	(5)	mississippi$	0
sippi$	(6)	pi$	9
ippi$	(7)	ppi$	8
ppi$	(8)	sippi$	6
pi$	(9)	sissippi$	3
i$	(10)	ssippi$	5
$	(11)	ssissippi$	2

Figure 4-1. *Example of a suffix array*

The memory officiency of one word per input character is only for the actual array. The algorithm that we use to construct it can take up more space, of course, similar to how we saw that we needed extra pointers for the suffix trees to get the linear running times.

The representation of a suffix array is simple. We have a pointer to the string (we need it in addition to the array to compare patterns against the suffixes), the length of the string/array, and then the array. In the following structure, I have included two additional arrays that we will not use yet, so you can ignore them for now.

```
struct suffix_array {
    uint8_t *string;
    uint32_t length;
    uint32_t *array;
```

```
    uint32_t *inverse;
    uint32_t *lcp;
};
```

When we construct a suffix array, we allocate the memory for the array and hardly more (the extra arrays are not always used so by default we set them to null—we can compute them when we need them).

```
static struct suffix_array *allocate_sa(uint8_t *string)
{
    struct suffix_array *sa =
        malloc(sizeof(struct suffix_array));
    sa->string = string;
    sa->length = (uint32_t)strlen((char *)string) + 1;
    sa->array = malloc(sa->length * sizeof(*sa->array));

    sa->inverse = 0;
    sa->lcp = 0;

    return sa;
}
```

Deallocating a suffix array is equally simple: we free the memory we allocated and that is that.

```
void free_suffix_array(struct suffix_array *sa)
{
    free(sa->array);
    if (sa->inverse) free(sa->inverse);
    if (sa->lcp)     free(sa->lcp);
    free(sa);
}
```

In each section of this chapter, I will present code that you have to compile in different files. I use macros liberally, and there are some overlaps between macros and variables in the algorithms, as I have tried to present the algorithms with variables that are typically used in the literature. Two of the algorithms are recursive, which means that you have to define prototypes for the functions you use. I have not done this everywhere, but only when it makes the text easier to read. However, for each section, I link to a file

141

on GitHub where you can download the full implementation. You can find the header file with the definition of the preceding structs at `https://github.com/mailund/stralg/blob/master/stralg/suffix_array.h` and the allocation/deallocation code here: `https://github.com/mailund/stralg/blob/master/stralg/suffix_array.c`. You need these two files for all the code in this chapter.

Constructing suffix arrays

Suffix arrays, like suffix trees, can be computed in linear time. This shouldn't surprise since we have already seen how they can be computed using a suffix tree and we know that a suffix tree can be computed in linear time. However, one of the benefits of using suffix arrays is the smaller memory footprint, and if we are pressed for memory, then using a suffix tree to build a suffix array is not useful. We want to construct the array directly from the string and not via a suffix tree.

Trivial constructions—Comparison-based sorting

Since the suffix array is simply the indices of the suffixes sorted in alphabetical order, an immediate approach to computing is to consider each suffix an independent string and explicitly sort them. Such an approach, using C's `qsort()` function, would look like this:

```
static // Wrapper of strcmp needed for qsort
int construction_cmpfunc(
    const void *a,
    const void *b
) {
    return strcmp(*(char **)a, *(char **)b);
}

struct suffix_array *qsort_sa_construction(
    uint8_t *string
) {
    struct suffix_array *sa = allocate_sa(string);

    uint8_t **suffixes =
        malloc(sa->length * sizeof(uint8_t *));
```

```
    for (int i = 0; i < sa->length; ++i)
        suffixes[i] = string + i;

    qsort(suffixes, sa->length, sizeof(char *),
            construction_cmpfunc);

    for (int i = 0; i < sa->length; i++)
        sa->array[i] = (uint32_t)(suffixes[i] - string);

    free(suffixes);

    return sa;
}
```

We build an array containing all our suffixes. Each suffix is represented by a pointer into the full string, which works since C strings are nothing more than pointers. When we point into the middle of our string, we get the string that starts at the position we point to. Then we call qsort() to sort the suffixes. The qsort() function uses a comparison function that gets a pointer to two keys to be compared. In our case, the keys are strings, that is, char *, so we need to get what the pointer is pointing to when we call strcmp().

When we have sorted the suffixes, we can get the indices of them for array by computing their offset from the string.

The expected running time of qsort() is $O(k \cdot n \log n)$ where k is the time it takes to compare keys. In our case, keys are strings, and comparing them takes worst-case time $O(n)$. So the expected running time for the quick sort solution is $O(n^2 \log n)$. This is the expected running time, a probabilistic running time assuming that strings are random. If they are not, the worst-case running time can be $O(kn^2)$, or $O(n^3)$, for constructing suffix arrays this way. The worst-case comparison time happens if we have a string consisting of a single character. Then all comparisons continue to the end of the shortest string, which is on average $n/2$. The cases where we hit the worst-case running time for quick sort depend on its implementation. The algorithm picks a *pivot* element in a range and splits the keys there into two subranges based on the pivot. It puts the keys smaller than the pivot in one range and the keys that are larger in the other. We get the best performance if it splits the range in two equal sizes. We get the worst case if it splits them such that one element goes in one of the subranges and all the others in the other subrange. If we create a suffix array from a string with a single character, the array of suffixes we just made is inversely sorted (shorter strings always go before longer strings). If the quick sort implementation uses the first or last element in the range as a pivot, we get the worst-case behavior. The pivot is either the largest or the smallest key in the range, so it will go in one subrange and all the other keys in the other. I will refer you to a textbook on fundamental algorithms to study the quick sort algorithm, if you are not already familiar with it.

The analysis is more pessimistic than what we will see in practice, though. We only see the worst-case complexity if the comparisons are very long. If there are few long repeats of substrings in our string, we will terminate the comparisons fast. With natural language strings or DNA strings, for example, we do not expect to see the worst case and the algorithm will in practice run in expected $O(n \log n)$. String comparisons run until we see the first mismatching character, and this length has a geometric distribution if the string is random, so k is $O(1)$.[3] The suffixes in the array we sort will have a random order, so quick sort will have the expected running time, $O(n \log n)$.

It is possible to do a radix sort instead of a comparison-based sort—do a stable bucket sort starting at the end of the suffixes and move to the beginning. This approach will have a worst-case running time of $O(n^2)$. It is better than quick sort both when it has its worst case, cubic running time, and when it has its expected running time but the string comparisons take linear time. With random strings, however, we expect that the quick sort algorithm will be faster.

The memory consumption in the construction is $2w$ per character. We need the array of pointers to the suffix strings to sort them, and then we need the actual suffix array.

The key takeaway from the analysis is that the running time with this approach is that for random strings, we might get an $O(n \log n)$, but it could be as bad as $O(n^3)$. For long strings, this is prohibitive, so we are motivated to find faster construction algorithms, and we will see two linear-time algorithms in the next following sections.

---

[3]If you pick two random letters from an alphabet of size h, they are equal with probability $1/h$ and different with probability $1 - 1/h$. The expected number of times you have to draw pairs of letters until they are different—corresponding to the number of characters you have to compare in random strings—is $\dfrac{1}{1-1/h}$. This depends on the alphabet size, which we assume is a constant, so a comparison of random strings takes constant time. If the alphabet is not uniformly distributed, you still have a probability for picking the same or different letters, and the formula is the same except for the value that goes in the denominator. The analysis is not entirely correct because we do not have random strings; they are all suffixes of the same string. When the strings are not independent, we cannot argue exactly this way, but with a long random string, the suffixes are sufficiently independent that it doesn't matter in practice.

The skew algorithm

The Kärkkäinen-Sanders, DC3, or skew algorithm—it has many names—is a divide-and-conquer approach to building a suffix array. It splits the string into two parts, one containing one-third of the suffixes and one containing the rest. It constructs a shorter string from the two-thirds suffixes and recursively sort it and then use it to combine the two initial array of suffixes into the correct array.

You can find the full source code for the algorithm at `https://github.com/mailund/stralg/blob/master/stralg/skew.c`. Let us dig into the details. Given an initial string, split it into the suffixes that have index i with $i \% 3 = 0$, those that have modulus one or two, $i \% 3 \neq 0$. Let us call these arrays `sa3` and `sa12`. We put all the suffix indices into them such that those indices $i \% 3 \neq 0$ go into `sa12` and the rest into `sa3`. We first construct `sa12` and sort it lexicographically according to the suffixes it holds. We do this recursively using the method we are building now (as one does in divide-and-conquer algorithms). Once we have `sa12`, we can then construct a sorted `sa3` from the result. All indices $i \% 3 = 1$ are sorted in `sa12`, so if we insert $i \% 3 = 0$ in the order that $i + 1$ appear in `sa12`, we have the indices in `sa3` sorted with respect to the suffix *following* their index. If we then do a stable sort of the first letters of the suffixes in `sa3`, we will have binned these suffixes, so the first letters are in order, and within each bin, the suffixes are sorted with respect to the suffix following the first letter. This means that we have sorted the suffixes in `sa3`. We can sort `sa3` in linear time if we use a radix sort. I go into details about this in a few pages.

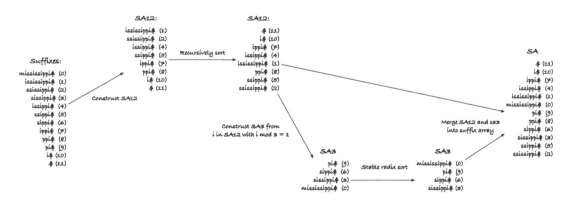

Figure 4-2. *Overview of the skew algorithm*

Once we have both `sa12` and `sa3` sorted, we can merge them into the suffix array we want. See Figure 4-2 for an overview of the steps in the algorithm.

We do not sort sa12 directly with a recursion. It isn't a string which is what our method should take as input. Instead, we create another string from the array, get the suffix array from that string, and from this suffix array, we extract the sorted suffixes in sa12.

I go into more details a little later, but this idea is this: first, do a radix sort based on the first three characters in the suffixes in sa12. We can do this in linear time for any constant-sized prefix of the suffixes in sa12, not just the first character as for sa3, so we can sort based on the first three characters in constant time. Now map each triple to a number such that the smallest lexicographically triplet gets zero, the second smallest 1, and so on. If all the triplets are unique, we have sorted sa12 completely, and we are done. If not, we build a string u of length m12 + 1, where m12 is the length of sa12. We put a sentinel, #, in the middle of it (which is why we need the length to be one more than m12). Then we run through the suffixes in sa12 and put the triplet number at the front of each suffix into u, those $i \% 3 = 2$ in the first half and those $i \% 3 = 1$ in the second half.[4] Insert them in the order they are found in sa12, not the sorted order; see Figure 4-3.

If we construct u this way, then you have an implicit representation of all the suffixes in sa12, just in a different alphabet. We cannot see the letters inside each triplet, but we have the order they should be sorted in from the way we mapped triplets into numbers. We have the $i \% 3 = 1$ suffixes in the first half and the others in the second half, and the sentinel ensures that we will not mix them up. We use the zero character for our sentinel. That way C will consider the strings before the sentinel as separate from the strings after it, even though we put them in the same buffer. If we are in the first half, the string only goes to the sentinel, and we never look at it farther than this. The way we have mapped triplets, the triplet representations of suffixes are ordered in the same way as the original strings. This, combined with the sentinel that takes care of the end of $i \% 3 = 1$ strings, means that if we sort u we have sorted the sa12 suffixes. The only thing we need to get sa12 is to map the indices in u to indices in sa12. There is a tiny bit of arithmetic here, but in essence, we check whether we are below or above the middle. If we are below, we add one because these are the $i \% 3 = 2$ indices that are at the odd places in sa12. If we are above the middle, we subtract the first half and the sentinel from the index.

```
uint32_t m = m12 / 2;
uint32_t k = (i < m) ? (2 * i + 1) : (2 * (i - m - 1));
```

---

[4]You could also insert the modulus one strings first. I chose not to, because the number of modulus two indices varies whether there are an even or uneven number of suffixes in sa12. If I put the modulus two suffixes at the beginning of the string, I can always use integer division to get the middle of the string; otherwise, I had to check the length. Conceptually it doesn't matter.

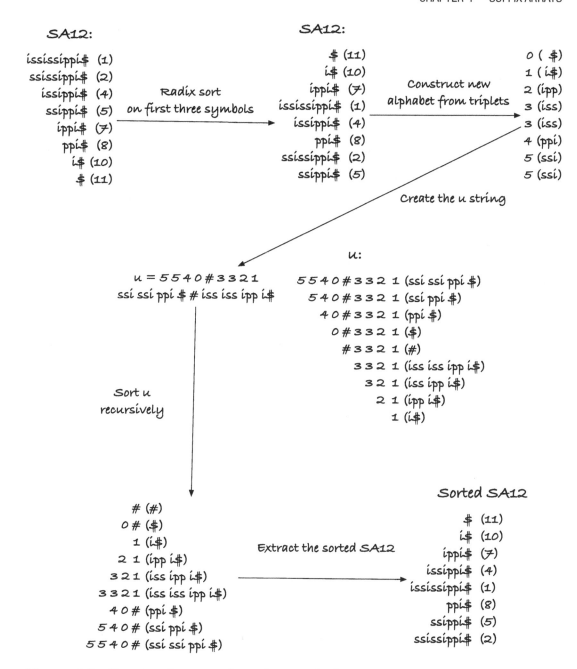

Figure 4-3. *Constructing u and sort it recursively*

Here m is the middle of the string and k is the index in the larger string that index i should map to. That is, i is an index into the *u* string and k is where that index is in sa12.

While you do not need to do so if you have an index into sa12—that contains the suffix indices—it is possible to map from a sa12 index into the suffixes it contains using

```
k + k / 2 + 1;
```

Once we have both sa12 and sa3, we need to merge them into the true suffix array. Again, I will go into more details later, but this is the intuition that should help you see the overall picture. It follows a typical merge algorithm: we move indices *i* and *j* through the two arrays and pick the smallest of the suffixes we compare in each iteration. The trick is to determine which suffix is the smallest. If the first letter in the suffixes differs, we can directly determine this, but if they do not, there is more work to do. There are two cases. If *i*, the index into sa12, is a $i \% 3 = 1$ index, then both $i + 1$ and $j + 1$ will be in sa12, and we can get their relative order from the array. If *i* is a $i \% 3 = 2$ index, then $i + 1$ and $j + 1$ will be in different arrays (see Figure 4-4). If the letters at index $i + 1$ and $j + 1$ are different, we can directly determine which suffix is the smallest. If not, we can move one step further, to $i + 2$ and $j + 2$. There, the indices are both in sa12. It is here that it is crucial that we do not split the data into two equal parts but one and two-thirds. This prevents the indices from repeatedly jumping to different tables. Here, we will never have to move beyond a third table lookup.

Constructing SA3

The simplest step in the skew algorithm is constructing sa3, so this is where we start. Recall that we construct the array from the indices modulus one in the already sorted sa12 and then radix sort on the first character. We have used uint8_t for our alphabet so far, and our final function for constructing suffix arrays will have strings over this alphabet as input, so we can use the same strings with our different algorithms. However, during the execution of the skew algorithm, we need to make new alphabets, when we handle s12, as we shall see later. Those alphabets can be larger than the 256 we can fit into a byte, so we should implement the algorithm so it can handle arbitrarily large alphabets (though bounded by *n* in size). But to simplify, and for speed reasons, we assume that we can hold all alphabets in uint32_t. We use the variable alph_size for the alphabet size. We use the alphabet size when radix sorting. All strings are therefore of type uint32_t *. It is a simple matter to translate the uint8_t * strings to uint32_t *.

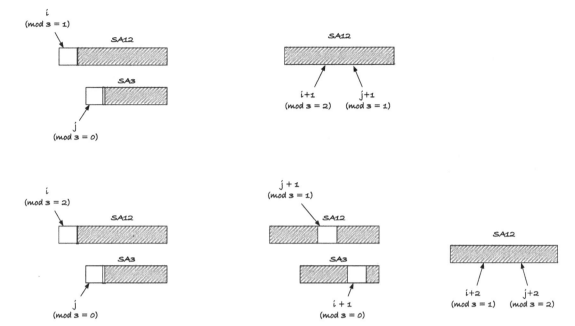

Figure 4-4. *Merging SA12 and SA3*

The construction function looks like this:

```
static void construct_sa3(
    uint32_t m12,
    uint32_t m3,
    uint32_t n,
    uint32_t *s,
    uint32_t alph_size,
    struct skew_buffers *shared_buffers
) {
    uint32_t j = 0;

    // If the last position divides 3, we don't
    // have information in sa12, but we know it
    // should go first.
    if ((n - 1) % 3 == 0) {
        SA3(j++) = n - 1;
    }
```

```
for (uint32_t i = 0; i < m12; ++i) {
    uint32_t pos = SA12(i);
    if (pos % 3 == 1) {
        SA3(j++) = pos - 1;
    }
}

radix_sort(s, n, shared_buffers->sa3, m3,
           0, alph_size, shared_buffers);
}
```

The m12 variable is the length of the sa12, m3 is the length of sa3, n is the length of the string we are building the suffix array over, and s is the string. We use alph_size in the radix sort, but you can ignore it for now. The shared_buffers variable points to a structure of type struct skew_buffers. This structure holds several arrays and buffers we will use to avoid heap-allocating arrays when running the algorithm. Its structure looks like this:

```
struct skew_buffers {
    uint32_t *sa12;              // 2/3n +
    uint32_t *sa3;              // 1/3n = n

    uint32_t current_u;
    uint32_t *u;                // 3*(2/3n+1)
    uint32_t *sau;              // 3*(2/3n+1)

    uint32_t radix_buckets[256];
    uint32_t radix_accsum[256];
    uint32_t *helper_buffer0;   // 2/3n +
    uint32_t *helper_buffer1;   // 2/3n = 4/3 n
    uint32_t *lex_remapped;     // alias for helper 0
};
```

The comments are the number of words we need to allocate for the arrays when the input string has length n. Remember that by "words" I mean the space we need for pointers or integers. In this case they are all integers, and with this implementation, each word is 4 bytes. If you change the integer types, then the space requirements will change as well, of course. When there are fractions, you have to round them up. So $1/3n$ means that you have to allocate a number of words that are equal to one-third of the input size, rounded up.

I will explain each buffer as we get to where they are used; in the sorting of sa3, we only use sa12 and sa3. We access them with SA12() and SA3(), which are macros.

```
#define SA12(i) (shared_buffers->sa12[(i)])
#define SA3(i)  (shared_buffers->sa3[(i)])
```

Since sa12 contains two-thirds of the input, that is what we must allocate for it, and sa3 contains a third so this is what we must allocate for that array.

I will use several macros in this algorithm to make the code more readable. The macros assume that shared_buffers and s are the variables we use in the functions, but we use that for consistency anyway. As you can see, the SA12() and SA3() look up in the sa12 and sa3 arrays in the shared buffers. This is where we have the indices of the suffixes for the two arrays.

We use these two macros for the sort:

```
#define B(i)    (shared_buffers->radix_buckets[(i)])
#define AS(i)   (shared_buffers->radix_accsum[(i)])
```

We use the first to pick a bucket. As we sort, we count how many elements we need to put into each bucket, rather than put the elements in there. We just count. Then we compute the cumulative sum of the buckets, that is, an array that for each bucket tells us how many elements there are in the buckets before it. We can now copy the actual elements into a result array. For each element, we look up its bucket and use AS(key) as the index we insert into. Each time we insert an element in a bucket, we increment its corresponding accumulative sum, so at this point AS(key) works as a pointer to the current position where elements in that bucket should be inserted; see Figure 4-5.

The radix sort function looks like this:

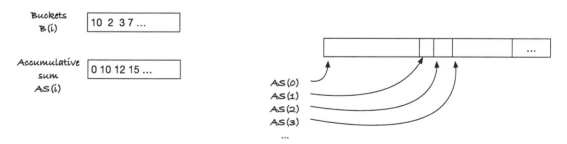

Figure 4-5. *Buckets and radix sort*

```c
#define RAWKEY(i) ((input[(i)] + offset >= n) ? 0 : s[input[(i)] + offset])
#define KEY(i)     ((RAWKEY((i)) >> shift) & mask)

static void radix_sort(
    uint32_t *s, uint32_t n,
    uint32_t *sa, uint32_t m,
    uint32_t offset, uint32_t alph_size,
    struct skew_buffers *shared_buffers)
{
    const int32_t mask = (1 << 8) - 1;
    bool radix_index = 0;

    uint32_t *input, *output;

    memcpy(shared_buffers->helper_buffer0, sa, m * sizeof(uint32_t));
    uint32_t *helper_buffers[] = {
        shared_buffers->helper_buffer0,
        shared_buffers->helper_buffer1
    };

    for (uint32_t byte = 0, shift = 0;
         byte < sizeof(*s) && alph_size > 0;
         byte++, shift += 8, alph_size >>= 8) {

        memset(shared_buffers->radix_buckets, 0,
               256 * sizeof(uint32_t));

        input = helper_buffers[radix_index];
        output = helper_buffers[!radix_index];
        radix_index = !radix_index;

        for (uint32_t i = 0; i < m; i++) {
            // Count keys in each bucket
            B(KEY(i))++;
        }
        uint32_t sum = 0;
        for (uint32_t i = 0; i < 256; i++) {
            // Get the accumulated sum for offsets
            AS(i) = sum;
```

```
            sum += B(i);
        }
        assert(sum == m);
        for (uint32_t i = 0; i < m; ++i) {
            // Move input to their sorted position
            output[AS(KEY(i))++] = input[i];
        }
    }

    memcpy(sa, output, m * sizeof(uint32_t));
}
```

The arguments are s, the string we will sort, and its length n; sa is the output, that is, the sorted indices, and m is its length. The offset is used to sort more than one computer word; it looks to the right of the index to get the index there rather than the character at the actual index. It is used later, but for sorting sa3, it is zero. The alph_size and shared_buffers arguments are the same as before. We use the alph_size to avoid extra work when the alphabet size does not use all 32 bits in uint32_t. You can try leaving it out of the outer loop to see the performance difference.

The function looks more complicated than it is. It sorts integers according to their bytes, and it uses two arrays for this, helper_buffer0 and helper_buffer1, accessed through the shared_buffers variable. We put these in an array, helper_buffers, so we can switch them using a Boolean, radix_insert. We use them to insert indices consecutively into their bucket. The input vector will hold the indices and the output contains partially filled buckets. We flip between the two helper buffers in the iterations of the radix sort using the shared_buffer array, so input always refers to the values we just sorted and output to where we will place the next sorted values. The accumulative sum starts with pointers to the beginning of each buffer and is incremented each time we insert an index into output.

The macro RAWKEY() gets the word in s we need to sort and the KEY() macro extracts the byte we are currently sorting by.

The size of the two helper buffers is two-thirds of the length of the initial string. This is because the longest string we will sort is the initial sa12; all other arrays we sort are shorter.

Recursively sorting sa12

Sorting sa3 is the easy part, and we can do it without recursion. But we need a sorted sa12 to do it. Sorting sa12 is the main part of the algorithm, and it is here we need the recursion in our divide-and-conquer algorithm. I've listed the recursive function first, in the following text, and I will go into the details later. To construct the suffix array, we first create a new string from sa12, recursively get the suffix array from that, and use it to get the sorted sa12. Everything except for the last two lines in the function handles this. The second to last line constructs sa3 from sa12, as we just saw earlier, and the last line merges the two sorted arrays—we will see how to do this and write the merge_suffix_arrays() function after we handle sa12.

I will present the algorithm top-down, since I think it will be easier to see how the pieces fit together that way. It does mean that you will see calls to functions you haven't seen the definition of yet. They will come later. If I presented all the minor functions that you need before we use them, I don't think it would be clear how they fit in. This does mean that you will not be able to copy the code into your editor and compile it as you read along. If you want to, you can fetch the code from GitHub (https://github. com/mailund/stralg/blob/master/stralg/skew.c), where the functions are in the right order for compilation. Otherwise, you have to be patient until you have seen all the function definitions.

As shown in Figure 4-3, the first step is to sort the suffixes by their first three symbols so we can create *u* from the mapped letters. In the following function, we do this using the remap_lex3() function that we will write shortly. The function returns the size of the alphabet of triplets and the mapping from indices in sa12 to their lexicographical number. If this alphabet size matches the entire number of suffixes, then they are already sorted, and we are done, but if they do not, we construct the *u* string with construct_u(); we will also see how to write that function shortly. We sort *u* recursively, and when we have the suffix for that, we construct sa12 by mapping indices in u to indices in sa12. For this, we use the function map_u_s(). You will see this function soon.

```
static void skew_rec(
    uint32_t *s, uint32_t n,
    uint32_t alph_size,
```

```
    uint32_t *sa,
    struct skew_buffers *shared_buffers
) {

    // When we index from zero, these are the number of
    // indices modulo 3. We have n - 1 to adjust for
    // the zero index and +1 because the zero index is
    // included in the array for m3.
    uint32_t m3 = (n - 1) / 3 + 1;
    uint32_t m12 = n - m3;

    uint32_t mapped_alphabet_size =
        remap_lex3(s, n, m12, alph_size, shared_buffers);

    // The +1 here is because we leave space for the sentinel.
    if (mapped_alphabet_size != m12 + 1) {
        uint32_t *u =
            shared_buffers->u + shared_buffers->current_u;
        uint32_t *sau =
            shared_buffers->sau + shared_buffers->current_u;
        shared_buffers->current_u += m12 + 1;

        // Construct the u string and solve the suffix array
        // recursively.
        construct_u(shared_buffers->lex_remapped,
                    m12, u);
        skew_rec(u, m12 + 1,
             mapped_alphabet_size,
              sau, shared_buffers);

        int32_t mm = m12 / 2;

        for (uint32_t i = 1; i < m12 + 1; ++i) {

            SA12(i - 1) = map_u_s(sau[i], mm);
        }
    }
```

```
    construct_sa3(m12, m3, n, s, alph_size, shared_buffers);
    merge_suffix_arrays(s, m12, m3, sa, shared_buffers);
}
```

We use the u and sau pointers for the *u* string and its suffix array. We could dynamically allocate them with malloc() and free(), but we know ahead of time how much space we need for them in total, so we have allocated all of the buffers already. We have a pointer to the head of the buffers we have used, current_u, and we set u and sau to point there, and then we update the current_u by incrementing it by m12 + 1, which is the space we need for u (we need all indices in sa12 plus a sentinel).

In each recursive call, we use u and sau of size m12 + 1 which is $\frac{2}{3}n+1$, two-thirds of the problem size. The sum $\sum_{i=0}^{\infty}\left(\frac{2}{3}\right)^{i}$ converges to 3, and we will never recurse deeper than *n*, so an upper bound of the total memory we need for u and sau is $3(2/3n + 1)$.

Given the suffix array for *u*, we map the indices there into indices in sa12 to get that array. We already saw the arithmetic needed for this, and we have wrapped it in this function:

```
// Map from an index in u to an index in s
inline static uint32_t map_u_s(uint32_t i, uint32_t m)
{
    // first: u -> s12
    uint32_t k = (i < m) ? (2 * i + 1) : (2 * (i - m - 1));
    return k + k / 2 + 1; // then s12 -> s
}
```

Once we have sorted sa12, we construct sa3 as shown earlier and merge the two arrays (as discussed below).

It is in the map_lex3() function, which I will list shortly, that we construct the sa12 array by running through the string, s, and inserting indices that are not zero modulo three. It then sorts the array according to the first three letters with the call to radix_sort_3(). The sorted array is in the shared_buffers struct as sa12, so it is a side effect of radix_sort_3() that gives us the result. Next, we need to map the indices in s to their lexicographical numbers. We have the sorted sa12 and can get the numbers from there, but we need to construct u in the order the suffixes appear in s.

If we iterate through the sorted sequence, we will go through different bins and each bin will correspond to a lex number. To remap to these numbers, we look up the numbers in each bin and assign the bin number to them (see Figure 4-6 A). We cannot quite do this since the indices in sa12 are into the s string and not into sa12 itself. So we need to get the index into s, SA12(i), and then map that back to an index in the shorter array using the map_s_s12() function (see Figure 4-6 B).

```
// Map from indices in s to indices in s12
inline static uint32_t map_s_s12(uint32_t k) {
    return 2 * (k / 3) + (k % 3) - 1;
}
```

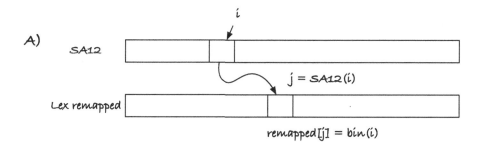

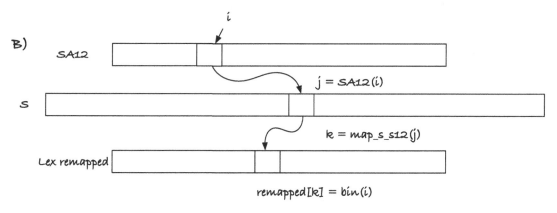

Figure 4-6. *Mapping array to lex3 bins*

The LEX3() macro maps directly from the sorted array to the remapped array.

```
#define LEX3(i) \
    (shared_buffers->lex_remapped[map_s_s12(SA12(i))])
```

The full remap function looks like this:

```
static int32_t remap_lex3(
    uint32_t *s, uint32_t n, uint32_t m12,
    uint32_t alph_size,
```

```
    struct skew_buffers *shared_buffers
) {
    // Set up s12
    for (uint32_t i = 0, j = 0; i < n; ++i) {
        if (i % 3 != 0) {
            SA12(j) = i;
            j++;
        }
    }

    // Sort s12
    radix_sort_3(s, n, m12, alph_size, shared_buffers);

    uint32_t no = 1; // Reserve 0 for sentinel
    LEX3(0) = 1;

    for (uint32_t i = 1; i < m12; ++i) {
        if (!equal3(s, n, SA12(i), SA12(i - 1))) {
            no++;
        }
        LEX3(i) = no;
    }

    return no + 1;
}
```

You haven't seen the functions radix_sort_3() and equal3() yet, but they are coming. Don't worry.

As a side effect of this function, we overwrite the shared sa12 array. We don't take sa12 as a parameter, but it sits in the sa12 array in the shared_buffers. We access it with the SA12() and write indices into it. Overwriting data in the array has no consequence for the algorithm. In skew_rec(), we call recursively after remapping, and we are not looking at this array until we return and reconstruct it using the result from the recursion.

The radix sort used in remap_lex3(), radix_sort3(), uses the radix_sort() function we saw earlier, calling it three times. It uses the offsets to sort for three different positions, starting two to the right of the suffix, then one, and then offset zero. Since the sort is stable, the result is an array sorted by the first three letters. The result is put in the shared_buffers->sa12 array. It is the third parameter to the radix_sort() function, and that is where radix_sort() writes its result.

```
inline static void
radix_sort_3(
    uint32_t *s, uint32_t n, uint32_t m,
    uint32_t alph_size,
    struct skew_buffers *shared_buffers
) {
    radix_sort(s, n, shared_buffers->sa12, m,
               2, alph_size, shared_buffers);
    radix_sort(s, n, shared_buffers->sa12, m,
               1, alph_size, shared_buffers);
    radix_sort(s, n, shared_buffers->sa12, m,
               0, alph_size, shared_buffers);
}
```

The equal3() function that we use to determine when we move from one bin to the next in the sorted array is straightforward. We run through the three symbols at index *i* and *j* and answer no if we see different characters (or if one reaches the end of the string). If we get through the loop without seeing any differences, the two triplets are equal and we return true.

```
inline static bool equal3(
    uint32_t *s, uint32_t n,
    uint32_t i, uint32_t j
) {
    for (int k = 0; k < 3; ++k) {
        if (i + k >= n) return false;
        if (j + k >= n) return false;
        if (s[i + k] != s[j + k]) return false;
    }
    return true;
}
```

Once we have the array of remapped letters, constructing u is trivial. Run through the indices that are two modulo three and insert their remapped symbol, insert the sentinel, and then run through the indices that are one modulo three.

```
static void construct_u(
    uint32_t *lex_remapped,
    uint32_t m12,
    uint32_t *u
) {
    uint32_t j = 0;
    // First put those mod 3 == 2 so the first "half"
    // is always m12 / 2 (the expression rounds down).
    for (uint32_t i = 1; i < m12; i += 2) {
        u[j++] = lex_remapped[i];
    }

    u[j++] = 0; // Add center sentinel.

    // Insert mod 3 == 1.
    for (uint32_t i = 0; i < m12; i += 2) {
        u[j++] = lex_remapped[i];
    }
}
```

Merging arrays

The final step in the algorithm is merging the two arrays. For this, we need to run through the indices in sa12 and sa3. These contain the suffixes in s, represented by their indices, sorted by their lexicographical order. So for all indices into s, we have those $i \% 3 = 0$ in sa3 and those $i \% 3 \neq 0$ in sa12.

When we merge, we have an index ii into sa12 that tells us how far we have gotten there, and an index jj into sa3. To compare letters there, which is the first thing we do, we need to get the corresponding indices in the string s, which we can do using ii = sa12[i] and jj = sa3[j], respectively. This macro does that.

```
#define CHECK_INDEX(ii,jj) {              \
if ((ii) >= n) return true;               \
if ((jj) >= n) return false;              \
if (s[(ii)] < s[(jj)]) return true;   \
if (s[(ii)] > s[(jj)]) return false; \
}
```

We use it in a function, less(), that we define below. Notice that it has return statements. It will make less() return true if suffix ii comes before suffix jj when we can determine this by only looking at the first character. The two first lines handle the special cases where one of the indices falls outside the string. Shorter strings always go before longer strings, so the index that is beyond the string is the smaller. If the first character for the two suffixes is the same, the macro falls through all the if statements and does not return. When this happens, the less() function will handle the next step in the comparison.

To decide if one suffix comes before another, we cannot merely look at the first character. If we could, we wouldn't be using a complicated algorithm—we could just use a bucket sort. We built the sa12 and sa3 algorithms so we could decide which suffix comes before another when they *agree* on the first character, and in that case, we need to determine if suffix ii+1 comes before jj+1 (and maybe if ii+2 comes before jj+2).

We write a function, less(), to handle the comparison. If the two indices come from different arrays, we compare characters. That is all we can do, because we do not know the relative order of indices in different arrays—that is, after all, what we are trying to work out. If the characters are the same, we add one to the indices to see if we can determine the order there. If we add one, then both indices could be different from zero modulo three, and they can be found in sa12. The order there gives us the information we want. Otherwise, we can add one more to them, and now they must be in sa12 if they weren't the first time. So how do we determine the order of two indices into sa12?

The indices ii and jj are into the string, s, which is the smallest given by the order in which they appear in sa12? We cannot get this order directly from the indices. However, if we can map indices ii from s into indices in sa12, we can compare those indices. The suffix array gives us, at each position *i*, an index into s, the suffix with rank *i* in s. What we want is a map in the other direction, so we can go from an index ii into s to the rank it has. That is, we want to know, for each index ii, where it is found in sa12.

We can build such an *inverse suffix array (ISA)* like this:

```
for (uint32_t i = 1, j = 0; j < m12; i += 3, j += 2) {
    ISA(SA12(j)) = i;
}
for (uint32_t i = 2, j = 1; j < m12; i += 3, j += 2) {
    ISA(SA12(j)) = i;
}
for (uint32_t i = 0, j = 0; j < m3; i += 3, j++) {
    ISA(SA3(j)) = i;
}
```

where we use the first helper buffer to store the inverse suffix array this macro:

```
#define ISA(ii) (shared_buffers->helper_buffer0[(ii)])
```

To test if suffix ii is smaller than index jj, we can now use this macro:

```
#define CHECK_ISA(ii,jj) \
    (((jj) >= n) ? false : \
    ((ii) >= n) || ISA((ii)) < ISA((jj)))
```

It first handles cases where the indices look past the end of the string (they are special cases that can happen in the less() function below), and if the indices do not map out of the string, then it compares the two indices in the suffix array via the ISA() map.

The function below implements the "less than" we use when merging. Either the two suffixes differs on the first letter, in which case CHECK_INDEX() handles the comparison and returns from the less() function (remember that the macro has return statements when it can determine the order directly). Otherwise, we check ii + 1 vs. jj + 1. If ii % 3 == 1, then we can check directly with ii + 1 (which must be two modulo tree) and jj + 1 (which must be one modulo three as it comes from sa3). Otherwise, we check index ii + 1 and jj + 1 and then check the inverse suffix array for ii + 2 and jj + 2. If we do this, we must be in the case where ii % 3 == 2, so ii + 2 % 3 = 1, and jj + 1 % 3 = 2, and they are both in sa12. See Figure 4-4.

```
inline static bool less(
    uint32_t ii, uint32_t jj,
    uint32_t *s, uint32_t n,
```

```
    struct skew_buffers *shared_buffers
) {
    CHECK_INDEX(ii, jj);
    if (ii % 3 == 1) {
        return CHECK_ISA(ii + 1, jj + 1);
    } else {
        CHECK_INDEX(ii + 1, jj + 1);
        return CHECK_ISA(ii + 2, jj + 2);
    }
}

// Just for readability in the merge
#define LESS(i,j) less((i), (j), s, n, shared_buffers)
```

In the function for merging the suffix arrays, we first construct the inverse suffix array—the code for that should be self-evident—and then we move through the two arrays, get the indices from the suffix arrays, and test which is smaller of the two.

```
static void merge_suffix_arrays(
    uint32_t *s, uint32_t m12, uint32_t m3,
    uint32_t *sa, struct skew_buffers *shared_buffers
) {
    uint32_t i = 0, j = 0, k = 0;
    uint32_t n = m12 + m3;

    // We are essentially building sa[i] (although
    // not sorting between 12 and 3) and then doing
    // isa[sa[i]] = i. Just both at the same time.
    for (uint32_t h = 1, j = 0; j < m12; h += 3, j += 2) {
        ISA(SA12(j)) = h;
    }
    for (uint32_t h = 2, j = 1; j < m12; h += 3, j += 2) {
        ISA(SA12(j)) = h;
    }
    for (uint32_t h = 0, j = 0; j < m3; h += 3, j++) {
        ISA(SA3(j)) = h;
    }
```

```c
    while (i < m12 && j < m3) {
        uint32_t ii = SA12(i);
        uint32_t jj = SA3(j);

        if (LESS(ii,jj)) {
            sa[k++] = ii;
            i++;
        } else {
            sa[k++] = jj;
            j++;
        }
    }
    for (; i < m12; ++i) {
        sa[k++] = SA12(i);
    }
    for (; j < m3; ++j) {
        sa[k++] = SA3(j);
    }
}
```

Construction function

We want a function that can work with the same strings as we use in the previous chapters, that is, we want our strings to have type uint8_t *. In the recursive algorithm, we had to use integers. So we need to wrap the algorithm in a function that translates a uint8_t * string, *x*, into an integer string, *s*, and then calls the algorithm. This function is also perfect to allocate the buffers we need and deallocate them after we have constructed the suffix array. There isn't much else to say about it; it looks like this:

```c
static void skew(
    const uint8_t *x,
    uint32_t *sa
) {
    uint32_t n = (uint32_t)strlen((char *)x);
    // Trivial special cases
    if (n == 0) {
        sa[0] = 0;
        return;
```

```
} else if (n == 1) {
    sa[0] = 1;
    sa[1] = 0;
    return;
}

// During the algorithm we can have letters larger than
// those in the input, so we map the string to one
// over a larger alphabet. We assume that we can hold
// the largest letter in uint32_t so we do not need to
// handle integers of arbitrary sizes.

// We are not including the termination sentinel
// in this algorithm but we explicitly set it
// at index zero in sa. We reserve
// the sentinel for center points in u strings.

uint32_t *s = malloc(n * sizeof(uint32_t));
for (uint32_t i = 0; i < n; ++i) {
    s[i] = (unsigned char)x[i];
}

uint32_t m3 = (n - 1) / 3 + 1;
uint32_t m12 = n - m3;
struct skew_buffers shared_buffers;

shared_buffers.sa12 =
    malloc(m12 * sizeof(uint32_t));
shared_buffers.sa3 =
    malloc(m3 * sizeof(uint32_t));

shared_buffers.current_u = 0;
shared_buffers.u =
    malloc(3 * (m12 + 1) * sizeof(uint32_t));
shared_buffers.sau =
    malloc(3 * (m12 + 1) * sizeof(uint32_t));

shared_buffers.helper_buffer0 =
    malloc(2 * m12 * sizeof(uint32_t));
```

```
    shared_buffers.helper_buffer1 =
        shared_buffers.helper_buffer0 + m12;

    // We never use helper_buffer0 between
    // creating and using the
    // lexicographical mapping buffer. So we
    // use the same buffer for both.
    shared_buffers.lex_remapped =
        shared_buffers.helper_buffer0;

    // Do not include index zero.
    skew_rec(s, n, 256, sa + 1, &shared_buffers);
    // but set it to the sentinel here
    sa[0] = n;

    free(shared_buffers.sa12);
    free(shared_buffers.sa3);
    free(shared_buffers.u);
    free(shared_buffers.sau);
    free(shared_buffers.helper_buffer0);
    free(s);
}

struct suffix_array *
skew_sa_construction(
    uint8_t *x
) {
    struct suffix_array *sa = allocate_sa(x);
    skew(x, sa->array);
    return sa;
}
```

The divide-and-conquer algorithm uses linear time in each recursive call, and since we reduce the input size to two-thirds in each recursion, which is a geometric sum that is bounded by a constant, we have a linear-time algorithm. The faster we get unique letters when we create the alphabet for u, the faster the algorithm will be in practice. The worst-case scenario is a string consisting of only one letter. There, we will have a single lexicographical number (except for cases at the end of the string), so we recurse maximally.

If we add up the space we allocate in all the buffers, we see that we use 6.4 words per character in the input string. I will leave the counting to the reader. This is close to the memory we use for the nodes in a suffix tree, but a suffix tree can have up to $2n - 1$ nodes, where n is the length of the string, so the suffix array algorithm here still uses less memory than if we constructed a suffix tree.

The SA-IS algorithm

The SA-IS (sampling-induced sorting) algorithm by Nong, Zhang, and Chan is another divide-and-conquer algorithm. It is similar to the skew algorithm in the sense that it sorts some strings recursively and then induces the sorting of all strings based on those sorted suffixes. It differs in how it chooses the suffixes to sort recursively and how it combines the sorted sequences with the remaining suffixes. There are more definitions and concepts needed to understand the algorithm, but once those are there, the algorithm turns out to be both simpler to understand and to implement than the skew algorithm. Further, there is less overhead in the operations we need to do, so the algorithm is also faster. It is one of the fastest linear-time construction algorithms known.

You can get the full implementation from `https://github.com/mailund/stralg/blob/master/stralg/sa_is.c`.

The overall idea in the algorithm is to identify particular substrings in the input and replace them with numbers to create a shorter string, compute the suffix array from this string, and then induce the suffix array for the initial string from it.

For each index in our input string, we assign it a class, S or L, depending on whether the suffix starting at that index is smaller or larger than the suffix starting at the next index. That is, index i is class S if $x[i, n] < x[i + 1, n]$, that is, suffix i is lexicographically smaller than suffix i+1. An index is class L if $x[i, n] > x[i + 1, n]$, that is, suffix i is greater than i+1. No two suffixes are the same, so they cannot be equal. A special case is the last character, the sentinel. We define it to have class S.

For example, the string `mississippi$` has the classes:

```
mississippi$
LSLLSLLSLLLS
```

We can compute the classes in linear time with a sweep from right to left. When we compare suffixes $x[i, n]$ and $x[i + 1, n]$, we can immediately see the class if $x[i] \neq x[i + 1]$ but if $x[i] = x[i + 1]$, so they start with the same character; then it turns out that they must have the same class. The sentinel is a special case, we define it to be class S, and it doesn't share a first character with any other suffix.

So consider suffix i where $x[i] = x[i + 1]$. Since they start with the same letter, let's call it a, they must both start with a run of that character (of length at least one since both strings start with a). That run of as is one longer for $x[i, n]$ than for $x[i + 1, n]$. Let k be the length of the run of as for $x[i + 1, n]$. After the first a in $x[i, n]$, the suffix has the run of k as that it shares with $x[i + 1, n]$. After that run of as, they must have a different letter, b, and after that they share a string, y, that is whatever goes after the b and to the end of the suffixes. If y is empty, then b is the sentinel. There will always be a character after the run of as (remember that we handle the sentinel as a special case).

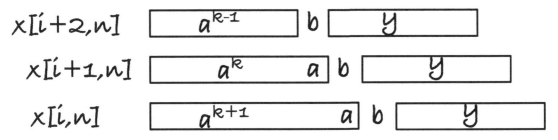

Figure 4-7. *Classifying strings into S and L (see the text for details)*

We can write the form of the suffixes like this: $x[i, n] = a^{k+1}by$, $x[i + 1, n] = a^k\,by$ and $x[i + 2, n] = a^{k-1}by$ (where the run of as for suffix $i + 2$ can be empty and it can start with the letter b); see Figure 4-7. The first difference we see when we compare suffix $i + 1$ with suffix $i + 2$, or when we compare suffix i with suffix $i + 1$, is the a against the b, and it is this comparison that determines which suffix is the smallest. If $a < b$, suffix $i + 1$ will be smaller than suffix $i + 2$, so class S, and since the comparison between i and $i + 1$ also ends with $a < b$, suffix i must be smaller than suffix $i + 1$, so suffix i is also class S. Symmetrically, if $a > b$, then suffix $i + 1$ has class L and so does suffix i. Whenever two consecutive suffixes start with the same character, they have the same class.

Let t be a vector that gives us the class of an index, that is, $t[i]$ is S if index i has class S and L if i has class L.

We define a *leftmost S* (LMS) index as an index of class S where the class to the left of it is class L, that is, i is an LMS $t(i) = S$ and $t(i - 1) = L$. We cannot look to the left of the first index in the string, but we define it not to be an LMS. The LMSs for `mississippi$` are shown below the classes here:

```
mississippi$
LSLLSLLSLLLS
*   *   *   *
```

If we can somehow sort the suffixes that start at LMS indices, then we can sort all the other suffixes. This is the induced sorting that gives us the final result. We recursively sort the LMS prefixes and then the rest using the sorted LMS strings.

The way we sort the strings can look a little complicated, but once you implement it, it will be three simple steps. Before the steps, though, we need to split the suffix array into bins based on the first character. It is a simple run through the string where we count how many occurrences we see of each character. We can get the beginning of the bins using an accumulative sum from left to right and the end of the bins using an accumulative sum from right to left. It is not unlike what we did in the skew algorithm except we are not using a radix sort but a bucketing.

We can split each bin into two parts: the first part will contain the L suffixes that go into the bin and the second part the S suffixes. We can do this because an L suffix $x[i, n]$ in the same bin as an S suffix, $x[j, n]$, will be lexicographically smaller than the S suffix, $x[i, n] < x[j, n]$.

To see this, consider their form. Since they are in the same bin, they start with the same letter. Let us call it a. So, a prefix of the strings must be some nonzero length run of a; let us say that suffix i starts with k as and suffix j with l as. After that, there is a character that is not a; call it b for suffix i and c for suffix j. We will call the remaining string for suffix i y and the remaining string for suffix j z. In other words, the suffixes have the form $x[i, n] = a^k by$ and $x[j, n] = a^l cz$. Because they have this form, and because the runs of as are nonempty, the suffixes that follow them, $i + 1$ and $j + 1$, have the form $x[i + 1, n] = a^{k-1} by$ and $x[j + 1, n] = a^{l-1} cz$ (where the runs of as can be empty). It means that when we compare suffix i with suffix $i + 1$, the first difference we see is when we compare a in suffix i with b in suffix $i + 1$, and it is this comparison that determines which of the two strings is the larger. Because $x[i, n]$ has class L, a must be larger than b. Otherwise, it would be smaller than $x[i + 1, n]$; see Figure 4-8. Similarly, we can analyze suffix j. When we compare suffix j with $j + 1$, the first difference we see is when we compare a with c. When j is of class S, a must be smaller than c.

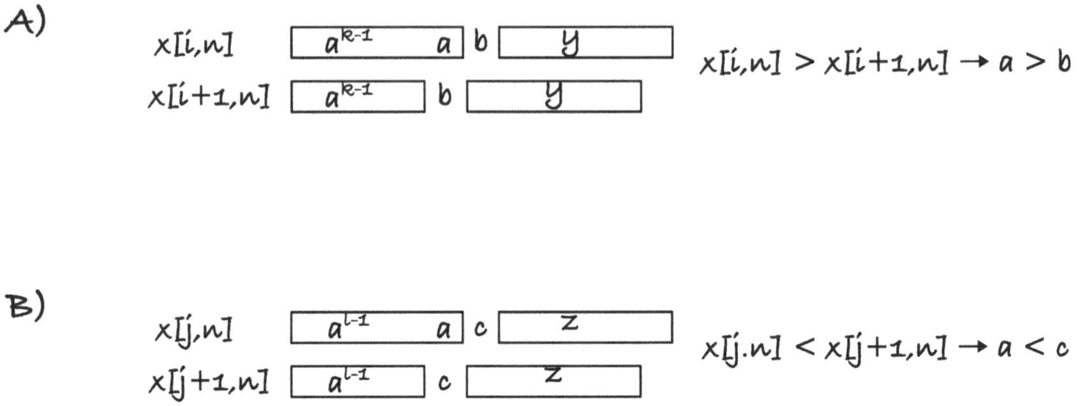

A)

$$x[i,n] \quad \boxed{a^{k-1} \quad a \,|\, b \boxed{y}}$$
$$x[i+1,n] \quad \boxed{a^{k-1} \quad b \boxed{y}}$$

$$x[i,n] > x[i+1,n] \rightarrow a > b$$

B)

$$x[j,n] \quad \boxed{a^{l-1} \quad a \,|\, c \boxed{z}}$$
$$x[j+1,n] \quad \boxed{a^{l-1} \quad c \boxed{z}}$$

$$x[j,n] < x[j+1,n] \rightarrow a < c$$

Figure 4-8. *The structure of L and S strings*

Now compare $x[i, n]$ and $x[j, n]$ and consider the three cases $l > k$, $l = k$, and $l < k$; see Figure 4-9. If $l > k$, then when we compare the two strings, we must match a b from $x[i, n]$ against an a from $x[j, n]$, and because $a > b$, we must have $x[i, n] < x[j, n]$. When $l = k$, we compare b against c and we know that $b < a$ and $c > a$ so again we have $x[i, n] < x[j, n]$. Thirdly, if $l < k$ we match an a from $x[i, n]$ against a c from $x[j, n]$, and since $c > a$ we have $x[i, n] < x[j, n]$. In short, within a bucket, the L strings come before the S strings.

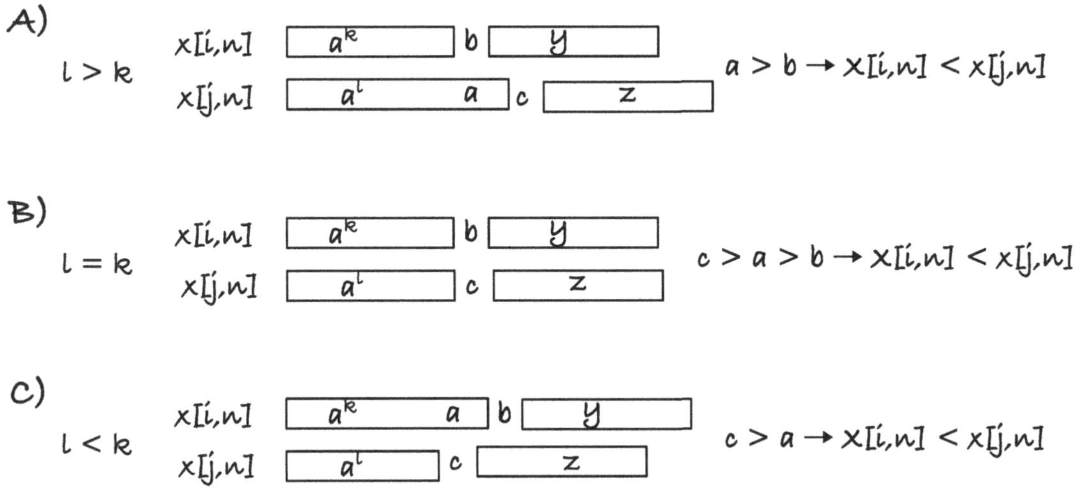

A)

$l > k$

$$x[i,n] \quad \boxed{a^k \quad |\, b \boxed{y}}$$
$$x[j,n] \quad \boxed{a^l \quad a \,|\, c \boxed{z}}$$

$$a > b \rightarrow x[i,n] < x[j,n]$$

B)

$l = k$

$$x[i,n] \quad \boxed{a^k \quad |\, b \boxed{y}}$$
$$x[j,n] \quad \boxed{a^l \quad |\, c \boxed{z}}$$

$$c > a > b \rightarrow x[i,n] < x[j,n]$$

C)

$l < k$

$$x[i,n] \quad \boxed{a^k \quad a \,|\, b \boxed{y}}$$
$$x[j,n] \quad \boxed{a^l \quad |\, c \boxed{z}}$$

$$c > a \rightarrow x[i,n] < x[j,n]$$

Figure 4-9. *L strings goes before S strings within buckets*

The structure of a bucket is as shown in Figure 4-10. We have the L strings on the left and the S strings on the right. If we have a pointer to the left of the bucket, we can insert L strings from that side by inserting them at the current pointer and increment it after each insertion. Likewise, we can insert S strings at the right by inserting them at the pointer and decrementing the pointer.

If we have the ordered LMS suffixes, we can sort all the suffixes in three simple steps:

1.   First, we go through the LMS suffixes from the end to the beginning, that is, in reverse order, and insert them at the end of their buckets. They are S strings, so they belong after L strings within their buckets. Putting them at the end doesn't mean we are putting them at the right position, LMS strings are not necessarily larger than other S strings in their buckets and don't all belong at the end of the bucket, but for now, we only need to have them in our suffix array in the right *order*, not the right *positions*, and we do that this way.

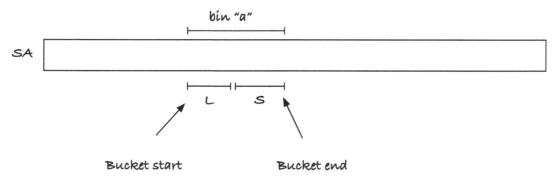

Figure 4-10. *Bucket structure*

2.   Now we are going to put all the L strings in the array in their correct position. Unlike the LMS strings, they will not only end up in the right order, but also in the right position. If we insert all the L strings in the L part of the bucket, and in the right order, they must also end up at their final position. What we will do is a scan from left to right in the bucket array, and when we see a string $x[i + 1, n]$ where $x[i, n]$ (the string before it) is an L string, we add $x[i, n]$ to its bucket. In our scan, we will see all such strings. We have the LMS strings so we will see L strings followed by an S, and as we insert L strings, we will always insert $x[i + 1, n]$ before we get to and need to insert $x[i, n]$. Because all L $x[i, n]$ strings must appear to the right of the suffix that follows them, $x[i + 1, n]$—this follows directly from the definition of the L class—we will always

171

have seen $x[i + 1, n]$ before $x[i, n]$ as we scan from left to right. So when we get to the point where we need to handle $x[i, n]$, we have already inserted it into the array. That we will insert the strings in the right order is something we can prove by induction. We start with the LMS strings in the right order, so the first string we insert must be at the correct position. So assume we have inserted k strings in the right order and consider $k + 1$. If that string is inserted incorrectly, then we have inserted $x[i, n]$ in a bin where there is a larger $x[j, n]$ already. But then consider $x[i + 1, n]$ and $x[j + 1, n]$—it is when we process these that we insert $x[i, n]$ and $x[j, n]$. If $x[j + 1, n]$ is already in the bin, we must have seen $x[j, n]$ before we now see $x[i, n]$. That cannot be right if the first k first strings were inserted correctly; we have a contradiction, so it must be true that we insert the strings in the right order. The base setup of the step is the LMS strings that ensures that the first set of strings are in the right order and kicks the induction off. The LMS strings are not in the right position, but this step doesn't need them to be. It only needs the order they appear in when we scan through the suffix array, and that order is correct. If they are in the right order, then we insert the suffixes before them in the right order into their respective buckets. The scan from left to right guarantees that all the other L strings are also added to the buckets in the right order.

3. As the final step, we place all the S strings based on the L strings we just inserted. Here, we scan from right to left, and each time we see suffix $x[i + 1, n]$ where $x[i, n]$ has class S, we insert $x[i, n]$ in its bucket. We can argue that this sorts them correctly similar to the earlier step. An S suffix will always appear to the left of the suffix that follows it in the suffix array. It follows from the dcfinition of S that it must be to the left. So when we get to suffix $x[i, n]$ in our scan, it is already inserted; we did so when we saw $x[i + 1, n]$ that is to the right of it. We have the L strings, so we will see S strings before L strings in the right order (the reverse order but this is the order we add them to the bucket, so that is what we want). S strings that are followed by S strings $x[i, n]$ must be to the

left of $x[i + 1, n]$—again by definition of S—and we have seen those strings before we get there. All in all, if the L strings are sorted, this scan will sort the S strings. Important to notice with this step is that we do not add strings to the end of the bucket pointers before the position where we have placed the LMS strings. We start back at the original end of the buckets. The LMS strings are not correctly placed in the first phase (it is only their order that is correct), but we place them correctly now.

If we start with knowing the order of the LMS suffixes, then these three steps give us the suffix array. The problematic step, of course, is getting the LMS suffixes sorted. Directly sorting them would take $O(n^2)$. We solve it recursively, but first, we need to create a reduced string.

We define LMS substrings as the strings that go from one LMS index to the next. The LMS substrings for `mississippi$` are `issi`, `issi`, and `ippi$`.

```
mississippi$
LSLLSLLSLLLS
 *   *   *    *
 |--|   |---|
    |--|
```

We will construct a new string that consists of the LMS substrings but where each substring is replaced by a number. That number should be the position the string has in a sorted list of LMS substrings—not unlike the LEX3 alphabet we constructed in the skew algorithm. The unique LMS substrings for `mississippi$` are `issi` and `ippi$` with `ippi$` < `issi`. Their lexicographical letters are therefore `ippi$` = 1 and `issi` = 2. The orders of the LMS substrings in `mississippi$` are `issi`, `issi`, and `ippi$`, so the reduced string for `mississippi$` is `221$`. This is the string we sort recursively.

Sorting the reduced string is only useful if the sorted suffixes there give us the order of the LMS suffixes. Not surprisingly, they do.

Let x be the original string and x' the reduced string. Let p be an array of pointers from the indices in x' to the start of the LMS substrings the characters in x' were taken from; see Figure 4-11. The indices in x' correspond to LMS substrings; the symbol at $x'[i]$ corresponds to the string $x[p[i], p[i + 1] + 1]$. Because of the way we defined equality between LMS substrings, if $x'[i] = x'[j]$, then the LMS strings that start at $p[i]$ and $p[j]$

have the same length, the same characters, and the same classes. Similarly, if $x'[i] < x'[j]$, then the LMS substring at $p[i]$ is smaller than the string at $p[j]$.

What we need to be able to use the reduced string to give us the sorted LMS suffixes is that the order of suffixes is preserved, that is, that if $x'[i, n] < x'[j, n]$, then $x[p[i], n] < x[p[j], n]$. If $x'[i] < x'[j]$, then the characters or classes in the LMS strings at $p[i]$ and $p[j]$ differ, and the order directly gives us that the suffix at $p[i]$ is less than the one at $p[j]$. If $x'[i] = x'[j]$, then the order of the suffixes is determined by $x'[i + 1, n]$ and $x'[j + 1, n]$, and we try comparing these, which we might, again, do from the first character. If not, we continue with the next suffixes, $i + 2$ and $j + 2$, and we continue until we have characters or classes that differ. The order is preserved, so if we sort the suffixes of x', we can get the order of the LMS suffixes from the suffix array of x' and the pointer to the original indices.

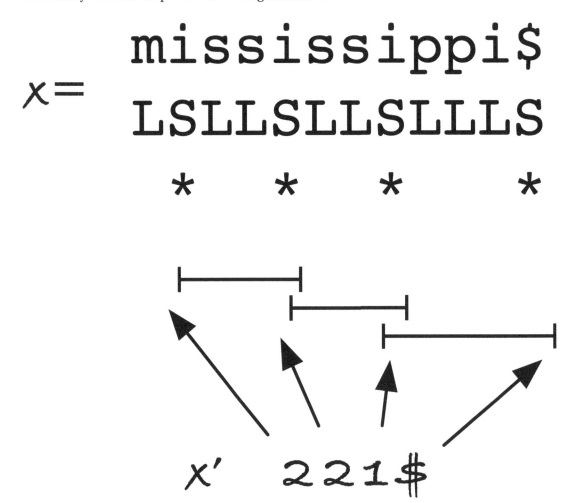

Figure 4-11. *Reduced string and the pointers to the original string*

So where we stand now is that if we can reduce our string, then we can recursively sort it, this gives us the order of the LMS suffixes, and from those, we can compute the original suffix array by three scans through the suffix array, one right to left, then one left to right, and then one right to left.

Reducing the string isn't hard either if we know the numbers for each LMS substring. Then it is just a scan through the string. Each number is unique, so we can put each string in its bucket. The tricky part is getting these numbers since they require sorting the LMS strings and scanning through them to give them names.

We can do the sorting using the exact three phases we used to induce the full suffix array from the ordered LMS suffixes. This time, we do not have the sorted LMS suffixes but put them at the end of their bins in any order. After inserting the LMS strings, we use steps 2 and 3 from the algorithm earlier to sort the L and S suffixes, respectively. We then end up with an array where the LMS substrings (but not suffixes) are in the correct order.

To see this, we define a set of strings, "LMS prefixes," where we include all single characters found at LMS indices, and then for each index i, we let $pre(i)$ be the string from i down to the first LMS index to the right of i (that means, if i is an LMS index, then $pre(i)$ is the entire LMS substring that starts at index i). We can show that by the three scans, we will sort the strings with respect to the prefixes longer than one.

When we insert strings in phase 1 of the sorting, we can think of it as sorting the length-one prefixes. The strings are put in bins for their initial character, so by inserting them thusly, we have sorted the length-one prefixes. In phase 2, we sort all the L prefixes. We can show this inductively by assuming we have inserted the first k correctly (and when we start, we will have the base case covered from phase 1). When we insert the $(k+1)$'s, $pre(i)$, we can assume that there is already a larger string in its bin, $pre(j)$. But that means that $pre(j+1)$ appeared before $pre(i+1)$ when we scanned from left to right, and that is a contradiction. So we insert the L prefixes in the right order, and since we insert all L prefixes, we must have sorted them with respect to the prefix order. When we scan through the S prefixes, the argument is the same. We overwrite the length-one strings because we fill the buckets from the back, where we put those strings, but all prefixes of length more than one will be sorted. The proof is entirely symmetric to the case for the L strings.

Since all the LMS strings are LMS prefixes (of length larger than one), the strings we have sorted in the preceding three phases must give us the right order for the LMS strings.

Summing the algorithm up: we can construct a reduced string by sorting the LMS strings and number them lexicographically. If this string doesn't have any duplicated characters, we can immediately sort it (similar to how we terminate the recursion in the skew algorithm). Otherwise, we sort it recursively. Once sorted, we construct the suffix array from it.

The scans before and after the recursive calls clearly take linear time. When we name the LMS strings, we need to iterate through them—this takes linear time—and compare contiguous strings. That comparison could potentially take linear time, but the total length of strings we compare cannot be more than linear. Each string is compared twice, to the string before and the string after, and the strings only overlap in a single character. So the running time, if we ignore the recursive call, is $O(n)$.

By construction of the LMS strings, we cannot have more than half as many characters as the full string (there is an L before each of the LMS indices that isn't an LMS index). Therefore, the reduced string is no longer than half the original string. If we let $T(n)$ be the running time for the algorithm with input length n, we have the recursive equation $T(n) = O(n) + T(n/2)$ for the running time. If we expand this equation, we get $n(1 + 1/2 + 1/4 + \cdots)$.

The sum $\sum_{i=0}^{\infty} 1/2^i = 2$, so the total running time is linear, $O(n)$.

Remapping

An essential part of the algorithm assumes that if we have a string with the same length as our alphabet size, then all letters are unique and can be mapped into bins numbered by their letter. This is not the case with natural language text. Many texts don't use the full character set, but the length of a string can be equal to the alphabet size. For example, assume that we have a character set with 8 bits, this could be latin-1 (ISO/IEC 8859-1). There, you have 256 characters, but few of them appear in any given text. If you have a text of length 256, chances are high that it doesn't contain all the characters, but instead have some characters appearing more than once. The assumptions about the alphabet and string length are guaranteed with all the strings constructed in the algorithm, but we must also ensure it with the initial string. So, we want to map our alphabet into indices 0, 1, ..., k where k is the number of unique characters found in the string (and we will use 0 for the sentinel as always). We use a table that maps characters and defines it like this:

```
struct remap_table {
    uint32_t alphabet_size;
    // I map from unsigned to signed for the table.
    // I do this to have a way of identifying letters
    // that were not found when building the map.
    // You cannot use this remapping if you have more than
    // 128 letters, if you do, use a larger table.
    signed char table[256];
    signed char rev_table[128];
};
```

We can use the table to map an original string to the reduced alphabet and back again.

We can build the table by scanning through the string and put a new index into the table each time we see a new character. If we do this, we will not necessarily preserve the lexicographical order of suffixes (the lexicographical order will depend on at which position we see a character rather than the order in the input). So instead, we can first collect the characters in the string and then assign indices to them in the sorting order the characters should have.

```
void build_remap_table(
    struct remap_table *table,
    const uint8_t *string
) {
    const uint8_t *x;

    // Collect existing characters.
    for (x = string; *x; x++) {
        if (table->table[*x] == -1) {
            table->alphabet_size++;
            table->table[*x] = 1;
        }
    }
```

```c
        // Now give the alphabet indices numbers in an
        // order that matches the input.
        for (int i = 0, char_no = 0; i < 256; i++) {
            if (table->table[i] != -1) {
                table->table[i] = char_no;
                table->rev_table[char_no] = i;
                char_no++;
            }
        }
}

void init_remap_table(
    struct remap_table *table,
    const uint8_t *string
) {
    table->alphabet_size = 1; // We always have zero.

    // Set table entries to -1. This indicates a letter
    // that we haven't seen.
    memset(table->table,     -1, sizeof(table->table));
    memset(table->rev_table, -1, sizeof(table->rev_table));
    // Sentinel is always the sentinel.
    table->table[0] = 0;
    table->rev_table[0] = 0;

    build_remap_table(table, string);
}

void dealloc_remap_table(
    struct remap_table *table
) {
    // We haven't allocated any resources.
}

void free_remap_table(
    struct remap_table *table
) {
    free(table);
}
```

Whenever you want to map a string s into a string rs, you can use this code:

```
init_remap_table(&remap_table, s);
rs = malloc(size + 1);
remap(rs, s, &remap_table);
```

where the remap() function could look like this:

```
void remap(
    uint8_t *output,
    const uint8_t *input,
    struct remap_table *table
) {
    // Since we map up to length + 1, we automatically
    // get a zero sentinel (the last character we copy from
    // input.
    const uint8_t *from = input;
    const uint8_t *to = input + strlen((char *)input) + 1;
    uint8_t *x = output;
    const uint8_t *y = from;
    for (; y != to; ++y, ++x) {
        *x = table->table[*y];
    }
}
```

We will assume that the input string to the algorithm is remapped this way.

A consequence of remapping the string we build the suffix array over is that you must also remap patterns you search for. If the two strings are in different alphabets, you will not find the patterns you are looking for.

Implementing the algorithm

We will need a bit per position class and we will need a value to indicate that an entry in an array is undefined. For this, we define these:

```
#define S true
#define L false
#define UNDEFINED ~0
```

For UNDEFINED I am using the largest number in our index type. It is unlikely that we will ever have *exactly* the same length as what we can index into, so this value should be free to use.

For classifying the position, we use a bool array, scan from right to left, and exploit the observation from earlier that when we cannot directly see which class an index has from comparing the character there and the next character, then we have the same character and then the class is the same as the index to the right. There is a special case when the string is empty. Then we cannot look at the character to the left of it. Otherwise, the function is simple:

```
static void classify_SL(
    const uint32_t *x,
    bool *s_index,
    uint32_t n
) {
    s_index[n] = S;
    if (n == 0) // empty string
        return;

    s_index[n - 1] = L;
    for (uint32_t i = n; i > 0; --i) {
        if (x[i - 1] > x[i]) {
            s_index[i - 1] = L;
        } else if (x[i - 1] == x[i] && s_index[i] == L) {
            s_index[i - 1] = L;
        } else {
            // either x[i - 1] < x[i] or
            // x[i - 1] == x[i] && s_index[i] == S
            s_index[i - 1] = S;
        }
    }
}
```

We will use a function for checking if an index is LMS. This function is equally simple. We have a special case with the leftmost index, where we cannot check the index to the left of it, but we handle this case explicitly and return that the index is L.

```
static bool is_LMS_index(
    bool *s_index,
    uint32_t n,
    uint32_t i
) {
    if (i == 0) return false;
    else return s_index[i] == S && s_index[i - 1] == L;
}
```

A large part of the algorithm involves putting suffixes in buckets determined by their first character. We can compute the bucket sizes by checking each character and incrementing a counter in the relevant bucket.

```
static void compute_buckets(
    uint32_t *x,
    uint32_t n,
    uint32_t alphabet_size,
    uint32_t *buckets
) {
    memset(buckets, 0, alphabet_size * sizeof(uint32_t));
    for (uint32_t i = 0; i < n + 1; ++i) {
        buckets[x[i]]++;
    }
}
```

Parameter x holds the string, n its length, alphabet_size—not surprisingly the number of letters in the alphabet—and buckets the array of bucket sizes.

We want to know the beginning or end index of each bucket, depending on which class we insert, and we can get those as an accumulative sum through the buckets.

```
static void find_buckets_beginnings(
    uint32_t *x,
    uint32_t n,
    uint32_t alphabet_size,
    uint32_t *buckets,
    uint32_t *beginnings
) {
```

```
    beginnings[0] = 0;
    for (uint32_t i = 1; i < alphabet_size; ++i) {
        beginnings[i] = beginnings[i - 1] + buckets[i - 1];
    }
}

static void find_buckets_ends(
    uint32_t *x,
    uint32_t n,
    uint32_t alphabet_size,
    uint32_t *buckets,
    uint32_t *ends
) {
    ends[0] = buckets[0];
    for (uint32_t i = 1; i < alphabet_size; ++i) {
        ends[i] = ends[i - 1] + buckets[i];
    }
}
```

The function for placing the LMS strings at first, at positions that might be incorrect but at least in their right buckets, looks like this:

```
void place_LMS(
    uint32_t *x,
    uint32_t n,
    uint32_t alphabet_size,
    uint32_t *SA,
    bool *s_index,
    uint32_t *buckets,
    uint32_t *bucket_ends
) {
    find_buckets_ends(x, n, alphabet_size, buckets, bucket_ends);
    for (uint32_t i = 0; i < n + 1; ++i) {
        if (is_LMS_index(s_index, n, i)) {
            SA[--(bucket_ends[x[i]])] = i;
        }
    }
}
```

In the expression SA[--(bucket_ends[x[i]])], we decrement the index of bucket x[i] *before* we insert index i in it. The bucket_ends array holds the indices *after* the buckets (or after the current bucket). This is for consistency with other subsequences in C where the first pointer is where values start, and the last pointer is one past the last value.

After inserting the LMS strings, we need to induce the L strings. Here, we scan from left to right, and where we see a string, that is, SA[i] is not undefined, we check if the index left of it has class L in which case we insert it at the beginning of its bucket. We increment the bucket pointer *after* we insert the index. The start pointers point at the first element and not one before.

```
static void induce_L(
    uint32_t *x,
    uint32_t n,
    uint32_t alphabet_size,
    uint32_t *SA,
    bool *s_index,
    uint32_t *buckets,
    uint32_t *bucket_starts
) {
    find_buckets_beginnings(x, n, alphabet_size, buckets, bucket_starts);
    for (uint32_t i = 0; i < n + 1; ++i) {
        // Not initialized yet.
        if (SA[i] == UNDEFINED) continue;

        // If SA[i] is zero, then we do not have
        // a suffix to the left of it.
        if (SA[i] == 0) continue;

        uint32_t j = SA[i] - 1;
        if (s_index[j] == L) {
            SA[(bucket_starts[x[j]])++] = j;
        }
    }
}
```

Inducing the S strings works similarly. In this case, we scan from right to left, and there is no need to check if elements are undefined. They will not be because the L classes are inserted, and because we scan from right to left, we have inserted S class strings before we get to them.

```
static void induce_S(
    uint32_t *x,
    uint32_t n,
    uint32_t alphabet_size,
    uint32_t *SA,
    bool *s_index,
    uint32_t *buckets,
    uint32_t *bucket_ends
) {
    find_buckets_ends(x, n, alphabet_size,
                        buckets, bucket_ends);
    for (uint32_t i = n + 1; i > 0; --i) {
        // We do not have a string to the left of the first.
        if (SA[i - 1] == 0) continue;
        uint32_t j = SA[i - 1] - 1;
        if (s_index[j] == S) {
            SA[--(bucket_ends[x[j]])] = j;
        }
    }
}
```

When we build the updated alphabet from LMS strings, we need to know if the two are equal. For this, we need to scan the two strings until we reach an LMS index. If we reach one in one string before the other, they are not the same, but if they reach one at the same point, and we have seen no mismatches along the way, they are. Mismatches, here, mean that characters or class differs. If we see that, we return false.

```
static bool equal_LMS(
    uint32_t *x,
    uint32_t n,
    bool *s_index,
```

```
    uint32_t i,
    uint32_t j
) {
    // The sentinel string is unique.
    if (i == n + 1 || j == n + 1) return false;
    uint32_t k = 0;
    while (true) {
        bool i_LMS = is_LMS_index(s_index, n, i + k);
        bool j_LMS = is_LMS_index(s_index, n, j + k);
        if (k > 0 && i_LMS && j_LMS) {
            // We reached the end of the strings.
            return true;
        }
        // If one string ends before another or we
        // have different characters, the strings are
        // different.
        if (i_LMS != j_LMS
            || x[i + k] != x[j + k]
          ) {
            return false;
        }
        k++;
    }
    return true;
}
```

It is the code that reduces a string where the real magic happens. In the function, we run through the strings in the order given by the input suffix array. In this array, the LMS strings are ordered, so every time we see one of these, we check if it is identical to the LMS string we saw before it, in which case it should have the same name, or if it is different, in which case it should have a name that is one larger. We store the names in a buffer where they will appear in the same order as they do in the string. We use this buffer to create the reduced string; it contains the names we have given the LMS strings in the same order as they appear in the input. Once we have the names buffer, we scan through it and construct the reduced string. The reduced string should be the LMS names in the order they appear in the input string, and that is exactly what we have in

the names buffer if we skip the undefined entries. We also collect the offsets at which the
LMS strings appear. We need them later for mapping the string in the other direction.

```
static void reduce_SA(
    uint32_t *x,
    uint32_t n,
    uint32_t *SA,
    uint32_t *names_buf,
    bool *s_index,
    uint32_t *new_alphabet_size,
    uint32_t *summary_string,
    uint32_t *summary_offsets,
    uint32_t *new_string_length
) {
    memset(names_buf, UNDEFINED,
            (n + 1) * sizeof(uint32_t));

    // Start names at one so we save zero for sentinel.
    uint32_t name = 0;

    names_buf[SA[0]] = name;
    uint32_t last_suffix = SA[0];

    for (uint32_t i = 1; i < n + 1; i++) {
        uint32_t j = SA[i];
        if (!is_LMS_index(s_index, n, j)) continue;
        if (!equal_LMS(x, n, s_index, last_suffix, j)) {
            name++;
        }
        last_suffix = j;
        names_buf[j] = name;
    }

    // One larger than the largest name used.
    *new_alphabet_size = name + 1;

    uint32_t j = 0;
    for (uint32_t i = 0; i < n + 1; i++) {
        name = names_buf[i];
```

```
        if (name == UNDEFINED) continue;
        summary_offsets[j] = i;
        summary_string[j] = name;
        j++;
    }
    // We don't include sentinel in the length.
    *new_string_length = j - 1;
}
```

The next function is long, but there is very little complicated in it. It is the main sorting function. First, we classify the indices and compute buckets. After that, we place LMS strings and induce the indices. Then, we build the reduced string and sort it recursively (we haven't seen sort_SA() yet, but we will shortly). Once we have the array for the reduced string, we use it to place the LMS strings again, but this time in the correct order (see later where we define the function remap_LMS()), and then we induce the remaining indices before we return.

```
static void recursive_sorting(
    uint32_t *x,
    uint32_t n,
    uint32_t *SA,
    uint32_t *names_buf,
    bool * s_index,
    uint32_t *buckets,
    uint32_t *bucket_endpoints,
    uint32_t *reduced_string,
    uint32_t *reduced_offsets,
    uint32_t alphabet_size
) {
    classify_SL(x, s_index, n);
    compute_buckets(x, n, alphabet_size, buckets);

    memset(SA, UNDEFINED, (n + 1) * sizeof(uint32_t));
    place_LMS(x, n, alphabet_size, SA, s_index,
            buckets, bucket_endpoints);
    induce_L(x, n, alphabet_size, SA, s_index,
            buckets, bucket_endpoints);
```

```
    induce_S(x, n, alphabet_size, SA, s_index,
            buckets, bucket_endpoints);

  uint32_t new_alphabet_size;
  uint32_t new_string_length;
  reduce_SA(x, n, SA,
            names_buf,
            s_index,
            &new_alphabet_size,
            reduced_string,
            reduced_offsets,
            &new_string_length);

  // Move to next position in the buffers.
  uint32_t *new_SA = SA + n + 1;
  uint32_t *new_names_buf = names_buf + n + 1;
  bool *new_s_index = s_index + n + 1;
  uint32_t *new_summary_string =
            reduced_string + n + 1;
  uint32_t *new_summary_offsets =
            reduced_offsets + n + 1;
  uint32_t *new_buckets =
            buckets + alphabet_size;
  uint32_t *new_bucket_endpoints =
            bucket_endpoints + alphabet_size;

  sort_SA(reduced_string, new_string_length,
            new_SA,
            new_names_buf,
            new_summary_string,
            new_summary_offsets,
            new_buckets,
            new_bucket_endpoints,
            new_s_index,
            new_alphabet_size);

  memset(SA, UNDEFINED, (n + 1) * sizeof(uint32_t));
  remap_LMS(x, n,
```

```
                buckets, bucket_endpoints,
                alphabet_size,
                s_index,
                reduced_string,
                new_string_length, new_SA,
                reduced_offsets,
                SA);
    induce_L(x, n, alphabet_size, SA, s_index,
                buckets, bucket_endpoints);
    induce_S(x, n, alphabet_size, SA, s_index,
                buckets, bucket_endpoints);
}
```

In the recursive call, I do not allocate new strings or buffers. Similarly to the skew algorithm, I allocate all the buffers in the outermost function and update pointers into them when I recurse. Here, we are working with a string of length n, excluding the sentinel, that we shouldn't override so we move the pointers $n + 1$ to the right before we call recursively.

The sort_SA() function decides if we can get the sorted suffix array directly. We can do this if the alphabet size matches the string length. When it does, all the LMS strings are unique, and their names give us the order they should appear in. So, we run through the string and bucket them at the index that matches their name. If we cannot construct the suffix array directly, we sort it recursively.

```
void sort_SA(
    uint32_t *x,
    uint32_t n,
    uint32_t *SA,
    uint32_t *names_buf,
    uint32_t *summary_string,
    uint32_t *summary_offsets,
    uint32_t *buckets,
    uint32_t *bucket_endpoints,
    bool *s_index,
    uint32_t alphabet_size
) {
```

```
if (n == 0) {
    // Trivially sorted.
    SA[0] = 0;
    return;
}

// Mapping each letter into its bin.
// This code assumes that the letters
// are numbers from zero (the sentinel)
// up to the alphabet size.
if (alphabet_size == n + 1) {
    SA[0] = n;
    for (uint32_t i = 0; i < n; ++i) {
        uint32_t j = x[i];
        SA[j] = i;
    }
} else {
    recursive_sorting(
        x, n, SA,
        names_buf,
        s_index,
        buckets,
        bucket_endpoints,
        summary_string,
        summary_offsets,
        alphabet_size
    );
}
}
```

Once done with sorting the reduced string, we need to put the LMS strings in the right order into the current suffix array. To do this, we run through the indices in the reduced string and get their position in the reduced suffix array—that gives us the order we should insert them in. The index we need to insert is not the index in the reduced suffix array but the offset in the original string, so we get that. We insert the indices at the end of their respective buckets, so they won't be overwritten when we induce the L suffixes from them.

```
void remap_LMS(
    uint32_t *x,
    uint32_t n,
    uint32_t *buckets,
    uint32_t *bucket_ends,
    uint32_t alphabet_size,
    bool *s_index,
    uint32_t *reduced_string,
    uint32_t reduced_length,
    uint32_t *reduced_SA,
    uint32_t *reduced_offsets,
    uint32_t *SA
) {
    find_buckets_ends(x, n, alphabet_size,
                      buckets, bucket_ends);

    for (uint32_t i = reduced_length + 1; i > 0; --i) {
        uint32_t idx = reduced_offsets[reduced_SA[i - 1]];
        uint32_t bucket_idx = x[idx];
        SA[--(bucket_ends[bucket_idx])] = idx;
    }
    SA[0] = n;
}
```

The main function maps the input string, of type uint8_t *, to an integer string, of type uint32_t *. Then it allocates all the buffers we use and call sort_SA(). When we are done with sorting the suffix array, we copy the first half of it—the part that is sorted at the first-level recursive call—into the suffix array buffer we want. Finally, we free all the buffers.

```
struct suffix_array *
sa_is_construction(
    uint8_t *remapped_string,
    uint32_t alphabet_size
) {
    struct suffix_array *sa = allocate_sa(remapped_string);
    // We work with the string length without the sentinel
```

```
// in this algorithm.
uint32_t n = sa->length - 1;

// Create string of integers instead of bytes.
uint32_t *s = malloc((n + 1) * sizeof(uint32_t));
for (uint32_t i = 0; i < n; ++i) {
    s[i] = remapped_string[i];
}
s[n] = 0;

// Allocate all buffers.
uint32_t *SA =
            malloc(2 * (n + 1) * sizeof(uint32_t));
uint32_t *names_buf =
            malloc(2 * (n + 1) * sizeof(uint32_t));
uint32_t *summary_string =
            malloc(2 * (n + 1) * sizeof(uint32_t));
uint32_t *summary_offsets =
            malloc(2 * (n + 1) * sizeof(uint32_t));
bool *s_index =
            malloc(2 * (n + 1) * sizeof(bool));
uint32_t max_alphabet_size =
            (alphabet_size > n) ? alphabet_size : n + 1;
uint32_t *buckets =
            malloc(2 * max_alphabet_size * sizeof(uint32_t));
uint32_t *bucket_endpoints =
            malloc(2 * max_alphabet_size * sizeof(uint32_t));

// Sort in buffer and then move the result to the suffix array.
sort_SA(s, n, SA, names_buf,
        summary_string, summary_offsets,
        buckets, bucket_endpoints, s_index,
        alphabet_size);
memcpy(sa->array, SA, (n + 1) * sizeof(uint32_t));

// Free all buffers.
free(bucket_endpoints);
```

```
    free(buckets);
    free(s_index);
    free(summary_offsets);
    free(summary_string);
    free(SA);
    free(s);

    return sa;
}
```

We argued earlier that the algorithm runs in linear time, and we shall see at the end of the chapter that it is fast in practice, but what is the memory footprint? We can check the buffers we allocate in the outermost function and reuse in all the recursions. We have seven arrays where six of them take up $2n$ words (here that means integers), and then we have one bool array. If we assume that this takes up one byte, then we use $12n + n/2$ words—less than what we needed for McCreight's algorithm but only barely so.

Memory reduction

The algorithm, as we have implemented it, is very wasteful of memory. It is fast, as we shall see at the end of the chapter, but if the reason for using suffix array over suffix trees is the smaller memory footprint, then we cannot spend more space constructing the suffix array than we would constructing the suffix tree. We can, however, with some tricks, bring this down to $2n$ words (integers) and n bits for each character in the string. Of these words, half is used for the suffix array, so we only have a factor two overhead for constructing the array. It is possible to go down to just n bits on top of the resulting suffix array if we have a constant bound on the size of the alphabets, but we will not get that far here.

The tricks are not extremely difficult to understand, but they would certainly take the focus from the overall ideas in the algorithm—and the simplicity of it—so I explain them in this separate section. I only show the most important changes to the algorithm to reduce the memory—the parts I don't show are the same as those I have already shown except that they work on a bit array instead of a byte array. You will not be able to compile the following code in the same file as the code earlier. I redefine some macros and several functions, and that will cause problems. Use a different file.
My implementation is at https://github.com/mailund/stralg/blob/master/stralg/sa_is_mem.c.

There are two main tricks to it. First, we observe that when we call recursively, we use half the space on the suffix array and half the length of the original string on the reduced string. This means that we can pack the two into the same buffer and build the reduced suffix array in the first half of the input array and the reduced string in the other. We will use the suffix array buffer for this. This array has size n words (integers), and we cannot get rid of it in any way, because it is the output of the algorithm.

Second, we observe that we do not need to preserve any data from before a recursive call because we need it after the call. We can reconstruct the classes array and the buckets after the recursion. So, we can free the memory they use before the call and allocate it again when we are done with the call. If we free and reallocate, we only use the longest arrays possible in a recursion. For the classes, this is n bits. The longest array we have equals the length of the first string. After that, we have at most half the length in a recursion. For the buckets, the length in the first call is equal to the size of the original alphabet, which we assume is a constant. The alphabet in the next call can be half the size of the input string because that is the maximum number of LMS strings we can have, and all of those could be unique. So by allocating and deallocating buckets, we will use at most $n/2$ words on them. So, adding up, we use n words on the suffix array, $n/2$ words on the buckets, and n bits on the classes. Because we have a function that takes `uint8_t *` strings as input, and the algorithm works on integers, we also need to spend n words on the integer string. We end up with $2\frac{1}{2}n$ words and n bits.

In the implementation we cannot get rid of the integer string, but from an algorithmic point of view, we can. If we consider the integer string the input and the SA string the output, and only analyze what *extra* memory the algorithm uses, then we have $n/2$ words (for the buckets) and n bits (for the classes). Compared to any of the other algorithms we have seen, this is by far the most memory efficient. With a probabilistic argument that I give at the end of this section, we can get rid of the $n/2$ words for the buckets, so the algorithm uses only n bits in total. It is *extremely* memory efficient.

The first thing we do is getting rid of the bool array and replacing it with a bit array. If you have worked with bit arrays before, you will not be surprised by how we do this. When we index into one, we divide the index by eight to get the correct byte, and inside the byte, we apply a mask that picks out the relevant bit. Getting a bit is simply that, except that we translate the bit we get to true and false. Otherwise, we cannot compare them to S and L values; we can interpret them as truth values, the L value will match zero, but the S value will not match bits that are not the lowest in the byte. So we must convert bits to bools. Setting a bit is slightly more involved. We need to get the bit from the byte using a mask and then "OR" it with the existing bit to set it, or we must invert the bit and then "AND" that to the existing byte.

```
static uint8_t mask[] = {
    0x80, 0x40, 0x20, 0x10, 0x08, 0x04, 0x02, 0x01
};
#define sget(i) ((s_idx[(i) / 8] & mask[(i) % 8]) \
                    ? true : false)
#define sset(i, b) (                               \
    s_idx[(i) / 8] =                               \
    (b) ? (mask[(i) % 8] | s_idx[(i) / 8])     \
        : ((~mask[(i) % 8]) & s_idx[(i) / 8]) \
```

The bit array macros assume that we have the byte array in a variable called s_idx. To use the array, we need to use the macros for getting and setting bits. Aside from that, most of the functions in the algorithm are the same as those we have already seen.

When we find buckets' beginnings and ends, we do not put them in separate buffers but reuse the buckets buffer. This means that we need to recompute the buckets every time we call find_buckets_beginnings() and find_buckets_ends(). The find_buckets_beginnings() looks like this:

```
static void find_buckets_beginnings(
    uint32_t *x,
    uint32_t n,
    uint32_t alphabet_size,
    uint32_t *buckets
) {
    compute_buckets(x, n, alphabet_size, buckets);
    uint32_t sum = 0;
    for (uint32_t i = 0; i < alphabet_size; ++i) {
        sum += buckets[i];
        buckets[i] = sum - buckets[i];
    }
}
```

When we reduce a string, we do not use a names buffer. Instead, we scan through the input suffix array and pack the LMS indices into the first half of the input. Then we collect the names in the second half. We exploit that there cannot be more names than half the input length, so we can pack the names in there by taking half their index and putting them after the reduced string. We can construct the reduced string as before—we scan through the names and insert them into the reduced string in the order that they appear. It doesn't matter that their indices are half what they were before; we only want their order.

```
static bool is_LMS_index(
    uint8_t *s_idx,
    uint32_t n,
    uint32_t i
) {
    if (i == 0) return false;
    else return sget(i) == S && sget(i - 1) == L;
}

static bool equal_LMS(
    uint32_t *x,
    uint32_t n,
    uint8_t *s_idx,
    uint32_t i,
    uint32_t j
) {
    // The sentinel string is unique.
    if (i == n + 1 || j == n + 1) return false;
    uint32_t k = 0;
    while (true) {
        bool i_LMS = is_LMS_index(s_idx, n, i + k);
        bool j_LMS = is_LMS_index(s_idx, n, j + k);
        if (k > 0 && i_LMS && j_LMS) {
            // We reached the end of the strings.
            return true;
        }
```

```c
        // If one string ends before another or we
        // have different characters, the strings are
        // different.
        if (i_LMS != j_LMS
            || x[i + k] != x[j + k]
            ) {
            return false;
        }
        k++;
    }
    return true;
}

static void reduce_SA(
    uint32_t *x,
    uint32_t n,
    uint32_t *SA,
    uint8_t *s_idx,
    uint32_t *new_alphabet_size,
    uint32_t *new_string_length
) {
    // Pack the LMS strings into the first half of the
    // SA buffer. After that we are free to use the
    // second half of the array.
    uint32_t *compacted = SA;
    uint32_t n1 = 0;
    for (uint32_t i = 0; i < n + 1; ++i) {
        if (is_LMS_index(s_idx, n, SA[i])) {
            compacted[n1++] = SA[i];
        }
    }

    // Now collect the names in the upper half of the array.
#define half_pos(pos) (pos % 2 == 0) ? pos / 2 : (pos - 1) / 2
    uint32_t *names = SA + n1;
    memset(names, UNDEFINED, sizeof(uint32_t) * (n + 1 - n1));
```

```
    uint32_t name = 0;
    names[half_pos(compacted[0])] = name;
    uint32_t last_suffix = compacted[0];

    for (uint32_t i = 1; i < n1; i++) {
        uint32_t j = compacted[i];
        if (!equal_LMS(x, n, s_idx, last_suffix, j)) {
            name++;
        }
        last_suffix = j;
        names[half_pos(j)] = name;
    }

    // Finally, construct the reduced string
    // by shifting the names down. They are in order
    // now, so we really only need the right number of
    // copies and we get them this way.
    uint32_t *reduced = SA + n1;
    uint32_t j = 0;
    for (uint32_t i = 0; i < n + 1 - n1; ++i) {
        if (names[i] != UNDEFINED) {
            reduced[j++] = names[i];
        }
    }

    // One larger than the largest name used.
    *new_alphabet_size = name + 1;
    // We don't include sentinel in the length.
    *new_string_length = n1 - 1;
}
```

The recursive sorting function doesn't change much. We allocate, deallocate, reallocate, and free the buffers, but otherwise, we do the same as before. We have fewer arguments to the reduce_SA() function because we do not use preallocated buffers but do our computation in SA, though.

```c
static void classify_SL(
    const uint32_t *x,
    uint8_t *s_idx,
    uint32_t n
) {
    sset(n, S);
    if (n == 0) // empty string
        return;
    sset(n - 1, L);

    for (uint32_t i = n; i > 0; --i) {
        if (x[i - 1] > x[i]) {
            sset(i - 1, L);
        } else if (x[i - 1] == x[i] && sget(i) == L) {
            sset(i - 1, L);
        } else {
            sset(i - 1, S);
        }
    }
}

void place_LMS(
    uint32_t *x,
    uint32_t n,
    uint32_t alphabet_size,
    uint32_t *SA,
    uint8_t  *s_idx,
    uint32_t *buckets
) {
    find_buckets_ends(x, n, alphabet_size, buckets);
    for (uint32_t i = 0; i < n + 1; ++i) {
        if (is_LMS_index(s_idx, n, i)) {
            SA[--(buckets[x[i]])] = i;
        }
    }
}
```

```
static void induce_L(
    uint32_t *x,
    uint32_t n,
    uint32_t alphabet_size,
    uint32_t *SA,
    uint8_t *s_idx,
    uint32_t *buckets
) {
    find_buckets_beginnings(x, n, alphabet_size, buckets);

    for (uint32_t i = 0; i < n + 1; ++i) {
        if (SA[i] == UNDEFINED) continue; // Not initialized yet

        // If SA[i] is zero, then we do not have
        // a suffix to the left of it.
        if (SA[i] == 0) continue;

        uint32_t j = SA[i] - 1;
        if (sget(j) == L) {
            SA[(buckets[x[j]])++] = j;
        }
    }
}

static void induce_S(
    uint32_t *x,
    uint32_t n,
    uint32_t alphabet_size,
    uint32_t *SA,
    uint8_t  *s_idx,
    uint32_t *buckets
) {
    find_buckets_ends(x, n, alphabet_size, buckets);
    for (uint32_t i = n + 1; i > 0; --i) {
        // We do not have a string to the left of the first.
        if (SA[i - 1] == 0) continue;
        uint32_t j = SA[i - 1] - 1;
```

```
        if (sget(j) == S) {
            SA[--(buckets[x[j]])] = j;
        }
    }
}

void sort_SA(
    uint32_t *x,
    uint32_t n,
    uint32_t *SA,
    uint32_t alphabet_size
) {
    if (n == 0) {
        // Trivially sorted
        SA[0] = 0;
        return;
    }

    // Mapping each letter into its bin.
    // This code assumes that the letters
    // are numbers from zero (the sentinel)
    // up to the alphabet size.
    if (alphabet_size == n + 1) {
        SA[0] = n;
        for (uint32_t i = 0; i < n; ++i) {
            uint32_t j = x[i];
            SA[j] = i;
        }
    } else {
        recursive_sorting(
            x, n, SA,
            alphabet_size
        );
    }
}
```

```
static void recursive_sorting(
    uint32_t *x,
    uint32_t n,
    uint32_t *SA,
    uint32_t alphabet_size
) {
    uint8_t *s_idx =
        malloc(((n + 1)/8 + 1) * sizeof(uint8_t));
    uint32_t *buckets =
        malloc(alphabet_size * sizeof(uint32_t));
    classify_SL(x, s_idx, n);

    memset(SA, UNDEFINED, (n + 1) * sizeof(uint32_t));
    place_LMS(x, n, alphabet_size, SA, s_idx, buckets);
    induce_L(x, n, alphabet_size, SA, s_idx, buckets);
    induce_S(x, n, alphabet_size, SA, s_idx, buckets);
    free(buckets);

    uint32_t new_alphabet_size;
    uint32_t new_string_length;
    reduce_SA(x, n, SA,
              s_idx,
              &new_alphabet_size,
              &new_string_length);
    uint32_t *reduced_string = SA + new_string_length + 1;

    // Don't use space on this for the recursive call.
    free(s_idx);

    sort_SA(reduced_string,
            new_string_length,
            SA,
            new_alphabet_size);

    // Get arrays back.
    s_idx = malloc(((n + 1)/8 + 1) * sizeof(uint8_t));
    classify_SL(x, s_idx, n);
    buckets = malloc(alphabet_size * sizeof(uint32_t));
```

```
remap_LMS(x, n,
          buckets,
          alphabet_size,
          s_idx,
          new_string_length,
          SA);
induce_L(x, n, alphabet_size, SA, s_idx, buckets);
induce_S(x, n, alphabet_size, SA, s_idx, buckets);

free(buckets);
free(s_idx);
}
```

There is more work to do in remap_LMS() now. We compute the offsets in this function now. Doing so is not hard, however. The offsets are the positions where LMS strings appear, so we scan through the string and find these. Once we have the reduced suffix array, we do not need the reduced string any longer, so we can put the offsets there.

The reduced suffix array, which is at the beginning of the input suffix array, gives us the sorted order of the offsets. We scan through the suffix array, get the offset of an index, and put that into the suffix array at the same index. It gives us the offsets in the right order at the beginning of the suffix array.

Finally, we set the upper half of the suffix array to UNDEFINED—we need all positions where we do not have LMS strings to be UNDEFINED—and then we scan from right to left through the lower half, where all the offsets are. We get the position of each offset from the suffix array, it holds the order in which we need to insert offsets, and then we put the offset in the right bucket and clear the old position by setting it to UNDEFINED. Offsets belong at an index that is higher than or equal to where they are packed in the array, so we do not risk overwriting one with UNDEFINED when we insert them in buckets.

```
void remap_LMS(
    uint32_t *x,
    uint32_t n,
    uint32_t *buckets,
    uint32_t alphabet_size,
    uint8_t *s_idx,
    uint32_t reduced_length,
    uint32_t *SA
```

```
) {
    // Compute the offsets we need to map
    // the reduced string to the original.
    uint32_t *offsets = SA + reduced_length + 1;
    uint32_t j = 0;
    for (uint32_t i = 1; i < n + 1; ++i) {
        if (is_LMS_index(s_idx, n, i)) {
            offsets[j++] = i;
        }
    }

    // Move the offsets into the first part of SA, sorted
    // by the SA of the reduced problem, so we have them
    // when we update SA.
    for (uint32_t i = 0; i < reduced_length + 1; ++i) {
        SA[i] = offsets[SA[i]];
    }

    // Reset the upper part of SA.
    memset(SA + reduced_length + 1,
           UNDEFINED,
           sizeof(uint32_t) * (n + 1 - (reduced_length + 1)));

    // Now we can insert the LMS strings in their buckets.
    // Scanning right to left this way ensures that we see
    // an LMS after we have zeroed its position, so we don't
    // risk removing one when we set a position to UNDEFINED.
    find_buckets_ends(x, n, alphabet_size, buckets);
    for (uint32_t i = reduced_length + 1; i > 0; --i) {
        uint32_t j = SA[i - 1]; SA[i - 1] = UNDEFINED;
        SA[--(buckets[x[j]])] = j;
    }
}
```

Finally, there is not much change to sa_is_construction(). We construct the string s, but we don't allocate any buffers and we call sort_SA() directly with the suffix array's array—we don't need to copy the result from a buffer now.

```
struct suffix_array *
sa_is_construction(
    uint8_t *remapped_string,
    uint32_t alphabet_size
) {
    struct suffix_array *sa = allocate_sa(remapped_string);
    // We work with the string length without the sentinel
    // in this algorithm.
    uint32_t n = sa->length - 1;

    // Create string of integers instead of bytes.
    uint32_t *s = malloc((n + 1) * sizeof(uint32_t));
    for (uint32_t i = 0; i < n; ++i) {
        s[i] = remapped_string[i];
    }
    s[n] = 0;

    // Sort in buffer and then move the
    // result to the suffix array.
    sort_SA(s, n, sa->array, alphabet_size);

    free(s);

    return sa;
}
```

In the preceding analysis, we saw that we would use $n/2$ words for buckets, n for the suffix array, n for the integer string, and n bits for the classes array. This is true for the worst case where the alphabet we build in the recursion has one letter per LMS string, but this is unlikely to happen. If your strings are random, the distance between LMS indices is geometrically distributed, so the length is expected to be constant. Then we use $O(1)$ space for the buckets. Which means that, besides the input string and output suffix array, we only use $O(n)$ bits. We always need to use n words for the suffix array—we cannot save away the output of the algorithm. We cannot get rid of the input string either, but always when we analyze an algorithm; we do not count input and output as part of the complexity. They can be handled by the caller of the algorithm. The one thing that we do not do efficiently in our current implementation is handling the input string. We use n words more than we need to, because we must translate a byte string into an integer string. If you dare assume that the alphabet size never grows larger than 256 (you can check how likely it will be, given your alphabet and character probabilities), then you can use a uint8_t array for strings and then there is no need to build an integer string before you can run the algorithm. In that case, the only overhead with using the algorithm is n bits. In the worst case, however, the alphabet can have a size that is one half of the input string, so I have not done this.

Searching using suffix arrays

Our suffix array would be a little use—except perhaps as a way to construct suffix trees—if we couldn't search for strings using them. Which, of course, we can. You can find the code for this section at https://github.com/mailund/stralg/blob/master/stralg/suffix_array.c.

Binary search

The most straightforward way to search using a suffix array is a binary search. The suffix array has our suffixes in sorted order, and for each index, we can get the corresponding suffix index from the array. In a binary search, we have an interval of the suffixes where the key we search for is found if it is in the string. We can compare the key to the middle of the interval and from there decide whether we must search in the first or second half. This idea can be implemented like this:

```
static uint32_t binary_search(
    const uint8_t *p,
    uint32_t key_len,
    struct suffix_array *sa
) {
    uint32_t low = 0;
    uint32_t high = sa->length;

    while (low < high) {
        uint32_t mid = low + (high - low) / 2;
        int cmp = strncmp(
            (char *)p,
            (char *)(sa->string + sa->array[mid]),
```

```
            key_len
        );
        if (cmp < 0) {
            high = mid - 1;
        } else if (cmp > 0) {
            low = mid + 1;
        } else {
            // If cmp is 0, we have a match.
            return mid;
        }
    }

    // This must be the lowest point where
    // a hit could be if we didn't catch it above.
    return low;
}
```

In the iterator for the search, we have the interval where the keys are found. When we have found the key in the string, we search backward and forward to get the interval where it matches, and we use this interval when we iterate through the matches.

```
struct sa_match_iter {
    struct suffix_array *sa;
    uint32_t L;
    uint32_t R;
    uint32_t i;
};
struct sa_match {
    uint32_t position;
};

void init_sa_match_iter(
    struct sa_match_iter *iter,
    const uint8_t *p,
    struct suffix_array *sa
) {
    iter->sa = sa;
```

```c
    uint32_t key_len = (uint32_t)strlen((char *)p);
    assert(key_len > 0); // I cannot handle empty strings!
    uint32_t mid = binary_search(p, key_len, sa);

    if (mid == sa->length ||
        strncmp((char *)(sa->string + sa->array[mid]),
                (char *)p, key_len)
            != 0) {
        // This is a special case where the lower bound is
        // the end of the array. Here we cannot check
        // the strcmp to figure out the interval
        // (or whether we have a hit at all)
        // but we know that the key is not in the
        // string.
        iter->L = iter->R = 0;
        iter->i = 1;
        return;
    }

    // Find lower and upper bound.
    uint32_t lower = mid;
    while (lower > 0 &&
            strncmp((char *)(sa->string + sa->array[lower]),
                    (char *)p, key_len) >= 0) {
        lower--;
    }
    iter->i = iter->L = lower + 1;
    uint32_t upper = mid;
    while (upper < sa->length &&
            strncmp((char *)(sa->string + sa->array[upper]),
                    (char *)p, key_len) == 0) {
        upper++;
    }
    iter->R = upper - 1;
}
```

```
bool next_sa_match(struct sa_match_iter *iter,
                   struct sa_match     *match)
{
    if (iter->i > iter->R)
        return false;
    match->position = iter->sa->array[iter->i++];
    return true;
}

void dealloc_sa_match_iter(struct sa_match_iter *iter)
{
    // Nothing to be done here.
}
```

We don't free anything in the deallocation function, but we need it to match the usage pattern we have for all our iterators.

The running time is $O(m(\log n + k))$, where m is the length of the key, n is the length of the string we search in, and k is the number of occurrences we find. The log n comes from the binary search, and the m is multiplied to it because the worst time comparison between the key and a suffix takes that long.

When setting up the iterator, we do a linear search for the beginning and end of the interval. You can also use a binary search here to find the lower and upper bound. The functions for that are listed as follows. The lower_bound_search() function finds the first occurrence of a key, or the position where that key should be inserted if it isn't in the list (i.e., the first suffix larger than the key). The upper_bound_search() finds one past the last occurrence of the key or the point where the string should be inserted, that is, if the key isn't in the string, then the upper and lower bound returns the same index. In the upper bound search, we need to check if we have a match or are below a match when the interval gets empty. This is to make sure that we get an index just past the right position in those cases. Otherwise, the two implements should be fairly straightforward.

```
uint32_t lower_bound_search(
    struct suffix_array *sa,
    const uint8_t *key
) {
    uint32_t L = 0, R = sa->length;
    uint32_t key_len = strlen((char*)key);
```

```c
    uint32_t mid;
    while (L < R) {
        mid = L + (R - L) / 2;
        int cmp = strncmp(
            (char *)key,
            (char *)(sa->string + sa->array[mid]),
            key_len
        );
        if (cmp <= 0) {
            R = mid;
        } else if (cmp > 0) {
            L = mid + 1;
        }

    }
    return (L <= R) ? L : R;
}

uint32_t upper_bound_search(
    struct suffix_array *sa,
    const uint8_t *key
) {
    uint32_t L = 0, R = sa->length;
    uint32_t key_len = strlen((char*)key);
    uint32_t mid;
    while (L < R) {
        mid = L + (R - L) / 2;
        int cmp = strncmp(
            (char *)key,
            (char *)(sa->string + sa->array[mid]),
            key_len
        );
        if (cmp < 0) {
            R = mid - 1;
        } else if (cmp >= 0) {
            L = mid + 1;
        }
```

```
    }
    R = (R > L) ? R : L;
    if (R == sa->length) return R;

    int cmp = strncmp(
        (char *)key,
        (char *)(sa->string + sa->array[R]),
        key_len
    );
    return (cmp >= 0) ? R + 1 : R;
}

void init_sa_match_iter(
    struct sa_match_iter *iter,
    const uint8_t *key,
    struct suffix_array *sa
) {
    iter->sa = sa;

    // Find lower and upper bound
    uint32_t lower = lower_bound_search(sa, key);
    uint32_t upper = upper_bound_search(sa, key);

    // No match
    if (lower == upper) {
        iter->L = iter->R = 0;
        iter->i = 1;
    }

    iter->i = iter->L = lower;
    iter->R = upper - 1;
}
```

With this approach, we do not pay a cost of m for each occurrence of the key, so we get the running time $O(m \log n + k)$.

There is another trick we can use to speed up the search. It doesn't change the asymptotic running time, it is still $O(m \log n + k)$, but it uses a faster approach to the binary search. The critical observation behind the idea is that when we have matched a prefix of the pattern against the suffix array, we have an interval, $[L, R]$, where all the suffixes that start with that prefix sit. If we want to extend the prefix by the next character, then we will get a subinterval where that additional character matches. To get that interval, we do not need to compare the key against the entire suffixes; we know that it matches the prefix we have searched for so far. Instead, we can do a binary search inside the interval where we match the next character in the pattern against characters at an offset that skips the prefix we know matches.

We will use a lower and an upper bound function to get one interval from the previous. These functions are very similar to the ones earlier, but they match a single character at an offset, *k*, into the suffixes.

```
uint32_t lower_bound_k(
    struct suffix_array *sa,
    uint32_t k, uint8_t a,
    uint32_t L, uint32_t R
) {
    while (L < R) {
        uint32_t mid = L + (R - L) / 2;
        uint32_t b_idx = sa->array[mid] + k;
        if (b_idx >= sa->length) {
            // b is less if it is past the end.
            L = mid + 1;
            continue;
        }
        uint8_t b = *(sa->string + b_idx);
        if (b < a) {
            L = mid + 1;
        } else {
            R = mid;
        }
    }
    return (L <= R) ? L : R;
}

uint32_t upper_bound_k(
    struct suffix_array *sa,
    uint32_t k, uint8_t a,
```

```
        uint32_t L, uint32_t R
) {
    uint32_t orig_R = R;
    while (L < R) {
        uint32_t mid = L + (R - L) / 2;
        uint32_t b_idx = sa->array[mid] + k;
        if (b_idx >= sa->length) {
            // b is less if it is past the end.
            L = mid + 1;
            continue;
        }
        uint8_t b = *(sa->string + b_idx);
        if (a < b) {
            R = mid - 1;
        } else {
            L = mid + 1;
        }
    }
    R = (R > L) ? R : L;
    if (R == orig_R) return R;

    uint8_t b = *(sa->string + sa->array[R] + k);
    return (a >= b) ? R + 1 : R;
}
```

In the upper bound calculations, we have to stay inside the original interval, so where we made sure that R would stay inside the suffix array, we tested it against sa->length; we now test it against the original R the function was called with.

In the match function—the function where we initialize the iterator—we run through the key and update the interval for each new index:

```
void init_sa_match_iter(
    struct sa_match_iter *iter,
    const uint8_t *key,
    struct suffix_array *sa
) {
```

```
    iter->sa = sa;

    uint32_t key_len = strlen((char*)key);
    uint32_t L = 0, R = sa->length;

    for (uint32_t i = 0; i < key_len; i++) {
        L = lower_bound_k(sa, i, key[i], L, R);
        R = upper_bound_k(sa, i, key[i], L, R);
        if (L >= R) break;
    }
    if (L == R) {
        iter->L = iter->R = 0;
        iter->i = 1;
    }
    iter->L = L;
    iter->R = R - 1;
    iter->i = L;
}
```

There are further improvements possible for a binary search based on precomputing possible intervals, but the result will still be a search that is logarithmic in the suffix array. It is possible to improve the approach to $O(m + \log n)$. We will skip those methods and move on to an approach that gives us a search algorithm that runs linear in the patterns we search for, $O(m)$.

Burrows-Wheeler transform–based search

The Burrows-Wheeler transform (BWT) is a transformation of a string that was originally used as a heuristic to make compression more efficient. We will not use it like that, and I will save you much discussion of it. All we need for the search algorithm is to know that for an index i in a string x, it is $x[SA[i]-1]$, with a special case for suffix zero. We can get it in for suffix array sa like this:

```
static inline unsigned char bwt(
    const struct suffix_array *sa,
    uint32_t i
)
```

```
{
    uint32_t suf = sa->array[i];
    return (suf == 0) ? '\0' : sa->string[suf - 1];
}
```

Contrary to what you might expect from the algorithm's name, it isn't an essential part of the search, but we use it to compute one of two tables that are essential.

Again, you need to compile the code in this section in a separate file, and you can find the implementation at `https://github.com/mailund/stralg/blob/master/stralg/bwt.c`.

C and O tables

We define two tables, the first indexed by symbols in our alphabet and the second by both a symbol and an index:

- $C(a)$ is the number of symbols smaller than a in x.

- $O(a, i)$ is the number of indices $j < i$ where $x[SA[j]]-1 = a$ (this is where we use the Burrows-Wheeler transform).

What the C table contains is self-evident, but the O table is less obvious, from the way I just defined it. Another way to define it, which is harder to capture mathematically but is the critical property we use in the algorithm, is this: $O(a, i)$ counts the number of suffixes lexicographically smaller than suffix $SA[i]$ that have an a before them in x.

These tables let us move from a string u in the suffix array to the string au (where a is a character), or one past where it would be in case it isn't in the array. If u is at index i, then au will be at index $C(a) + O(a, i)$; see Figure 4-12. To see this, observe that before au in the suffix array, we must have all the suffixes that start with a letter smaller than a, $C(a)$. Inside the sequence of strings that start with a, the suffixes are sorted with respect to the strings that follow a, and before u, there are $O(a, i)$ other suffixes.

In the BWT search algorithm, we will search for a pattern starting at the end of the pattern and prepending characters until we are done. Each time we prepend a letter, we will use this jump rule. Before we get that far, however, we need to build the tables.

Both tables have a dimension with a length that depends on the alphabet size. We have used `uint8_t` for our alphabet so far, but using 256 symbols is excessive in memory usage, especially for the O table that also has a dimension of length n. Therefore, we want to reduce the alphabet as much as possible, so we must remap the input string before we construct the tables.

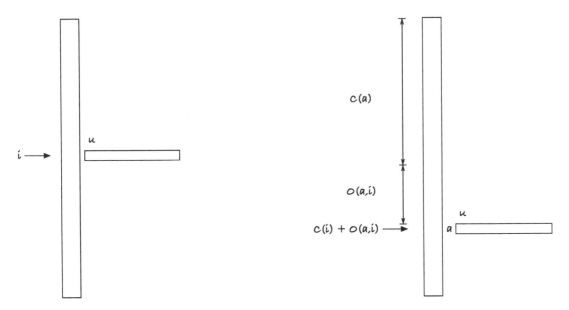

Figure 4-12. *Jump using the BWT tables*

Building the C and O tables

We store the two tables in a structure with a pointer to the remapped table and the (remapped) suffix array, and we define two macros to make access to the tables easier to read.

```
struct bwt_table {
    struct remap_table  *remap_table;
    struct suffix_array *sa;
    uint32_t *c_table;
    uint32_t *o_table;
    uint32_t **o_indices;
};

#define C(a)     (bwt_table->c_table[(a)])
#define O(a,i)   (bwt_table->o_indices[i][a])
```

I use two arrays for the O table. I put all the data in o_table and use o_indices to precompute offsets into the o_table array. You can compute the index into o_table from a letter a and index i as a * (table->sa->length + 1) + i, but I found that setting the offset, a * (table->sa->length + 1), into a separate array

o_indices[i] == o_table + i * alphabet_size

and then looking up using bwt_table->o_indices[i][a] was substantially faster.

To compute the *C* table, we first count how often we see each character *a* in the string. We get *C* as the accumulative sum of these. That will give us the count of characters less than *a*.

```
C(a) = C(a-1) + char_counts[a - 1];
```

For the *O* table, at index *i*, we either have the same number of smaller suffixes or one more, if the previous index has an *a* before it.

$$O(a,i) = \begin{cases} O(a,i-1) + 1 \; x \left[SA[i-1]-1 \right] = a \\ O(a,i-1) \quad \text{otherwise} \end{cases}$$

Putting these two observations together, we can compute the tables like this:

```c
void init_bwt_table(
    struct bwt_table    *bwt_table,
    struct suffix_array *sa,
    struct remap_table  *remap_table
) {
    bwt_table->remap_table = remap_table;
    bwt_table->sa = sa;

    // ---- COMPUTE C TABLE
    uint32_t char_counts[remap_table->alphabet_size];
    memset(char_counts, 0,
            remap_table->alphabet_size * sizeof(uint32_t));
    for (uint32_t i = 0; i < sa->length; ++i) {
        char_counts[sa->string[i]]++;
    }

    bwt_table->c_table =
        calloc(remap_table->alphabet_size,
                sizeof(*bwt_table->c_table));
    for (uint32_t i = 1; i < remap_table->alphabet_size; ++i) {
        C(i) = C(i-1) + char_counts[i - 1];
    }
```

```
// ---- COMPUTE O TABLE
// The table has indices from zero to n, so it must
// have size Sigma x (n + 1).
uint32_t o_size =
    remap_table->alphabet_size *
    (sa->length + 1) *
    sizeof(*bwt_table->o_table);
bwt_table->o_table = malloc(o_size);
bwt_table->o_indices =
    malloc((sa->length + 1) *
            sizeof(*bwt_table->o_indices));
for (uint32_t i = 0; i < sa->length + 1; ++i) {
    uint32_t *ptr = bwt_table->o_table + alphabet_size * i;
    bwt_table->o_indices[i] = ptr;
}
for (uint8_t a = 0; a < remap_table->alphabet_size; ++a) {
    O(a, 0) = 0;
}
for (uint8_t a = 0; a < remap_table->alphabet_size; ++a) {
    for (uint32_t i = 1; i <= sa->length; ++i) {
        O(a, i) = O(a, i - 1) + (bwt(sa, i - 1) == a);
    }
}
}
```

Building the tables is clearly done in linear time (assuming the alphabet size is a constant).

Deallocating the table is relatively straightforward:

```
void dealloc_bwt_table(
    struct bwt_table *bwt_table
) {
    free(bwt_table->c_table);
    free(bwt_table->o_table);
    free(bwt_table->o_indices);
}
```

Searching

As mentioned earlier, when we search for a pattern using the BWT algorithm, we start from the end and move forward. In the search we keep track of two pointers, L and R, that spans the interval in the suffix array where the suffixes have the pattern so far as a prefix. The L pointer points to the first suffix in the interval and the R pointer points one past the last. When we prepend a character to the pattern, we update the pointers using the jump rule from earlier; see Figure 4-13. This gives us another interval where the suffixes have the new pattern as prefixes. Once we reach the start of the pattern, that is, once we have the interval where all suffixes have the pattern as a prefix, we are done.

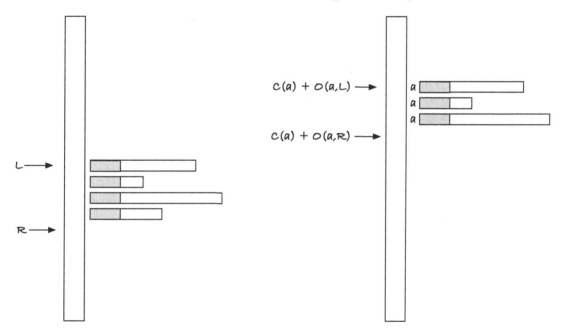

Figure 4-13. *Searching using the BWT*

Each time we update the interval, we do constant work, and we only update intervals m times, so searching is done in linear time in the length of the pattern.

We do the entire search in the search iterator. This will give us the L and R interval, and when we iterate over the hits, we scan through it.

```
void init_bwt_exact_match_iter(
    struct bwt_exact_match_iter *iter,
    struct bwt_table *bwt_table,
    const uint8_t *remapped_pattern
);
```

```
void init_bwt_exact_match_iter(
    struct bwt_exact_match_iter *iter,
    struct bwt_table *bwt_table,
    const uint8_t *remapped_pattern
) {
    const struct suffix_array *sa = iter->sa = bwt_table->sa;

    uint32_t n = sa->length;
    uint32_t m = (uint32_t)strlen((char *)remapped_pattern);

    uint32_t L = 0;
    uint32_t R = n;

    // If the pattern is longer than the string, then
    // there won't be a match.
    if (m > n) {
        R = 0; L = 1;
    }
    // We need i to be signed, so we use int64_t.
    // This gives us a signed integer that can
    // easily index all of uint32_t.
    int64_t i = m - 1;

    while (i >= 0 && L < R) {
        uint8_t a = remapped_pattern[i];
        L = C(a) + O(a, L);
        R = C(a) + O(a, R);
        i--;
    }
    iter->L = L;
    iter->R = R;
    iter->i = L;
}
```

The variable i in the iterator is used when we report hits. It starts at the first index in the interval (L) and will be incremented for each hit. When we report hits, we need to map the index i the suffix array to the index in the string, but that is just a lookup in the suffix array.

```
struct bwt_exact_match {
    uint32_t pos;
};

bool next_bwt_exact_match_iter(
    struct bwt_exact_match_iter *iter,
    struct bwt_exact_match       *match
) {
    // Cases where we never had a match.
    if (iter->i < 0)        return false;
    // Cases where we no longer have a match.
    if (iter->i >= iter->R) return false;

    // We still have a match.
    // Report it and update the position
    // to the next match (if any).
    match->pos = iter->sa->array[iter->i];
    iter->i++;

    return true;
}
```

We do not allocate any resources in the iterator, so deallocating it is trivial.

```
void dealloc_bwt_exact_match_iter(
    struct bwt_exact_match_iter *iter
) {
    // Nothing to free
}
```

Getting the longest common prefix (LCP) array

For the LCP algorithm in the previous chapter, we (obviously) needed the LCP array (or longest common prefix array). We saw how to get it from a depth-first traversal of the tree, and in this section, we see how to compute it from the suffix array.

The linear-time algorithm iterates through the suffixes and compares each suffix with its predecessor in the suffix, but fast because of the observation in Figure 4-14. If we know the LCP for some index ii, it means that we know the longest prefix shared between

SA[ii] and SA[ii-1] (see Figure 4-14 A). Let i = SA[ii] and consider suffix i+1. This suffix shares a prefix with SA[ii-1]+1 that has length LCP[ii]-1 (see Figure 4-14 B). If we go back to the suffix array where i+1 sits, call it jj=ISA[i+1], then the previous suffix, jj-1, shares a prefix of length LCP[jj] that must be at least LCP[ii] - 1 long (see Figure 4-14 C). The suffixes come in blocks of shared prefixes in the suffix array, and since there is at least one suffix that shares a length LCP[ii]-1 prefix with jj, the longest must be at least that long. To get the actual length, we need to compare suffixes SA[jj-1] and SA[jj], but we can skip the first LCP[ii]-1 characters in the comparison because we know these match.

The ii and jj indices are related in the way illustrated in the figure, but notice that it is also a relationship between the LCPs of suffixes i and $i + 1$. The figure also tells us that the longest common prefix of ISA[i+1] is at least LCP[ISA[i]]. The prefixes are clustered in the suffix array so this tells us that there is a shared prefix there. Further, the suffix before ISA[i+1] must be smaller than ISA[i+1] because SA[ii-1] is smaller than SA[ii]. This is what we exploit in the algorithm. We run through the suffixes in x and keep track of how much we can skip when comparing suffixes using the preceding observation. The reason that the algorithm runs in linear time is an argument similar to the one we had for computing the border array back in the chapter on classical algorithms. If we consider the interval we can skip in each iteration, then it gets one smaller because we skip LCP[ii]-1 and then it increases when we scan LCP[jj] vs. LCP[jj-1]. The maximum length we can get is n, and we cannot increase beyond this and what we decrease, which is bounded by n. Thus the algorithm runs in linear time.

We can implement the computation of the inverse suffix array like this

```
void compute_inverse(struct suffix_array *sa)
{
    if (sa->inverse) return; // only compute if it is needed

    sa->inverse = malloc(sa->length * sizeof(*sa->inverse));
    for (uint32_t i = 0; i < sa->length; ++i)
        sa->inverse[sa->array[i]] = i;
}
```

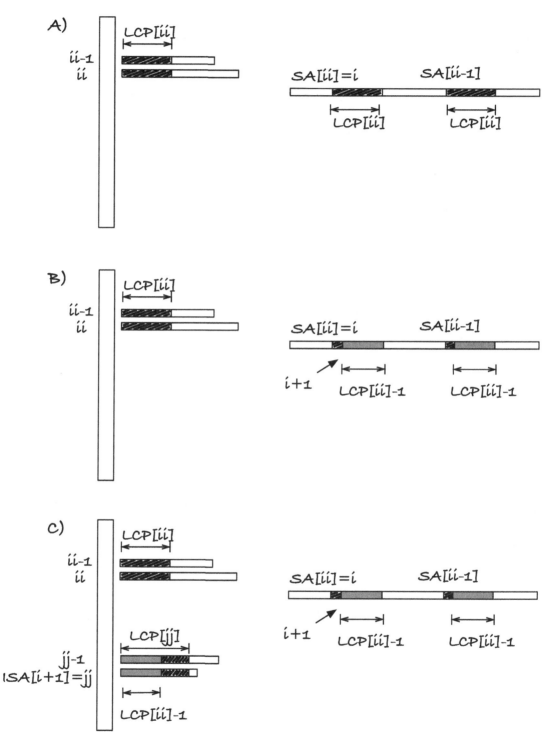

Figure 4-14. *Key observation for computing the LCP*

and the LCP array like this

```c
void compute_lcp(struct suffix_array *sa)
{
    if (sa->lcp) return; // only compute if we have to

    sa->lcp = malloc((sa->length) * sizeof(*sa->lcp));

    compute_inverse(sa);
    sa->lcp[0] = 0;
    uint32_t l = 0;
    for (uint32_t i = 0; i < sa->length; ++i) {
        uint32_t j = sa->inverse[i];

        // Don't handle index 0; lcp[0] is always zero.
        if (j == 0) continue;

        uint32_t k = sa->array[j - 1];
        while (sa->string[k + l] == sa->string[i + l])
            ++l;
        sa->lcp[j] = l;
        l = l > 0 ? l - 1 : 0;
    }
}
```

We do not compute the two arrays when we build the suffix array—because we do not always need them—so in each function, we check if it is already built. and if not we construct the array. In the function that computes LCP, the variable l keeps track of the length of comparison we can skip. We increase it when we match in the comparison and decrease it by one when we are done.

Comparisons

So what is the running time for constructing suffix arrays in practice? In Figure 4-15, you can see the construction time for each algorithm for three alphabets, all equal characters, a four-letter alphabet, and full 8-bit character set. I have also shown McCreight's suffix tree construction algorithm for comparison.

Consistently the SA-IS algorithm is the fastest, followed by the memory-efficient SA-IS algorithm. All the recomputing takes some time, and the memory-efficient algorithm thus runs slower than the memory-hungry version.

The worst-case input for both the naïve sorting algorithm and the skew algorithm is strings of a single repeated character. For explicit sorting, string comparison takes linear time in the length of the shortest string; on average, this is half the original string. For the skew algorithm, the triplet character alphabet we make in each recursive call will contain a single character until the very bottom of the recursion so that the algorithm will do maximal work. Once we have random strings with more characters, both algorithms are faster. The explicit sorting remains the slowest, though.

Building the suffix tree with McCreight's algorithm takes time somewhere in the middle of the suffix array construction algorithms except for the large 8-bit alphabet, which, as we saw in the previous chapter, shows the large fan-out of children in each node slows down the algorithm substantially. With a large alphabet, McCreight's algorithm is still increasing the node's fan-out when the suffix array algorithms are long done with building their arrays.

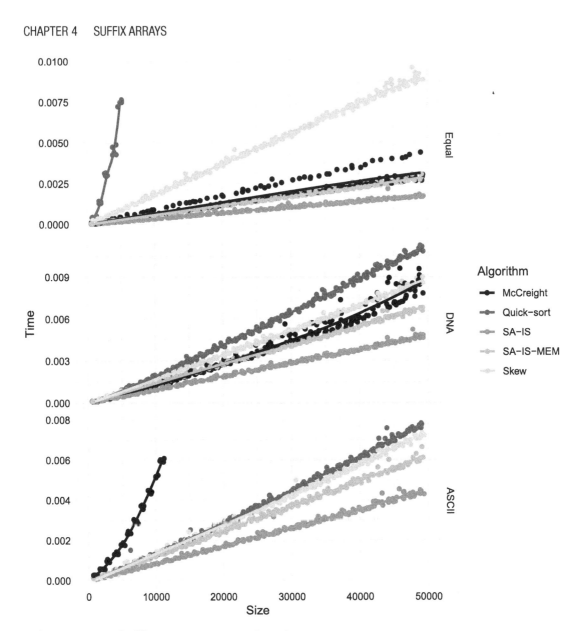

Figure 4-15. *Suffix array construction time*

In Figure 4-16, I have plotted the construction time for a suffix array (using the SA-IS algorithm) and the additional time it takes to build the BWT tables. It takes extra time to create the BWT tables, but the overhead is slight if we consider cases where the tables are constructed only once and after that used for thousands of linear-time searches.

However, is it worthwhile to search using BWT compared to searching directly in the suffix array? After all, the logarithm function grows very slowly, so the difference between $O(m)$ and $O(m \log n)$ might not matter in practice until we have incredibly long strings. Add to this that the suffix array search only performs simple lookups in the string and suffix array, while the BWT algorithm needs additional lookups in the C and O tables. When looking for a value in the O table, we also need to compute the offset using multiplication with the alphabet size. It is therefore conceivable that each step in the linear BWT search is more expensive than the steps in the $O(m \log n)$ suffix array search.

In Figure 4-17, I have plotted the running time of the BWT search (BWT), the binary search in a suffix array (SA), and the search in a suffix tree (ST), for n up to 1000 and m up to 50, so relatively short strings. The string that we search in, x, is a random DNA string, and the pattern, p, is selected from a random position in x, so all searches continue to the end of the pattern. I have fitted lines to the data points, although the suffix array binary search is not linear in n (you can see a curve in the plot if you look closely). The line illustrates the growth of the functions. We observe that the algorithms behave as they are expected to, BWT and ST are constant in n while SA is not, and all algorithms are linear in m. The binary search is slower than the two linear-time algorithms, maybe surprising and maybe not, considering the small data size, but it is more complex code. The BWT algorithm is substantially slower than the suffix tree search. Since the suffix tree needs to both search through children in the nodes of the tree and down edges, this would not be obvious, but the reason is to some degree that the strings are random. This means that there is a large fan-out near the root of the tree, but after that, the search runs down a long edge and searching through an edge consists of comparing strings character by character, which is much faster than the table lookups in BWT.

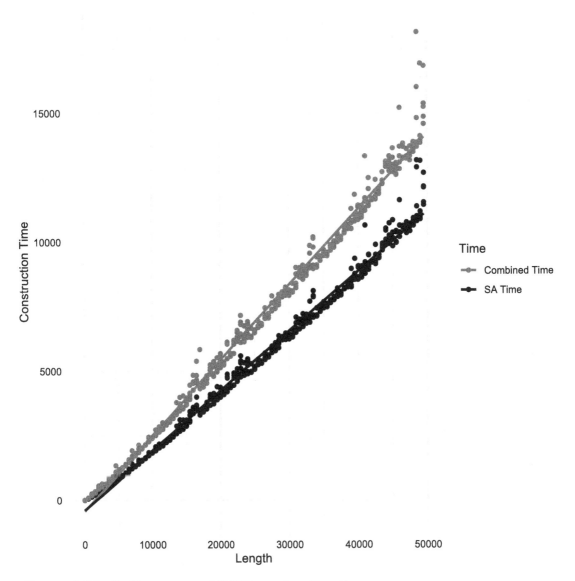

Figure 4-16. *Suffix array and BWT construction time*

The results will not be representative of strings that have a structure very far from random, but most strings are not far from random in their character sequences. Natural language texts will also have a large fan-out near the root, and then long edges to leaves, since sentences in a book rarely share more than a few words in a row. It is hard to think of pathological strings, such as strings with a single character repeated, that are found in real applications that do not give a suffix tree a similar structure.

Figure 4-17 shows results for very short strings, and there the algorithms behave as we expect from theory, but if we increase the string lengths slightly (see Figure 4-18), we see an unexpected explosion in the BWT algorithm's performance. Many of the experiments for n between 20,000 and 25,000 have exceedingly long running times, so the suffix array search algorithm beats BWT for large m. What we see here is something that the theory doesn't predict but is a real concern in practice—memory efficiency, specifically data locality. The theoretical model for computations used in this book is the RAM model, and it assumes that we can access all memory positions in the same running time. On a real computer, this is far from true.

When you access memory, it is pulled into a cache, so it is more efficient to get it again. The cache also pulls in memory adjacent to what you accessed, so this will also be faster to access. There are several levels of caches, so when you cannot get the data you want from the cache that is closest to the CPU, you need to go some levels out to get it. When you cannot find it in a cache, you have to go all the way out to get it in RAM. Each time you move from one level to the next, you spend orders of magnitude more time getting your data. Each time you miss the cache, you get a massive jump in access time. For the experiments, it is evened out over many memory accesses, but it is clear that we have more misses when the data is larger, and this effect drowns the expected running time based on the RAM model.

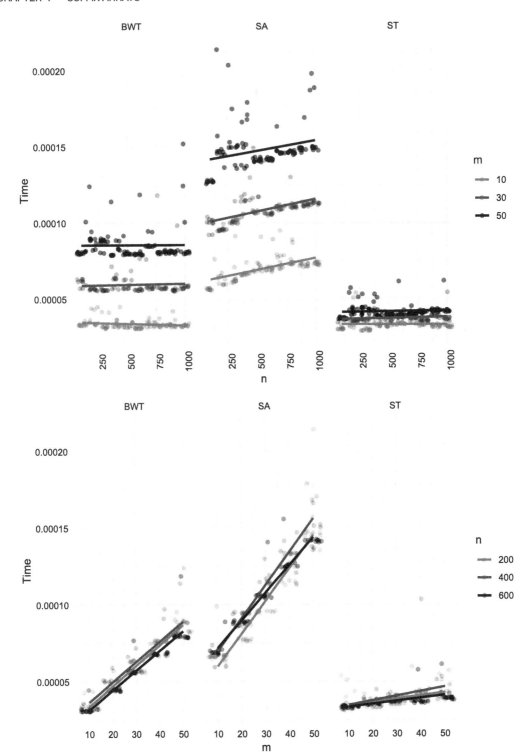

Figure 4-17. *Search time with n up to 1000 and m up to 50*

The character-by-character search down the edges in the ST algorithm is cache-efficient. We are looking at consecutive memory addresses, and that is ideal for caching. We do not see a worsening of the running time. We do not see the effect for the SA algorithm either. The suffix array takes up less memory than the BWT tables, and with random strings, the search interval shrinks rapidly. Before long, the algorithm is searching down a single string, similar to how the suffix tree algorithm search down a single edge.

If we continue with n up to 10 million, Figure 4-19, we see the effect more dramatically. None of the algorithms run in linear time for n. The ST algorithm is close (if we ignore the data points for the highest n that I will get back to). The BA algorithm isn't supposed to be. The surprising results are for BWT. We see a steep growth up to around a million, then it flattens out, but not entirely, and then there is an explosion in the running time, one we see for all three algorithms. What is happening is that for the BWT algorithm, more and more of the memory accesses misses the cache, and as the number of misses increases, so does the running time. When it levels off, it is because practically all access to the table involves a cache miss. There is still an increase because some of the memory access needs to go all the way to RAM, and that access is vastly slower than going to the cache. To the far right of the plot, where there is a massive jump for all the algorithms, my test program runs out of RAM entirely, and the operating system has to swap memory in and out of the disk. When that happens, the performance deteriorates quickly.

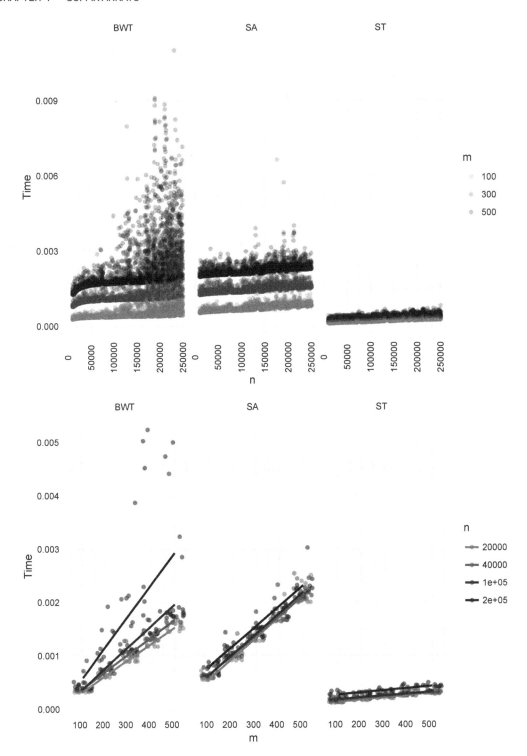

Figure 4-18. *Search time with n up to 25,000 and m up to 600*

The computer runs out of memory faster for the data structures that take up more memory, but what we see in the runtime experiments is the memory access patterns more than when the program will need to be swapped. The random access with the suffix array, and even more with the BWT tables, requires more swapping than the access to consecutive characters for the suffix tree.

Admittedly, the comparisons made here are not entirely fair. It is possible to compress suffix arrays and BWT tables, so they use less memory, so they can reach larger n before there are memory issues with swapping. But with the algorithms that I have presented in this chapter, the memory access patterns matter, and if you use these algorithms, the suffix tree is more efficient for searching than the other two approaches.

You can find the code I have used for my experiments here:

```
https://github.com/mailund/stralg/blob/master/
performance/suffix_array_construction.c
```

```
https://github.com/mailund/stralg/blob/master/
performance/bwt_construction.c
```

```
https://github.com/mailund/stralg/blob/master/
performance/suffix_array_search.c
```

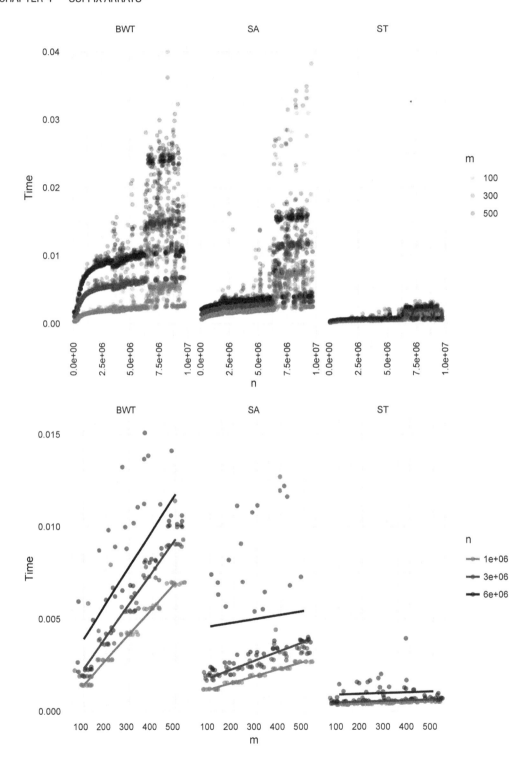

Figure 4-19. *Search time with n up to 10 million and m up to 600*

CHAPTER 5

Approximate search

We are not always satisfied with finding locations where a pattern matches exactly. Sometimes we could, for example, want to find all occurrences of a word and include occurrences where the word is misspelt. Searching for "almost matches" is called approximate search. We will look at a suffix tree–based approach and a BWT-based approach. Considering the experimental results from the last chapter, it might seem odd to consider a BWT approach instead of a suffix array approach, but there is a reason for this: we can add a trick to the BWT approach to make it faster than the suffix tree solution that was the most efficient for exact search.

Local alignment and CIGAR notation

An approximative match is one where we can edit the key to make it match at a given location. The operations we can do are

- Substitute, or replace, one character for another

- Insert a character

- Delete a character

If we have a match of such an edited pattern at a given location, we say that we can *align* the pattern there. The idea is that we conceptually put the pattern on top of the reference string at the location where we have an approximative match. We then describe how the reference string should be edited to become the reference string, that is, whether we should change a character in the reference, a substitution, delete a character that is in the reference but not the pattern, or insert a character in the pattern string that is not in the reference.

For matching and substitution strings, we have one character on top of another. When we insert a character, we show it as a dash in the reference string (the inserted character does not match any of the characters in the reference, but this is where it

© Thomas Mailund 2020
T. Mailund, *String Algorithms in C*, https://doi.org/10.1007/978-1-4842-5920-7_5

should be inserted). If we delete a character, we put a dash in the reference string (the character would have been at this position if we hadn't deleted it). The following are two examples:

```
      AACTTTCTGAA
...TTAAAAAATTTCT-AACAACA...
        *       *
```

```
      AACTTTCTG-AA
...TGGAAAA-TTTCTGGAATGGAT...
        *       *
```

The first alignment has a substitution where A should replace the C in the pattern, and it has an insertion of G (shown as a dash in the string we align to; it isn't at that position but it is where we must insert it). The second alignment has an insertion of C (also shown as a dash in the string below) and a deletion of G.

This type of alignment is also called a *local* alignment. A *global* alignment is one where we edit one string to match the entirety of another string. We will not consider global alignments in this book.

When we report an occurrence of an approximative match, we want to report both the position of the occurrence and how the pattern must be edited to get the match. Reporting an alignment is not convenient but what we can do is to report the transformations needed on the pattern. For example, we can report matches as M, substitutions as S, insertions as I, and deletions as D as a string. The sequence of operations we perform for the alignments earlier is MMSMMMMMIMM and MMIMMMMMMDMM. The *CIGAR* format is a compressed form of this sequence of events. Whenever there is a sequence of the same operation, it contains the length of the sequence followed by the operation. It does not distinguish between M and S; if we know that one character should go above another, we can always check if we have a match or substitution anyway. The CIGAR for the first alignment above is 8M1I2M and the CIGAR for the second is 2M1I6M1D2M. The reason that there are 8 Ms in the first CIGAR, although there are only two Ms in the string of operations, is that we use M for substitutions as well in CIGARs.

When matching a pattern, I find it easiest to collect each transformation step individually, that is, the first format earlier, and then transform it into a CIGAR string to report once I am done. The following edits_to_cigar() function will take a string where each edit is represented by a letter and produce the corresponding CIGAR string:

```
static const char *scan(
    const char *edits
) {
    const char *p = edits;
    while (*p == *edits)
        ++p;
    return p;
}

void edits_to_cigar(
    char *cigar_buffer,
    const char *edits
) {
    while (*edits) {
        const char *next = scan(edits);
        cigar_buffer = cigar_buffer + sprintf(
            cigar_buffer, "%d%c",
            (int)(next - edits), *edits
        );
        edits = next;
    }
    *cigar_buffer = '\0';
}
```

The code might be a little hard to decipher. The sprintf() function writes to the front of the cigar_buffer and returns the length of the string it writes. When we add that length to cigar_buffer, we get a pointer to where we should continue writing next time we call sprintf(). The (int)(next - edits) expression gives us the number of characters we have scanned past, and *edits is the operation we repeated for this number of times.

```
cigar_buffer = cigar_buffer + sprintf(
    cigar_buffer, "%d%c",
    (int)(next - edits), *edits
);
```

Brute force approach

The straightforward way to do approximative matching is to construct all the patterns at a certain edit distance (number of changes) from the pattern and then do an exact search. We call all such strings the *edit cloud* around the pattern, and we can construct it recursively.

Building an edit cloud

An easy way to build a string and a CIGAR from a pattern is to recursively handle the three operations (four if you separate matching into (actual) matchind and mismatching). Assume we have processed the pattern up to some point, for example, a `pattern_front` pointer. Put the modified string in a buffer and have a pointer, `string_front`, pointing at the next position we should add characters to, and have the edits so far in a buffer where pointer `edit_fronts` points to the next position where we should add to the buffer. The situation is shown in Figure 5-1.

If we want to add an insertion to the pattern, we skip past the current symbol in the pattern, we do not add anything to the string, but we record the operation in the edits. The `pattern_front` and `edits_front` are incremented. If it seems odd to you that we do not add a symbol to the string in an insertion operation, then remember that insertion is something we do to transform the string into the pattern. The symbol we skip past in the pattern is the one we have inserted there. Substitutions and matching are the same operation (except that substitutions increase the edit distance). We add a character to the string and increment `string_front`, increment `pattern_front` past the character matched or substituted to, and record the operation in the edits buffer. For deletion, we do almost the same as for matching. We add a character to the string and increment `string_front`, and we add a D to the edits buffer. The difference to matching is that we do not increment `pattern_front`. The character we insert into the string is deleted in the pattern so we should continue the recursion from the current position.

The idea is implemented in the following function; I will explain the `at_beginning` variable after the code listing.

```
void recursive_generator(
    const uint8_t *pattern_front,
    const uint8_t *alphabet,
    // To avoid initial deletions.
```

```c
    bool at_beginning,
    // Write the edited string here.
    uint8_t *string_front,
    // Holds the beginning of full buffer
    // so we can report the string.
    uint8_t *string,
    // We write the output cigar here.
    char *cigar,
    // We build the edit string here.
    char *edits_front,
    // and use the beginning of the edits buffer
    // when we report
    char *edits,
    int max_edit_distance)
{
    if (*pattern_front == '\0') {
        // No more pattern to match...
        // Terminate the buffer and report.
        *string_front = '\0';
        *edits_front = '\0';
        edits_to_cigar(cigar, edits);
        report(string, cigar);

    } else if (max_edit_distance == 0) {
        // We can't edit anymore, so just move the
        // pattern to buffer and report.
        uint32_t rest = strlen((char *)pattern_front);
        for (uint32_t i = 0; i < rest; ++i) {
            string_front[i] = pattern_front[i];
            edits_front[i] = 'M';
        }
```

```
        string_front[rest] = cigar[rest] = '\0';
        edits_to_cigar(cigar, edits);
        report(string, cigar);

    } else {
        // RECURSION
        // Insertion
        *edits_front = 'I';
        recursive_generator(pattern_front + 1,
                            alphabet,
                            false,
                            string_front, string,
                            cigar,
                            edits_front + 1, edits,
                            max_edit_distance - 1);
        // Deletion
        if (!at_beginning) {
            for (const uint8_t *a = alphabet; *a; a++) {
                *string_front = *a;
                *edits_front = 'D';
                recursive_generator(pattern_front,
                                    alphabet,
                                    at_beginning,
                                    string_front + 1,
                                    string,
                                    cigar,
                                    edits_front + 1, edits,
                                    max_edit_distance - 1);
            }
        }
        // Match/substitution
        for (const uint8_t *a = alphabet; *a; a++) {
            if (*a == *pattern_front) {
                *string_front = *a;
                *edits_front = 'M';
```

```
        recursive_generator(pattern_front + 1,
                             alphabet,
                             false,
                             string_front + 1,
                             string,
                             cigar,
                             edits_front + 1, edits,
                             max_edit_distance);
    } else {
        *string_front = *a;
        *edits_front = 'M';
        recursive_generator(pattern_front + 1,
                             alphabet,
                             false,
                             string_front + 1,
                             string,
                             cigar,
                             edits_front + 1, edits,
                             max_edit_distance - 1);
    }
  }
 }
}
```

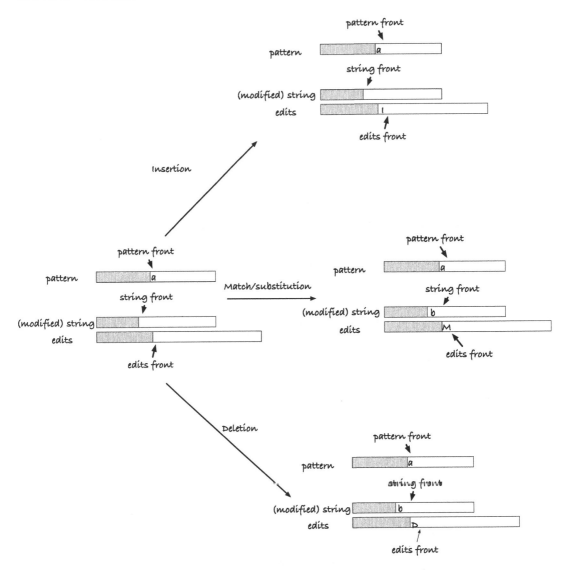

Figure 5-1. *Recursion for constructing an edit cloud*

I use the at_beginning variable to avoid initial deletions. We cannot easily avoid that many sequences of edits can lead to the same string, but we know that all edits that start or end with deletions will have the same string as the edits that do not include them. Whenever we reach the end of the pattern, we report the result, and we do not add possible deletions as results as well. So terminal deletions are naturally avoided. We can avoid initial deletions if we never do a deletion unless we have already done an insertion or a match. The at_beginning parameter ensures exactly that.

To get an iterator version of the recursion, we need an explicit stack. Stack frames will contain the information we need for an operation and information about which operation to do. I found it easiest to have four operations: one that creates the recursive calls and three operations for insertion, deletion, and matches. Stack frames look like this:

```
enum edit_op {
    RECURSE,
    INSERTION,
    DELETION,
    MATCH
};
struct deletion_info {
    char a;
};
struct match_info {
    char a;
};

struct edit_iter_frame {
    enum edit_op op;

    // The character we should delete or match
    uint8_t a;
    // Have we inserted or matched yet?
    bool at_beginning;

    // Fronts of buffers
    const uint8_t *pattern_front;
    uint8_t *string_front;
    char *cigar_front;

    // Number of edits left
    int max_dist;

    // The rest of the stack
    struct edit_iter_frame *next;
};
```

Deletion and match operations need to know which character to add to the string. In the recursive function, we put those characters into the buffer before we called recursively. With the explicit stack, we need to iterate through the alphabet to push operations, and if we just update the string buffer, we would override all but the last character we put there. Instead, we remember the character in the stack frame and add it to the string when we get to the operation.

Pushing information to the stack is straightforward.

```
static struct edit_iter_frame *
push_edit_iter_frame(
    enum edit_op op,
    bool at_beginning,
    const uint8_t *pattern_front,
    uint8_t *string_front,
    char *cigar_front,
    int max_dist,
    struct edit_iter_frame *next
) {
    struct edit_iter_frame *frame =
        malloc(sizeof(struct edit_iter_frame));
    frame->op = op;
    frame->at_beginning = at_beginning;
    frame->pattern_front = pattern_front;
    frame->string_front = string_front;
    frame->cigar_front = cigar_front;
    frame->max_dist = max_dist;
    frame->next = next;
    return frame;
}
```

An iterator will hold the beginning of the buffers, a `cigar` buffer that we use to translate the edits string into a CIGAR representation, and a pointer to the remainder of the stack below the frame.

```
struct edit_iter {
    const uint8_t *pattern;
    const char *alphabet;
```

```
    uint8_t *string;
    char *edits;
    char *cigar;

    struct edit_iter_frame *frames;
};
```

When we initialize an iterator, we allocate the buffers we need. We can never have more than twice the string length edits—regardless of the maximum edit distance, we will explore. If we remove all characters and then insert them again, we get this maximum, and that is the most distant string we can ever create. So that is an upper bound on the size of the buffers we need. After allocating the buffers, we push the first recursion unto the stack.

```
void init_edit_iter(
    struct edit_iter *iter,
    const uint8_t *pattern,
    const char *alphabet,
    int max_edit_distance
) {
    uint32_t n = 2 * (uint32_t)strlen((char *)pattern);

    iter->pattern = pattern;
    iter->alphabet = alphabet;

    iter->string = malloc(n); iter->string[n - 1] = '\0';
    iter->edits = malloc(n);  iter->edits[n - 1] = '\0';
    iter->cigar = malloc(n);

    iter->frames = push_edit_iter_frame(
        RECURSE,
        true,
        iter->pattern,
        iter->string,
        iter->edits,
        max_edit_distance,
        0
    );
}
```

When we increment the iterator, we check if we have reached the end of the pattern or the total number of edits allowed. In either case, we report an occurrence. If not, we perform the operation from the frame and then proceed to the next frame in a recursive call. There is not much more to say about the function; it closely follows the recursive version.

```
struct edit_pattern {
    const uint8_t *pattern;
    const char *cigar;
};

bool next_edit_pattern(
    struct edit_iter *iter,
    struct edit_pattern *result
) {
    if (iter->frames == 0) return false;

    // Pop top frame
    struct edit_iter_frame *frame = iter->frames;
    iter->frames = frame->next;

    const uint8_t *pattern = frame->pattern_front;
    uint8_t *buffer = frame->string_front;
    char *cigar = frame->cigar_front;

    if (*pattern == '\0') {
        // No more pattern to match...
        *buffer = '\0';
        *cigar = '\0';
        edits_to_cigar(iter->cigar, iter->edits);
        result->pattern = iter->string;
        result->cigar = iter->cigar;
        free(frame);
        return true;

    } else if (frame->max_dist == 0) {
        // We can't edit anymore, so just move
        // pattern to the string and report.
```

```
    uint32_t rest = (uint32_t)strlen((char *)pattern);
    for (uint32_t i = 0; i < rest; ++i) {
          buffer[i] = pattern[i];
          cigar[i] = 'M';
    }
    buffer[rest] = cigar[rest] = '\0';
    edits_to_cigar(iter->cigar, iter->edits);
    result->pattern = iter->string;
    result->cigar = iter->cigar;
    free(frame);
    return true;
}

switch (frame->op) {
    case RECURSE:
        for (const char *a = iter->alphabet; *a; a++) {
            if (!frame->at_beginning) {
                iter->frames = push_edit_iter_frame(
                    DELETION,
                    false,
                    frame->pattern_front,
                    frame->string_front,
                    frame->cigar_front,
                    frame->max_dist,
                    iter->frames
                );
                iter->frames->a = *a;
            }
            iter->frames = push_edit_iter_frame(
                MATCH,
                false,
                frame->pattern_front,
                frame->string_front,
                frame->cigar_front,
```

```
                    frame->max_dist,
                    iter->frames
                );
                iter->frames->a = *a;
            }
            iter->frames = push_edit_iter_frame(
                INSERTION,
                false,
                frame->pattern_front,
                frame->string_front,
                frame->cigar_front,
                frame->max_dist,
                iter->frames
            );
            break;

        case INSERTION:
            *cigar = 'I';
            iter->frames = push_edit_iter_frame(
                RECURSE,
                false,
                frame->pattern_front + 1,
                frame->string_front,
                frame->cigar_front + 1,
                frame->max_dist - 1,
                iter->frames
            );
            break;

        case DELETION:
            if (frame->at_beginning) break;
            *buffer = frame->a;
            *cigar = 'D';
            iter->frames = push_edit_iter_frame(
                RECURSE,
                false,
```

```
                frame->pattern_front,
                frame->string_front + 1,
                frame->cigar_front + 1,
                frame->max_dist - 1,
                iter->frames
            );

        break;
    case MATCH:
        if (frame->a == *pattern) {
            *buffer = frame->a;
            *cigar = 'M';
            iter->frames = push_edit_iter_frame(
                RECURSE,
                false,
                frame->pattern_front + 1,
                frame->string_front + 1,
                frame->cigar_front + 1,
                frame->max_dist,
                iter->frames
            );
        } else {
            *buffer = frame->a;
            *cigar = 'M';
            iter->frames = push_edit_iter_frame(
                RECURSE,
                false,
                frame->pattern_front + 1,
                frame->string_front + 1,
                frame->cigar_front + 1,
                frame->max_dist - 1,
                iter->frames
            );
        }
```

```
            break;
    }

    free(frame);
    return next_edit_pattern(iter, result); // recurse...
}
```

When we are done with the iterator, we need to remove what might remain of the stack (in case we stop iterating before we reach the end of it) and free the buffers.

```
void dealloc_edit_iter(
    struct edit_iter *iter
) {
    struct edit_iter_frame *frame = iter->frames;
    while (frame) {
        struct edit_iter_frame *next = frame->next;
        free(frame);
        frame = next;
    }

    free(iter->string);
    free(iter->edits);
    free(iter->cigar);
}
```

Once you have created the edit cloud for a pattern, you can use any exact pattern-matching algorithm of your choosing. The number of strings grows exponential with the maximum edit distance, however. We cannot get around this in general; the recursion works that way. But if we do the search at the same time as we explore edits, we can break when we know that we cannot match a pattern further. With suffix trees and BWT search, we can do exactly that.

Suffix trees

If we search for approximative matches in a suffix array, we can stop our search if we exceed the number of edits we allow, simply by aborting the recursive search. In my implementation, I collect all CIGARs and roots of a matching hit when I initialize the iterator. It is possible to iterate one hit at a time, but the code gets substantially harder to read, so I have chosen this approach. I have also decided to write the search as a recursive function. I do not expect that patterns are very long, so the recursion doesn't get too deep. It is trivial to replace the recursion stack with an explicit stack if the recursion depth becomes a problem. I collect the hits in two vectors, one that holds the root of the tree where we have hits and one that holds the CIGAR used for this hit. I need to copy the CIGARs the function generates when I store the hits, and for that, I use this function:

```c
uint8_t *str_copy(const uint8_t *x)
{
    uint32_t n = strlen((char *)x);
    uint8_t *copy = malloc(sizeof(uint8_t) * n + 1);
    strncpy((char *)copy, (char *)x, n);
    copy[n] = 0;
    return copy;
}
```

The iterator will hold the suffix tree, so we have access to it when we needed it. It also holds the two vectors we collect hits in. For iterating through the hits, we have a flag, processing_tree, that tells us if we are in the middle of traversing a tree or not. Finally, it holds an index that tells us which tree we are processing and a leaf iterator for doing the actual processing.

```c
struct st_approx_match_iter {
    struct suffix_tree *st;

    struct pointer_vector nodes;
    struct string_vector cigars;

    bool processing_tree;
    uint32_t current_tree_index;
    struct st_leaf_iter leaf_iter;
};
```

When searching for the hits, we also need three string buffers—one that contains the operations we have so far, a pointer to the beginning of this buffer for when we need to construct a CIGAR from it, and then a buffer in which we construct the CIGAR.

```
struct collect_nodes_data {
    struct st_approx_match_iter *iter;
    char *edits_start;
    char *edits;
    char *cigar_buffer;
};
```

The iterator initialization closely follows the recursion we used in the previous section. A difference is that we search along an edge in the suffix tree using a pointer x to look at the current character we are processing and another, end, that is the end of the edge. We also have a pointer to where we currently are in the patter, p, and a pointer to where we are in the edits string, edits. Then, we have a flag, at_beginning, that tells us if we have seen insertions or matches yet so we avoid initial deletions (similar to what we did earlier). Finally, we have a counter that keeps track of how many edit operations we have left.

The function should be relatively easy to read. We will terminate the search if we reach the end of the string the suffix was built from.

If we reach that point, we know we cannot continue matching. If we do not have any edits left, we also terminate the search. If we have reached the end of the pattern, we report the result by adding the current CIGAR and the current node to the vectors. If we reach the end of the edge we are scanning, we will continue searching from the node's children. If none of the previously discussed applies, then we recurse with the different edit operations.

```
static void collect_approx_hits(
    struct collect_nodes_data *data,
    struct suffix_tree_node *v,
    bool at_beginning,
    const uint8_t *x, const uint8_t *end,
    const uint8_t *p,
    char *edits,
    int edits_left
) {
    struct suffix_tree *st = data->iter->st;
    // We need to know this one so we never move past the end
    // of the string (and access memory we shouldn't).
    const uint8_t *string_end = st->string + st->length;
```

```
if (x == string_end)
    return; // Do not move past the end of the buffer.

if (edits_left < 0) {
    // We have already made too many edits.
    return;
}
if (*p == '\0') {
    // A hit. Save the data in the iterator.
    *edits = '\0';
    edits_to_cigar(
        data->cigar_buffer,
        data->edits_start
    );
    string_vector_append(
        &data->iter->cigars,
        str_copy((uint8_t*)data->cigar_buffer));
    pointer_vector_append(
        &data->iter->nodes, (void *)v);
    return;
}

if (x == end) {
    // We ran out of edge: recurse on children.
    recurse_children(
        data, v,
        at_beginning,
        edits, p, edits_left);
    return;
}
if (edits_left == 0 && *x != *p) {
    // We cannot do any more edits and
    // we need at least a substitution.
    return;
}
```

```
    // Recursion
    int match_cost = *p != *x;
    *edits = 'M';
    collect_approx_hits(
        data, v,
        false,
        x + 1, end,
        p + 1,
        edits + 1,
        edits_left - match_cost,
    );
    if (!at_beginning) {
        *edits = 'D';
        collect_approx_hits(
            data, v,
            false,
            x + 1, end,
            p, edits + 1,
            edits_left - 1
        );
    }
    *edits = 'I';
    collect_approx_hits(
        data, v,
        false,
        x, end,
        p + 1, edits + 1,
        edits_left - 1
    );
}
```

I have moved the code for recursing on a node's children to a separate function that looks like this:

```
static void recurse_children(
    struct collect_nodes_data *data,
    struct suffix_tree_node *v,
```

```
    bool at_beginning,
    char *edits,
    const uint8_t *p,
    int max_edits
) {
    struct suffix_tree_node *child = v->child;
    while (child) {
        const uint8_t *x = child->range.from;
        const uint8_t *end = child->range.to;
        collect_approx_hits(data, child, at_beginning,
                            x, end, p, edits, max_edits);
        child = child->sibling;
    }
}
```

When we initialize the iterator, we allocate the strings we use to build CIGARs and the vectors we use to collect the hits, and then we collect the hits recursively. We also initialize the leaf iterator. This instantiation of the leaf iterator is not used for anything— we initialize it again in the next function—but by always keeping the iterator initialized, we know that the deallocation function can always release the resources in it. At the end of the initialization, we mark that we are not in the process of iterating through leaves— the first step in the next function will then start from the first tree—and we set the current tree index to zero so the next function will start there.

```
void init_st_approx_iter(
    struct st_approx_match_iter *iter,
    struct suffix_tree *st,
    const uint8_t *pattern,
    int edits
) {
    iter->st = st;

    uint32_t n = strlen((char *)pattern);
    struct collect_nodes_data data;
    data.iter = iter;
    data.edits_start = data.edits = malloc(2*n + 1);
    data.cigar_buffer = malloc(2*n + 1);
```

```
    init_pointer_vector(&iter->nodes, 10);
    init_string_vector(&iter->cigars, 10);
    collect_approx_hits(&data, st->root, true,
                        st->root->range.from, st->root->range.to,
                        pattern, data.edits, edits, 0);

    free(data.edits_start);
    free(data.cigar_buffer);

    // We only initialize this to make resource management
    // easier. We keep this iterator initialized at all
    // time except when we deallocate it and immediately initialize.
    // it again.
    init_st_leaf_iter(&iter->leaf_iter, st, st->root);

    iter->processing_tree = false;
    iter->current_tree_index = 0;
}
```

The information we want to report for each match is the position of the match and the CIGAR:

```
struct st_approx_match {
    uint32_t pos;
    const char *cigar;
};
```

When we increment the iterator, we check if we are in a leaf iteration. If not, we need to pick the next tree or terminate the iteration if we do not have any more trees. When we have a tree, we initialize the leaf vector and tag that we are now processing a tree. We then call the function recursively so it can handle the new situation. If we are processing a tree, we increment the leaf iterator. If we do have more trees, we initialize the leaf iterator so it can process the next tree. We call recursively to get the next tree and start processing it.

```
bool next_st_approx_match(
    struct st_approx_match_iter *iter,
    struct st_approx_match *match
) {
```

```
    if (!iter->processing_tree) {
        if (iter->current_tree_index == iter->nodes.used) {
            return false;
        }
        dealloc_st_leaf_iter(&iter->leaf_iter);
        init_st_leaf_iter(
            &iter->leaf_iter, iter->st,
            pointer_vector_get(
                &iter->nodes,
                iter->current_tree_index
            )
        );
        iter->processing_tree = true;
        return next_st_approx_match(iter, match);
    } else {
        struct st_leaf_iter_result res;
        bool more_leaves =
            next_st_leaf(&iter->leaf_iter, &res);
        if (!more_leaves) {
            iter->processing_tree = false;
            iter->current_tree_index++;
            return next_st_approx_match(iter, match);
        } else {
            uint32_t i = iter->current_tree_index;
            match->pos = res.leaf->leaf_label;
            match->cigar = (const char *)iter->cigars.data[i];
            return true;
        }
    }
}
```

The resources we need to free when the iterator is deallocated are the nodes vectors, the CIGAR strings and the CIGAR vector, and then the leaf iterator.

```
void dealloc_st_approx_iter(
    struct st_approx_match_iter *iter
) {
    dealloc_pointer_vector(&iter->nodes);
    for (uint32_t i = 0; i < iter->cigars.used; ++i) {
        free(iter->cigars.data[i]);
    }
    dealloc_string_vector(&iter->cigars);
    dealloc_st_leaf_iter(&iter->leaf_iter);
}
```

The Li-Durbin algorithm

You can take the same approach with the BWT search as you can with the suffix tree—write a recursion that explores all edits while you search until you cannot match any more with the edits you have available—but the Li-Durbin algorithm adds an idea to this. They build an additional table for the BWT search that they use to terminate a search early. The table gives a minimum number of edits you need to match the rest of a string, and if the number of edits is smaller than this, the recursion stops.

The BWT search algorithm processes a pattern from the end toward the beginning. If we build a suffix array from the reversed string and search in that, starting at the beginning of the pattern and moving toward the end, then we find out where the reversed pattern sits in the reversed string. It is not hard to see this. If we reversed both the string and the pattern and did the BWT search, then we would locate the reversed pattern in the reverse string. The BWT algorithm doesn't care that it is the reversed string we are searching in. Processing the pattern in the beginning-to-end order will give the algorithm the characters in the order it would get them if we reversed the pattern and went from end to beginning.

We can determine if a prefix of the pattern is in the string by searching from the beginning against the suffix array of the reversed string. The reversed pattern prefix is in the reversed string if and only if the prefix is in the original string. The same applies to any substring of the pattern. We can determine if that substring is in the string either by searching from the end to the beginning of the pattern using the original suffix array or by searching from the beginning to the end in suffix array of the reversed string. We are interested in prefixes when building the table that lets the Li-Durbin algorithm terminate early, so we will search from beginning to end in the reversed string.

The idea is to build a table with an entrance per index in the pattern, and at each index, we will record a lower bound in the number of edits we need. We do an exact matching search from left to right in the pattern, searching in the reversed string. Each time we get to a point where we do not have a match, we record that at least one edit is needed to match the prefix. We then start from the full range of the reversed string and the point we got to in the prefix and continue until we cannot match any longer. There, we record that at least two edits are needed. We continue like this until we have processed the entire pattern. Then, when we do an approximative match from right to left in the pattern, we always check how many edits are needed to match the rest of the pattern (the prefix remaining). If we do not have enough edit operations left to match the pattern, we stop the recursion.

To search in the reversed string, we add an O table from the suffix of the reversed string to our bwt_table data struct and add the suffix array to the initialization function. Rather than having separate tables and initializers, we take an argument for the suffix array of the reversed string that can be null. If it is, we do not use it, and if it is not, we build the O table from it.

```
struct bwt_table {
    struct remap_table  *remap_table;
    struct suffix_array *sa;
    uint32_t *c_table;
    uint32_t *o_table;
    uint32_t *ro_table;    // NEW TABLE
    uint32_t **ro_indices; // NEW TABLE
};

#define RO(a,i)  (bwt_table->ro_indices[i][a])

void init_bwt_table(
    struct bwt_table   *bwt_table,
    struct suffix_array *sa,
```

```
    struct suffix_array *rsa,
    struct remap_table  *remap_table
) {
    assert(sa);

    uint32_t alphabet_size = remap_table->alphabet_size;
    bwt_table->remap_table = remap_table;
    bwt_table->sa = sa;

    // ---- COMPUTE C TABLE -----------------------------------
    uint32_t char_counts[remap_table->alphabet_size];
    memset(char_counts, 0, remap_table->alphabet_size * sizeof(uint32_t));
    for (uint32_t i = 0; i < sa->length; ++i) {
        char_counts[sa->string[i]]++;
    }

    bwt_table->c_table = calloc(remap_table->alphabet_size, sizeof(*bwt_
    table->c_table));
    for (uint32_t i = 1; i < remap_table->alphabet_size; ++i) {
        C(i) = C(i-1) + char_counts[i - 1];
    }

    // ---- COMPUTE O TABLE -----------------------------------
    // The table has indices from zero to n, so it must have size.
    // Sigma x (n + 1)
    uint32_t o_size = remap_table->alphabet_size *
        (sa->length + 1) *
        sizeof(*bwt_table->o_table);
    bwt_table->o_table = malloc(o_size);
    bwt_table->o_indices =
        malloc((sa->length + 1) *
                sizeof(*bwt_table->o_indices));
    for (uint32_t i = 0; i < sa->length + 1; ++i) {
        uint32_t *ptr = bwt_table->o_table +
                        alphabet_size * i;
        bwt_table->o_indices[i] = ptr;
    }
```

```
    for (uint8_t a = 0; a < remap_table->alphabet_size; ++a) {
        O(a, 0) = 0;
    }
    for (uint8_t a = 0; a < remap_table->alphabet_size; ++a) {
        for (uint32_t i = 1; i <= sa->length; ++i) {
            O(a, i) = O(a, i - 1) + (bwt(sa, i - 1) == a);
        }
    }

    // NEW CODE
    if (rsa) {

        bwt_table->ro_table = malloc(o_size);
        bwt_table->ro_indices =
            malloc((sa->length + 1) *
                    sizeof(bwt_table->ro_indices));
        for (uint32_t i = 0; i < sa->length + 1; ++i) {
            bwt_table->ro_indices[i] =
              bwt_table->ro_table +
              alphabet_size * i;
        }

        for (uint8_t a = 0; a < remap_table->alphabet_size; ++a) {
            RO(a, 0) = 0;
        }

        for (uint8_t a = 0; a < remap_table->alphabet_size; ++a) {
            for (uint32_t i = 1; i <= rsa->length; ++i) {
                RO(a, i) = RO(a, i - 1) + (bwt(rsa, i - 1) == a);
            }
        }

    } else {
        bwt_table->ro_table = 0;
        bwt_table->ro_indices = 0;
    }
}
```

```
void dealloc_bwt_table(
    struct bwt_table *bwt_table
) {
    free(bwt_table->c_table);
    free(bwt_table->o_table);
    // NEW CODE
    if (bwt_table->ro_table) free(bwt_table->ro_table);
    if (bwt_table->ro_indices) free(bwt_table->ro_indices);
}
```

The approximative matching iterator looks like this:

```
struct bwt_approx_iter {
    struct bwt_table *bwt_table;
    const uint8_t *remapped_pattern;

    uint32_t L, R, next_interval;
    struct index_vector  Ls;
    struct index_vector  Rs;
    struct string_vector cigars;

    uint32_t m;
    char *edits_buf;
    uint32_t *D_table;
};
```

It contains pointers to the BWT tables and the (remapped) pattern. We need these for the recursive search. We use the L, R, and next_interval variables when we traverse the interval for a hit. The intervals for hits that we find are stored in the Ls and Rs vectors and the corresponding CIGARs in the cigars vector. The m variable will contain the length of the pattern. We will use it for allocating CIGAR strings; it tells us how long they can maximally be. The edits_buf variable points to the beginning of the string that holds our edits and the D_table variable holds the D table we use to terminate searches early.

When we initialize our approximative match iterator, we build the table of lower bounds, called D in the code. We only build it if we have the suffix array for the reversed string, so it is also possible to search without the D table if one so wishes. Building D is done as described earlier. We do a normal BWT search except it is in the ro_table suffix array and from the beginning to the end. We search until we get an empty interval and then record that we need one edit more.

In the initializer, we also handle the recursive search for hits. I have taken a different approach to avoid initial deletion here, just to show the alternative. We call the recursion after matches and insertions so we are never in the situation where we can have an initial deletion.

```
void init_bwt_approx_iter(
    struct bwt_approx_iter *iter,
    struct bwt_table      *bwt_table,
    const uint8_t         *remapped_pattern,
    int                    max_edits)
{
    // Initialize resources for the recursive search.
    iter->bwt_table = bwt_table;
    iter->remapped_pattern = remapped_pattern;
    init_index_vector(&iter->Ls, 10);
    init_index_vector(&iter->Rs, 10);
    init_string_vector(&iter->cigars, 10);

    if (bwt_table->ro_table) {
        // Build D table.
        uint32_t m = (uint32_t)strlen((char *)remapped_pattern);
        iter->D_table = malloc(m * sizeof(uint32_t));

        int min_edits = 0;
        uint32_t L = 0, R = bwt_table->sa->length;
        for (uint32_t i = 0; i < m; ++i) {
            uint8_t a = remapped_pattern[i];
            L = C(a) + RO(a, L);
            R = C(a) + RO(a, R);
            if (L >= R) {
                min_edits++;
                L = 0;
                R = bwt_table->sa->length;
            }
```

```
            iter->D_table[i] = min_edits;
      }
  } else {
      iter->D_table = 0;
  }

  // Set up the edits buffer.
  uint32_t m = (uint32_t)strlen((char *)remapped_pattern);
  uint32_t buf_size = 2 * m + 1;
  iter->m = m;
  iter->edits_buf = malloc(buf_size + 1);
  iter->edits_buf[0] = '\0';

  // Start searching.
  uint32_t L = 0, R = bwt_table->sa->length; int i = m - 1;

  struct remap_table *remap_table = bwt_table->remap_table;
  char *edits = iter->edits_buf;

  // M-operations
  unsigned char match_a = remapped_pattern[i];
  // Iterating alphabet from 1 so
  // I don't include the sentinel.
  for (unsigned char a = 1;
          a < remap_table->alphabet_size;
          ++a) {

      uint32_t new_L = C(a) + O(a, L);
      uint32_t new_R = C(a) + O(a, R);

      int edit_cost = (a == match_a) ? 0 : 1;
      if (max_edits - edit_cost < 0) continue;
      if (new_L >= new_R) continue;

      *edits = 'M';
      rec_approx_matching(iter, new_L, new_R, i - 1,
                          1, max_edits - edit_cost,
                          edits + 1);

  }
```

```
    // I-operation
    *edits = 'I';
    rec_approx_matching(iter, L, R, i - 1, 0,
                        max_edits - 1, edits + 1);

    // Make sure we start at the first interval.
    iter->L = m; iter->R = 0;
    iter->next_interval = 0;
}
```

The recursive function follows the suffix tree recursion closely. The main difference is in how we handle the CIGAR at a hit. We search for the pattern from the end to the beginning, so we build the edit operations in that order as well. To build the CIGAR for a match, we must first reverse the edits and then build the CIGAR. We cannot reverse the edits inside the edits buffer. This would affect all the recursive calls since it is a shared buffer. Instead, we allocate a new string, move the edits into it, reverse it, and then compute the CIGAR and store it in the vector for the hits.

```
static void rec_approx_matching(
    struct bwt_approx_iter *iter,
    uint32_t L, uint32_t R, int i,
    int edits_left,
    char *edits
) {
    struct bwt_table *bwt_table = iter->bwt_table;
    struct remap_table *remap_table = bwt_table->remap_table;

    int lower_limit =
        (i >= 0 && iter->D_table) ? iter->D_table[i] : 0;
    if (edits_left  < lower_limit) {
        return; // We can never get a match from here.
    }

    if (i < 0) { // We have a match.
        index_vector_append(&iter->Ls, L);
        index_vector_append(&iter->Rs, R);
```

```
    // Extract the edits and reverse them.
    *edits = '\0';
    char *rev_edits =
        (char *)str_copy((uint8_t *)iter->edits_buf);
    str_inplace_rev((uint8_t*)rev_edits);
    // Build the cigar from the edits.
    char *cigar = malloc(2 * iter->m);
    edits_to_cigar(cigar, rev_edits);
    // Free the reversed edits; we do not need them now.
    free(rev_edits);

    string_vector_append(&iter->cigars, (uint8_t *)cigar);

    return; // Done down this path of matching...
}

uint32_t new_L;
uint32_t new_R;

// M-operations
unsigned char match_a = iter->remapped_pattern[i];
// Iterating alphabet from 1 so
// I don't include the sentinel.
for (unsigned char a = 1;
        a < remap_table->alphabet_size;
        ++a) {

    new_L = C(a) + O(a, L);
    new_R = C(a) + O(a, R);

    int edit_cost = (a == match_a) ? 0 : 1;
    if (edits_left - edit_cost < 0) continue;
    if (new_L >= new_R) continue;

    *edits = 'M';
    rec_approx_matching(iter, new_L, new_R, i - 1,
                        edits_left - edit_cost,
                        edits + 1);
}
```

```
    // I-operation
    *edits = 'I';
    rec_approx_matching(iter, L, R, i - 1,
                        edits_left - 1, edits + 1);

    // D-operation
    *edits = 'D';
    for (unsigned char a = 1;
            a < remap_table->alphabet_size;
            ++a) {
        new_L = C(a) + O(a, L);
        new_R = C(a) + O(a, R);
        if (new_L >= new_R) continue;

        rec_approx_matching(
            iter, new_L, new_R, i,
            edits_left - 1, edits + 1
        );
    }
}
```

The expression checks if we can use the D table. We can only do this if we haven't reached the beginning of the pattern and the D table was calculated (it will only be if we have the suffix array of the reversed string).

```
int lower_limit = (i >= 0 && iter->D_table) ?
                    iter->D_table[i] : 0;
```

When we increment the iterator, we use the L and R variables to determine whether we are processing an interval or if we should move to the next interval. If R is less than L, the current interval is empty, and we move to the next. If there aren't any intervals left, we return false to report that we have iterated over all matches. If we are in an interval, we extract the CIGAR and the current position in the interval (where iter->L points).

```
bool next_bwt_approx_match(
    struct bwt_approx_iter  *iter,
    struct bwt_approx_match *match
) {
```

```
    if (iter->L >= iter->R) { // Done with current interval
        if (iter->next_interval >= iter->Ls.used)
            return false; // No more intervals
        // Start the next interval
        iter->L = iter->Ls.data[iter->next_interval];
        iter->R = iter->Rs.data[iter->next_interval];
        iter->next_interval++;
    }
    match->cigar =
        (char *)iter->cigars.data[iter->next_interval - 1];
    match->position = iter->bwt_table->sa->array[iter->L];
    iter->L++;

    return true;
}
```

When we deallocate the iterator, we deallocate all the vectors and the D table if it was computed.

```
static void free_strings(
    struct string_vector *vec
) {
    for (int i = 0; i < vec->used; i++) {
        free(string_vector_get(vec, i));
    }
}

void dealloc_bwt_approx_iter(
    struct bwt_approx_iter *iter
) {
    dealloc_index_vector(&iter->Ls);
    dealloc_index_vector(&iter->Rs);
    free_strings(&iter->cigars);
    dealloc_string_vector(&iter->cigars);
    free(iter->edits_buf);
    if (iter->D_table) free(iter->D_table);
}
```

Comparisons

I will not compare edit cloud–based exact search with the other algorithms in this chapter. Being able to build the edit cloud gives a good intuition about approximative searching, and using an edit cloud with an exact search is an excellent way to run tests of the more complex algorithms. In practice, though, the size of the edit cloud explodes when the pattern gets large, and in practice, it is not practical to use this approach. Instead, I will compare searching using the suffix tree and the BWT with and without the D table. The results are shown in Figure 5-2.

I have performed the experiments with a maximum edit distance of 1, 2, and 3 (shown at the top of the figure). The pattern lengths I have used are 50, 100, and 150; see the x axis. What we see is that for small edit distances, there is not much difference between the algorithms, but that the difference in running time increases with the edit distance. Using the BWT approach without the D table is the slowest. Then comes the suffix tree approach and, finally, the BWT approach with the D table. The latter is dramatically faster and should be your first choice if you need to do approximative searches.

Of course, there is also a penalty for building the D table. It takes roughly twice as long to build both the O and the RO table than just the O table; see Figure 5-3. You only construct the tables once and might search in the millions of times, so this extra construction time might not be an issue.

You can find the code I used for the experiments here:

https://github.com/mailund/stralg/blob/master/performance/bwt_search.c

https://github.com/mailund/stralg/blob/master/performance/bwt_construction.c

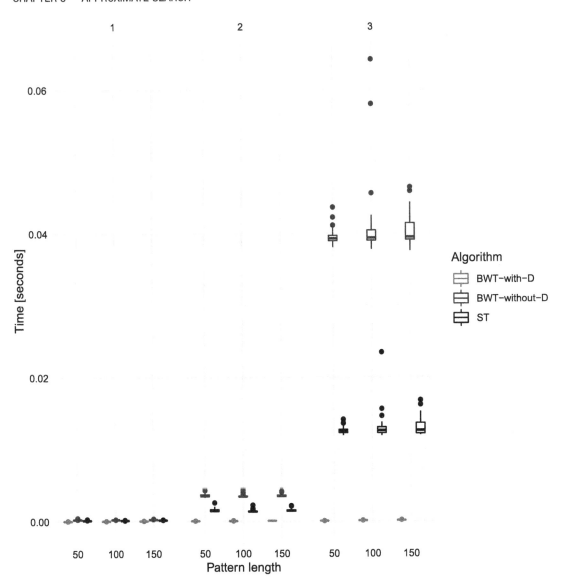

Figure 5-2. *Comparison of approximative search algorithms*

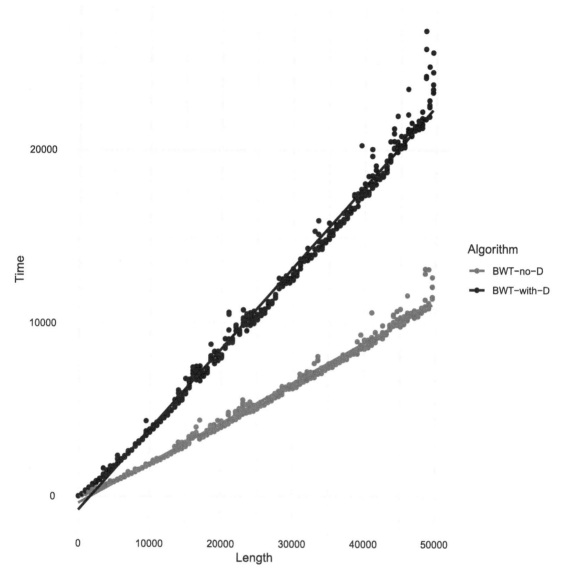

Figure 5-3. *BWT construction with and without D*

CHAPTER 6

Conclusions

You have now reached the end of *String Algorithms in C*. In the book, I have presented key algorithms and data structures for searching in strings and included implementation details often left out of textbooks on the topic. There are many more algorithms for exact search and for building, manipulating, and searching in suffix trees and suffix arrays that I could not fit into this book, but I encourage you to find them and implement them. After reading this book, you should have an idea about how you can effectively implement such algorithms, and use iterators to make it simple for a user to use your implementation. You can find all the algorithms in the book, plus example code in the form of tests and performance measurement programs, on GitHub: `https://github.com/mailund/stralg`. I hope you have enjoyed the book.

© Thomas Mailund 2020
T. Mailund, *String Algorithms in C*, https://doi.org/10.1007/978-1-4842-5920-7_6

Fundamental data structures

In several algorithms we have used fundamental data structures such as vectors and queues. I trust the reader to be familiar with these data structures, and rather than describing their implementation in the middle of the description of an algorithm, I have moved them to this appendix and made references to them when we encountered them the first time. We have needed some of the data structures for more than one type of elements, for example, a vector of strings and indices and a queue of pointers and indices. To avoid duplicated code, I have used a combination of functions and macros. Most of the smaller functions are most appropriately implemented as inline functions, so the compiler can optimize them. I have done this where I found for all short functions but not for longer functions. Without further ado, here are their implementations.

Vectors

```
#define vector_init(vec, init_size) {        \
  (vec)->data = malloc((init_size) * sizeof(*(vec)->data)); \
  (vec)->size = init_size;                    \
  (vec)->used = 0;                            \
}
#define dealloc_vector(vec) {                 \
  free((vec)->data);                          \
}
#define vector_append(vec, val) {             \
```

© Thomas Mailund 2020
T. Mailund, *String Algorithms in C*, https://doi.org/10.1007/978-1-4842-5920-7

```
  if ((vec)->used == vec->size) {                  \
    (vec)->data =                                  \
        realloc((vec)->data, 2 * (vec)->size \
                * sizeof(*(vec)->data));       \
    (vec)->size = 2 * (vec)->size;             \
  }                                                \
  (vec)->data[(vec)->used++] = (val);          \
}
#define vector_get(vec,idx) (vec)->data[(idx)]
#define vector_set(vec,idx,val) (vec)->data[(idx)] = (val)

struct index_vector {
    uint32_t *data;
    uint32_t size;
    uint32_t used;
};

static inline void init_index_vector(
    struct index_vector *vec,
    uint32_t init_size
) {
    vector_init(vec, init_size);
}
static inline void dealloc_index_vector(
    struct index_vector *vec
) {
    dealloc_vector(vec);
}
static inline struct index_vector *
alloc_index_vector(
    uint32_t init_size
) {
    struct index_vector *vec =
        malloc(sizeof(struct index_vector));
    init_index_vector(vec, init_size);
    return vec;
}
```

```c
static inline void free_index_vector(
    struct index_vector *vec
) {
    dealloc_index_vector(vec);
    free(vec);
}
static inline void index_vector_append(
    struct index_vector *vec,
    uint32_t index
) {
    vector_append(vec, index);
}

static inline uint32_t
index_vector_get(
    struct index_vector *vec,
    uint32_t i
) {
    return vector_get(vec, i);
}
static inline void
index_vector_set(
    struct index_vector *vec,
    uint32_t i,
    uint32_t val
) {
    vector_set(vec, i, val);
}

void sort_index_vector(
    struct index_vector *vec
);
bool index_vector_equal(
    struct index_vector *v1,
    struct index_vector *v2
);
```

```c
void print_index_vector(
    struct index_vector *vec
);

struct string_vector {
    uint8_t **data;
    uint32_t size;
    uint32_t used;
};

static inline void init_string_vector(
    struct string_vector *vec,
    uint32_t init_size
) {
    vector_init(vec, init_size);
}

static inline void dealloc_string_vector(
    struct string_vector *vec
) {
    dealloc_vector(vec);
}

static inline struct string_vector *
alloc string vector(
    uint32_t init_size
) {
    struct string_vector *vec =
        malloc(sizeof(struct string_vector));
    init_string_vector(vec, init_size);
    return vec;
}

static inline void free_string_vector(
    struct string_vector *vec
) {
    dealloc_string_vector(vec);
    free(vec);
}
```

```c
static inline uint8_t *string_vector_get(
    struct string_vector *vec,
    uint32_t idx
) {
    return vector_get(vec, idx);
}
static inline void string_vector_set(
    struct string_vector *vec,
    uint32_t idx,
    uint8_t *string
) {
    vector_set(vec, idx, string);
}
static inline void string_vector_append(
    struct string_vector *vec,
    uint8_t *string
) {
    vector_append(vec, string);
}

struct pointer_vector {
    void **data;
    uint32_t size;
    uint32_t used;
};

static inline void init_pointer_vector(
    struct pointer_vector *vec,
    uint32_t init_size
) {
    vector_init(vec, init_size);
}
static inline void dealloc_pointer_vector(
    struct pointer_vector *vec
) {
    dealloc_vector(vec);
}
```

```c
static inline struct pointer_vector *
alloc_pointer_vector(
    uint32_t init_size
) {
    struct pointer_vector *vec =
        malloc(sizeof(struct pointer_vector));
    init_pointer_vector(vec, init_size);
    return vec;
}
static inline void free_pointer_vector(
    struct pointer_vector *vec
) {
    dealloc_pointer_vector(vec);
    free(vec);
}

static inline void *pointer_vector_get(
    struct pointer_vector *vec,
    uint32_t idx
) {
    return vector_get(vec, idx);
}
static inline void pointer_vector_set(
    struct pointer_vector *vec,
    uint32_t idx,
    void *pointer
) {
    vector_set(vec, idx, pointer);
}
static inline void pointer_vector_append(
    struct pointer_vector *vec,
    uint8_t *pointer
) {
    vector_append(vec, pointer);
}
```

Lists

```c
struct index_linked_list {
    struct index_linked_list *next;
    uint32_t data;
};

static inline struct index_linked_list *
new_index_link(
    uint32_t val,
    struct index_linked_list *tail
) {
    struct index_linked_list *link =
        malloc(sizeof(struct index_linked_list));
    link->data = val; link->next = tail;
    return link;
}

void free_index_list(
    struct index_linked_list *list
) {
    while (list) {
        struct index_linked_list *next = list->next;
        free(list);
        list = next;
    }
}

struct pointer_linked_list {
    struct pointer_linked_list *next;
    void *data;
};

static inline struct pointer_linked_list *
new_pointer_link(
    void *val,
    struct pointer_linked_list *tail
) {
```

```
    struct pointer_linked_list *link =
        malloc(sizeof(struct pointer_linked_list));
    link->data = val; link->next = tail;
    return link;
}

void free_pointer_list(
    struct pointer_linked_list *list
) {
    while (list) {
        struct pointer_linked_list *next = list->next;
        free(list);
        list = next;
    }
}
```

Queues

```
#define init_queue(queue) {    \
    (queue)->front = 0;        \
    (queue)->back = 0;         \
}

#define alloc_queue(queue_type) {                       \
    queue_type *queue = malloc(sizeof(queue_type));     \
    init_queue(queue);                                  \
    return queue;                                        \
}

#define enqueue(list_type, link_constructor, queue, val) { \
    list_type *link = link_constructor(val, 0);            \
    if (queue->front == 0) {                               \
        queue->front = queue->back = link;                 \
    } else {                                               \
```

```
        queue->back->next = link;               \
        queue->back = link;                      \
    }                                            \
}
#define dequeue(list_type, queue) {              \
    assert(queue->front != 0);                   \
    list_type *link = queue->front;              \
    if (queue->front == queue->back) {           \
        queue->front = queue->back = 0;          \
    } else {                                     \
        queue->front = queue->front->next;       \
    }                                            \
    free(link);                                  \
}

#define dealloc_queue(list_type, queue) {        \
    while (!is_queue_empty(queue))               \
        dequeue(list_type, queue);               \
}
#define free_queue(list_type, queue) {           \
    dealloc_queue(list_type, queue);             \
    free(queue);                                 \
}

#define is_queue_empty(queue) \
  ((queue)->front == 0 && (queue)->back == 0)

#define queue_length(list_type, queue) {         \
    uint32_t i = 0;                              \
    for (list_type *link = queue->front;         \
      link;                                      \
      link = link->next) {                       \
      i++;                                       \
    }                                            \
    return i;                                    \
}
```

```c
struct index_queue {
    struct index_linked_list *front;
    struct index_linked_list *back;
};

static inline void init_index_queue(
    struct index_queue *queue
) {
    init_queue(queue);
}

static inline void dealloc_index_queue(
    struct index_queue *queue
) {
    dealloc_queue(struct index_linked_list, queue);
}

static inline struct index_queue *
alloc_index_queue(void) {
    alloc_queue(struct index_queue);
}

static inline void free_index_queue(
    struct index_queue *queue
) {
    free_queue(struct index_linked_list, queue);
}

static inline bool is_index_queue_empty(
    const struct index_queue *queue
) {
    return is_queue_empty(queue);
}

static inline uint32_t
index_queue_front(
    const struct index_queue *queue
) {
    assert(queue->front != 0);
    return queue->front->data;
}
```

```
static inline void enqueue_index(
    struct index_queue *queue,
    uint32_t index
) {
    enqueue(struct index_linked_list,
            new_index_link, queue, index);
}
static inline void dequeue_index(
    struct index_queue *queue
) {
    dequeue(struct index_linked_list, queue);
}

static inline uint32_t
index_queue_length(
    struct index_queue *queue
) {
    queue_length(struct index_linked_list, queue);
}

struct pointer_queue {
    struct pointer_linked_list *front;
    struct pointer_linked_list *back;
};

static inline void init_pointer_queue(
    struct pointer_queue *queue
) {
    init_queue(queue);
}
static inline void dealloc_pointer_queue(
    struct pointer_queue *queue
) {
    dealloc_queue(struct pointer_linked_list, queue);
}
static inline struct pointer_queue *
alloc_pointer_queue(void)
```

```
{
    alloc_queue(struct pointer_queue);
}
static inline void free_pointer_queue(
    struct pointer_queue *queue
) {
    free_queue(struct pointer_linked_list, queue);
}

static inline bool is_pointer_queue_empty(
    const struct pointer_queue *queue
) {
    return is_queue_empty(queue);
}
static inline void *pointer_queue_front(
    const struct pointer_queue *queue
) {
    assert(queue->front != 0);
    return queue->front->data;
}

static inline void enqueue_pointer(
    struct pointer_queue *queue, void *pointer
) {
    enqueue(struct pointer_linked_list,
            new_pointer_link, queue, pointer);
}
static inline void dequeue_pointer(
    struct pointer_queue *queue
) {
    dequeue(struct pointer_linked_list, queue);
}

static inline uint32_t pointer_queue_length(
    struct pointer_queue *queue
) {
    queue_length(struct pointer_linked_list, queue);
}
```

Index

W, X, Y

Z

Printed in the United States
By Bookmasters